THE MULTIPLE SELF

STUDIES IN RATIONALITY
AND SOCIAL CHANGE

Edited by Jon Elster

THE MULTIPLE SELF

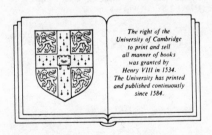

The right of the
University of Cambridge
to print and sell
all manner of books
was granted by
Henry VIII in 1534.
The University has printed
and published continuously
since 1584.

Cambridge University Press

Cambridge

New York – New Rochelle – Melbourne – Sydney

Published in collaboration with Maison des Sciences de l'Homme, Paris

126
M919

Published by the Press Syndicate of the University of Cambridge
The Pitt Building, Trumpington Street, Cambridge CB2 1RP
32 East 57th Street, New York, NY 10022, USA
10 Stamford Road, Oakleigh, Melbourne 3166, Australia
and in Scandinavia by Norwegian University Press, P.O. Box 2959 Tøyen, 0608, Oslo 6,
    Norway

First published 1986
Reprinted 1987

First paperback edition 1987

Printed in Great Britain at the University Press, Cambridge

British Library Cataloguing in Publication Data
The multiple self.–(Studies in rationality and
social change)–(Demokrati og samfunnstyring)
1. Self   2. Social psychology
I. Elster, Jon   II. Maison des sciences de
l'homme·   III. Series
302.5′4   HM251

Library of Congress Cataloguing in Publication Data
The multiple self.
(Studies in rationality and social change)
"Published in collaboration with Maison des sciences de l'homme."
Includes index
1. Self (Philosophy)–Addresses, essays,
lectures. 2. Self-deception–Addresses, essays,
lectures. 3. Decision-making–Addresses, essays,
lectures. I. Elster, Jon, 1940–   II. Maison
des sciences de l'homme (Paris, France)   III. Series.
BD450.M78 1986   126   85–26979

ISBN 0 521 26033 7 (hard covers, excluding Scandinavia)
ISBN 0 521 34683 5 (paperback)

WV

Contents

Preface

The papers in this volume, as in the companion volume on *Foundations of Social Choice Theory*, result from the discussions in a 'Working Group on Rationality' set up under the auspices of the Maison des Sciences de l'Homme (Paris). Most of the papers were presented at two meetings of the working group. The first, on 'Irrationality: explanation and understanding' took place in January 1980, the second, on 'The multiple self' in January 1982. Some additional papers have also been solicited. Jon Elster's contribution is reprinted with permission of All Souls College, Oxford.

J.E.

Notes on contributors

George Ainslie is a psychiatrist at the Veteran Administration Medical Center, Coatesville, Pennsylvania

Donald Davidson is Professor of Philosophy at the University of California, Berkeley

Jon Elster is Professor of Political Science and Philosophy at the University of Chicago

Serge-Christophe Kolm, an economist, is affiliated with the Ecole des Ponts et des Chaussées and the Ecole des Hautes Etudes en Sciences Sociales, Paris

Ulrich Krause is Professor of Mathematics at the University of Bremen

David Pears is Tutor in Philosophy at Christ Church, Oxford and Reader in Philosophy, Oxford University

George A. Quattrone is Professor of Psychology at Stanford University

Amélie Oksenberg Rorty is Professor of Philosophy at Rutgers University

Thomas Schelling is Professor of Economics at the Kennedy School of Government, Harvard University

Ian Steedman is Professor of Economics at Manchester University

Amos Tversky is Professor of Psychology at Stanford University

Introduction*

JON ELSTER

The idea that the individual person may be seen as – or actually is – a set of sub-individual, relatively autonomous 'selves' has a long history. The contributions to the present volume explore this idea in the light of recent developments in philosophy, psychology and economics. The conceptual strategies that have been used to make sense of this perplexing notion differ in many ways: with respect to how literally the notion of 'several selves' is taken, with respect to the principles of partition and with respect to the modes of interaction between the systems.

Some theories take the notion of a split self very literally, to the point of postulating different physical ('hardware') bases for the subsystems. Split-brain theories (Section VIII) are the most prominent example. Thomas Schelling (1983, pp. 95–6), in a speculative digression, suggests that 'the human being is not best modeled as a speculative individual but as several alternates according to the contemporary body chemistry. Tuning in and tuning out perceptual and cognitive and affective characteristics is like choosing which "individual" will occupy this body and nervous system.' This suggests a division of the self by different programmes ('softwares') using the same neuro-physiological substrate. Somewhat further down on the scale of literalness is the Freudian theory of id, ego and superego. In some readings of Freud these are understood to be distinct and autonomous entities in a very strong sense, but in Ainslie's version they turn out to be little more than a manner of speaking (Section VII). The theories of self-deception and weakness of will offered by Davidson, Pears and Rorty in this volume retain some of the literal connotations of the

*I am grateful to Amos Tversky for helpful discussions.

divided self, but do not suggest that the relatively autonomous systems are durable, stable entities that have distinct functions in the life of the mind. The concept employed by Steedman and Krause in their contribution is even weaker. Their 'selves' are, as they say, more like aspects than like agents.

The two main strategies for concept formation in this field rely on, respectively, interpersonal and intertemporal phenomena to make sense of the notion of several selves. The obvious first idea is to ask whether subsystems within a person can relate to one another in ways analogous to the relations between different persons. This may amount to postulating a set of selves with different interests but similar status or force (Section III) or to a more asymmetrical notion of a hierarchical self (Section IV). Special cases are Freud's theory (Section VII) and the idea that *homo economicus* and *homo sociologicus* cohabit our minds (Section IX). A different strategy is to look at different 'time-slices' of the same person as so many selves (Section V). Again, this may or may not involve a hierarchy of agents. Finally one may toy with the notion of 'parallel selves' (Section VI), a notion explored in the contributions by Ainslie, Elster and Schelling.

Another way of differentiating between the approaches is by looking at the form of interaction postulated between the subsystems. I shall be arguing that *deception* and strategic *manipulation* are the central forms of interaction, the former having as its immediate goal to induce a belief and the latter to induce an action. Since one way of inducing an action is by inducing a belief, the two categories do not exclude one another, but manipulation can also take place by acting on the motives or directly on the opportunity set. Self-deception has to be an asymmetrical relation, in the sense that one could hardly have two subsystems mutually deceiving one another (Section IV). By contrast, the possibility of mutual strategic interaction ought at least to be considered, although I shall conclude that it is hardly plausible. Indeed, the unity of the multiple self may stem from such asymmetries.

I begin and end by considering some borderline cases at opposite ends of the spectrum. Some cases of split selves turn out to be little more than lack of integration or coordination (Section I). The left hand may not know what the right hand is doing, but this is not to say that the latter is fooling it (cp. also Section VIII). An extreme version of the multiple-self theory, on the other hand, is that of the infinitely fragmented self (Section X). Hume had trouble finding more than a bundle of perceptions in his search for the self; a similar 'no self' theory is proposed in the Buddhist ideas discussed by Kolm in his contribution.

I. The loosely integrated self

Many apparent cases of a split or divided self turn out to be little more than failures of coordination and integration. Or what at any given occasion looks like a fissure in the unity of the self may only be a by-product of patterns that in the long run ensure the highest degree of unity. An analogy with the firm may be instructive.[1] Subunits within a firm may achieve considerable independence and autonomy. One subunit may proceed on the basis of information that another unit already knows to be outdated. In spite of the knowledge that this is liable to happen, the direction of the firm may still decide that the overall value of independent subunits outweighs the loss of efficiency. This may even hold if it anticipates that because of jealousy between subunits some of them may actively try to hide part of what they know in order to trap other units into making bad decisions. In the case of the self, one hypothetical analogue to the 'direction' is natural selection. That is, it might be the case that our cognitive and affective apparatus is an optimal package solution, given the constraints on what the nervous system could support and the goal of maximizing fitness.[2] This, however, is necessarily very speculative. Although one can tell a story of a sort to rationalize apparently suboptimal behaviour, both the existence of the alleged benefits and their explanatory power are often dubious.[3] Another possibility is that the direction could be a central planning agency within the person, delegating the less important tasks to habits and subroutines, knowing that this may occasionally lead one astray, but believing that on balance the outcome will be better than if the full power of the mind were brought to bear on every issue (since

---

[1] See Margolis (1982, pp. 42–3) for one use of this analogy. Classically, of course, the analogy was used the other way around. The firm was assumed to be a unitary actor with consistent goals, on the model of the rational individual agent.

[2] For some speculations along this line, see Nisbett and Ross (1980, pp. 191ff), citing Goldman (1978).

[3] For a spelling out of these doubts, see Elster (1983, pp. 157ff).

the full power would then at any given occasion be smaller).[4] This is close to what is argued by Amélie Rorty in her contribution below. Or, a third possibility, there may be no direction that bears responsibility for the lack of coordination. There might be less, or more, coordination than a rational direction would have chosen.

Let me survey some typical examples of coordination failures, beginning with beliefs. Contradictory beliefs may coexist peacefully for a long time, if they belong to different realms of life. As a child (and even a bit longer) I had two different beliefs concerning the origin of hot water in our house. On a practical level I believed, indeed knew, that the hot water came from a heater in the basement. There was not enough for everybody to have a bath in the morning, so we followed the operations of the heater with some attention. In addition I entertained the theoretical view that beneath the streets there ran two parallel sets of water pipes, one for hot and one for cold water. One day the two beliefs, hitherto separate, came into contact with each other, upon which one of them crumbled, never to be seen again.

Somewhat similar examples are provided by the child who believes in Santa Claus, yet asks the parents about the price of the Christmas gifts; by the Ethiopians who believe that leopards, being Christian animals, will never attack their domestic beasts on a day of fasting, yet do not fail to secure their enclosures on such days; by the Romans who believed in the divinity of their rulers, yet on important family occasions always turned to their traditional gods.[5] In such cases it is unclear whether we are dealing with different modalities of belief, or with separate beliefs that guide different spheres of life. On neither interpretation is there any need to postulate a split self. Nor do we need to make this strong assumption in cases where the formation of one belief, for which we have good evidence, is blocked by a strong a priori conviction incompatible with it. The television programme, *Candid Camera*, once recorded persons sitting on a bench in Central Park who suddenly saw a tree on the edge of their visual field walking towards them. Most reacted by shaking their head as if waking from a

[4] 'A system – any system, economic or other – that at *every* given point of time fully utilizes its possibilities to the best advantage may yet in the long run be inferior to a system that does so at *no* given point of time, because the latter's failure to do so may be a condition for the level or speed of long-run performance' (Schumpeter 1961, p. 83).

[5] For these and similar examples, see Veyne (1978, pp. 248, 561, 589, 669) and Veyne (1983, *passim*).

bad dream, and then went back to whatever they were doing. The thing couldn't happen, so it didn't happen. This is more like a sound piece of Bayesian reasoning than like self-deception. (But when the tree moved again, some left their bench to sit elsewhere, as if to escape from this persistent waking dream. This calls for a more complex analysis.)

Consider next some issues of motivation. An individual's preference can be inconsistent in various ways that do not imply any kind of split self. It is possible to make a person prefer A over B and C over D, even if A is essentially the same option as D, and B the same as C. For instance, 'Mr H. mows his own lawn. His neighbor's son would mow it for $8. He wouldn't mow his neighbor's same-sized lawn for $20' (Thaler 1980). The proposed explanation for this phenomenon is that people value out-of-pocket expenses differently from opportunity cost, thus creating a normatively unjustifiable presumption in favour of the status quo. Although this particular example may yield to another explanation (Section IX), many other cases certainly fit this distinction. Thus, credit card customers may be less deterred by a cash discount to non-users than by a surcharge to users, even if the two are substantively the same (Thaler 1980). If in such cases it is possible to induce preference reversal, it is not because two parts of the person have different preferences. Rather it is because *the* person reacts to the way in which the options are presented, and not simply to their substantive content.

Sometimes these phenomena occur as the result of mental compartmentalization, in the following sense. Whether as the outcome of deliberation or not, people often keep a mental account of their expenses and avoid spending too much in any given category. They may have, say, one attitude to money spent on going to the theatre and another to accidental losses of money. Thus if I go to the theatre to pick up a ticket costing $10 and on my way lose a ten-dollar bill, this may not stop me from going, but if I have bought the ticket and then lose it, I might not want to buy another one (Tversky and Kahneman 1981). Yet the two scenarios are substantively equivalent. Such 'framing' phenomena may seem irrational, yet some mental rules of thumb of this kind are often useful to facilitate decision-making. Compartmentalization allows for preference reversal, but this is not to say that the mind has separate compartments with different preferences.

II. Self-deception and weakness of will

In the philosophical literature these are the paradigmatic examples of a divided self (Davidson 1980, ch. 2; Pears 1984). In the present volume, four contributions deal with self-deception (Davidson, Elster, Pears, Quattrone–Tversky), one with weakness of will (Ainslie) and one with both (Rorty). Self-deception may also be involved in what, according to Ainslie, is the way in which people overcome their impulsiveness. This will be brought out by comparing his argument to the Quattrone–Tversky analysis of voting. Otherwise I shall not attempt to summarize the analyses, except for some classificatory remarks.

When philosophers refer to 'the problem or weakness of will' and 'the problem of self-deception', they usually have in mind the question how these phenomena are at all possible. Davidson and Pears have pioneered in offering non-mythical answers to that question. When non-philosophers refer to these problems, they are more likely to have in mind the question how weakness of will and self-deception can be overcome. Both questions turn upon the notion of the divided self. For these paradoxical phenomena to be possible, there must be some breakdown of internal communication in the mind. To restore communication, or to prevent the defective lines from doing serious damage, some further action is required. Whether this also needs a separate, further agent is more doubtful. While it might appear that a third party is needed to prevent the subversive action of one part of the self against another, it is more plausible to identify the referee with one of the parts – but operating at a different time. I return to this issue in several later sections.

Weakness of will, as traditionally conceived, is a problem of impulsive behaviour. It is clear, however, that impulsiveness is neither sufficient nor necessary for weakness of will. It is not sufficient, since the totally impulsive person, in whom there is no inner conflict, cannot be subject to weakness of will. That notion requires both that there is a conflict between two opposed wishes, and that the wish that the person himself judges to be the more decisive loses out. Nor does weakness of will always take the form of giving in to impulsive urges. As noted by Davidson (1980, p. 30), compulsive, rigid, rule-governed behaviour can also be a form of weakness of will, that is, acting against one's own better judgment. This establishes a conceptual connection by subsuming the apparently opposite concepts of impulsive and compulsive behaviour under a common heading. The important insight offered by Ainslie is that there is a causal connection as well, in that compulsive behaviour may be seen as the overly successful attempt to control impulsiveness (Section VI).

Self-deception is one of a family of notions that also includes wishful thinking and other forms of improper influence of wishes on belief formation. Let me make two distinctions here. The first is between the mental operations that, however irrational, at least provide some fleeting satisfaction or pleasure, and those that do not even have that redeeming feature. The pleasure principle may be second best to the reality principle, but it does at least provide some pleasure, however precarious and short-lived. But what shall we say about the congenital pessimist, who constantly believes the world to be different from what he would wish it to be? Here the wirings of the pleasure machine have gone seriously wrong. (A similar distinction can be made with respect to preference formation, see Elster 1983, pp. 111–12.) The other distinction concerns two different operations of the pleasure principle. In addition to self-deception, which necessarily requires some duality in the mind, there can be wishful thinking that is a form of 'motivated irrationality', yet does not involve any kind of duality. A person might entertain a belief out of wishful thinking, and yet *that very same* belief might also be justified by the evidence available to him, had he only considered it. If the will to believe is strong, the process of evaluating the evidence may never start up at all. Bias may give rise to beliefs that by accident turn out to be not only true (which is irrelevant here), but unbiased. I confess to some uncertainty here. The cases which I have elsewhere described as demonstrating this possibility (Elster 1983, pp. 150–1), might turn out to be better characterized by saying that the person forms the belief by considering the evidence, but that he would have formed the same belief even had the evidence pointed in a different direction.[6]

To see the connection between impulse control and self-deception in

[6] Pears (1984, pp. 94ff) points to the difference between irrational intervention and failure to intervene rationally, and argues that irrational belief formation is to be explained in terms of the latter. I believe this captures many central cases, but I am still not sure it covers all important instances.

Ainslie's contribution, it is useful to begin by considering a closely analogous phenomenon in Quattrone and Tversky's chapter. One of their findings is that people sometimes fool themselves into thinking that voting can be instrumentally justified, even when the terms of the problem are such that this manifestly cannot be the case. What operates is a confusion of diagnostic and causal reasoning that magically magnifies the consequences of an individual act of voting so as to make it worth while.[7] 'If I vote, others like me are likely to vote too, so let me vote in order to bring it about that they vote as well.' Needless to say, the belief could never be consciously articulated in this way; some sort of self-deception is needed.

Ainslie argues that the same reasoning can help an individual overcome the problem of impulsiveness, which may be seen as an intra-personal collective action problem. By making present decisions diagnostic of later ones, the individual can bunch his choices in a way that allows for more self-control. In this case, however, it is not clear that the thinking is magical or irrational; at least it can be articulated consciously without losing its force. It corresponds to the following, well-known chain of reasoning. '(1) If I take a drink just this one time, I can abstain on the next occasions and no harm will be done. (2) But do I really have any reason to think that I shall behave differently on future occasions, which will be essentially similar to the present one? (3) On reflection, therefore, I had better abstain now since otherwise I shall almost certainly yield to temptation the next time.'

Is this irrational? Observe first that we are not here talking about a genuine causal impact of the present choice on later choices, as in cases of habituation or addiction. In this respect it corresponds to the voting problem, in which it is similarly assumed that voters do not exert any causal influence upon one another by setting an example etc. Yet the first choice will typically be known to the person at the moment the later choices are made, unless he engages in a piece of genuine or self-deceptive forgetting. When he is about to make the later choice, the situation will differ from the earlier one in that he now has information about an earlier choice (or about more earlier choices). This information constrains his *self-image* in a way that may ease or obstruct the

---

[7] Note that this does not turn upon altruist motivation. Altruism can also act as a multiplier on the benefits from voting, but there is of course nothing irrational about this.

prudential decision.[8] If this is self-deception it is of a benign kind, since it turns out to be self-fulfilling.[9]

III. Faustian selves

'Two souls, alas, do dwell within his breast.' It is a common fact that people are often torn between different desires. They want to do several things that as a matter of fact or a matter of logic are mutually exclusive. It would be absurd to elevate all such cases to the status of 'split selves', but some of them may exemplify that notion as well as any. If the opposed desires are not sorted out by the person to yield a consistent series of choices, but lead to behavioural inconsistencies of some kind, there is a prima-facie reason to suspect a deep-seated split.

Intransitive choices – choosing A over B, B over C and C over A – is one form of inconsistent behaviour. Steedman and Krause argue that such choices could be due to an Arrow-like problem of aggregation, an analogue a social-choice problem within the individual. As they point out, the plausibility of this move turns crucially upon the ordinality of the underlying 'aspect preferences'. If there are at least three aspects that the individual finds himself unable to compare in cardinal terms, and thus has to treat 'democratically', he could find himself in a Condorcet paradox. A somewhat trivial example would be an internalized social-choice problem, for example, if the ordinal (transitive!) preference of each member of my family form one aspect of my preference structure. More generally, one would have to look for cases in which the 'aspect preference' is based on ordinal information only, even if there is an (unknown) cardinal structure.

Choice reversal – first choosing A over B and then B over A – is an even more dramatic form of inconsistency. As mentioned in Section I, some instances of this phenomenon can be explained without any reference to a divided self. This also holds in cases where two corner solutions are deemed equally and optimally good. And, if the choice reversal is itself irreversible, because the preferences of the person simply have changed, there is no paradox at all. Hence, as a necessary but not sufficient condition, we shall have to look for cases in which A and B are alternately chosen.

[8] Cp. Føllesdal (1981) for an interpretation of Sartre along these lines.
[9] For the relation between self-deceptive and self-fulfilling beliefs see Elster (1984, pp. 48, 177) and Pears (1984, pp. 33ff).

In several important articles Thomas Schelling has discussed the notion that different selves might alternately win out in 'the intimate contest for self-command'. Thus: 'People behave sometimes as if they had two selves, one who wants clean lungs and a long life and another who adores tobacco, or one who wants a lean body and another who wants dessert, or one who wants to improve himself by reading Adam Smith's theory of self-command (in *The Theory of Moral Sentiments*) and another who would rather watch an old movie on television' (Schelling 1980, p. 58). Or again: 'To plead in the night for the termination of an unbearable existence and to express relief at midday that one's gloomy night broodings were not taken seriously, to explain away the nighttime self in hopes of discrediting it, and then to plead again the next night for termination creates an awesome dilemma' (Schelling 1983, pp. 107–8).

In his earlier work Schelling (1963) had pioneered in exploring the idea that in strategic interactions one may improve one's prospects by eliminating certain options from the feasible set, as when one bargainer gets his way by making certain concessions physically impossible or extremely costly. In the intra-personal case this can be understood in two ways. First, most obviously, I may try to protect myself against weakness of will by removing the source of temptation; that is, one self may try to ensure that the other self will not be exposed to temptation. In this case, the language of several selves does not seem to have much purchase. Next, more interestingly, I may try to make myself invulnerable against the strategies that I might later use to get my way. Here the first person singular seems inadequate. If two or more parts of a person are really engaging in mutual strategic manipulation, there would seem to be good grounds for referring to several selves. Schelling argues that there are such cases.

Is he right? Do we observe that the self that wants to stay sober hides the bottle from the self who wants to drink, while the latter hides the Antabuse pills from the former? Or, to use the bargaining analogy, do we observe that the self who wants to drink makes sure that if he is deprived of alcohol he will die – something that the other self is not likely to want to happen? My contention is that we do not. There may be some examples of mutual manipulation;[10] I certainly do not think

[10] Aanund Hylland has provided me with an example. Going to a party, he overheard a conversation between a woman who was trying to quit smoking and her companion. It

there is any logical impossibility involved in this notion. But as far as I know such cases are few and far between, and not very important. Observe that this carries no implication about which self is the more 'authentic' or ethically valuable one. The asymmetry with respect to the capacity for strategic behaviour helps us to identify *the* person (Frankfurt 1971), but it does not tell us what goals are the most valuable or autonomous (Elster 1983, pp. 21–2). The observer could well be on the side of the easy-going spontaneous self that is constantly being repressed by the excessively far-sighted self that is in charge. The observer might plead unsuccessfully, 'Give yourself a break', meaning that the other self should get a break. Also, being in charge does not mean getting one's way – the horse may throw the rider even if the latter is in command. The capacity to form second-order intentions, the capacity to form autonomous intentions and the ability to get one's way – these may, but need not, go together.

IV. Hierarchical selves

The asymmetry just pointed out is a hierarchical one. The self that constitutes *the* person is not the stronger or more decisive self, the self that gets its way: it is the self that entertains higher-order intentions about other selves. Horizontal divisions would yield selves neither of which (as in Steedman and Krause) or both of which (as in Schelling) have higher-order intentions about the other. A remotely similar asymmetry obtains in self-deception, as discussed by Davidson and Pears. The part of the person that wants another part to have a certain belief, not justified by the evidence, must itself have some beliefs about the other part, but not vice versa. The deceived ignores the existence of the deceiver, not only of the deception. At least this is true in the absence of learning about one's tendency to deceive oneself. If such learning occurs, the deceived self might try to change the ways of the deceiver, or at least to minimize the harm it can do, by seeking advice etc. It would not, however, try to influence the deceiver by deceiving it in turn; at least I cannot attach any sense to this idea.

transpired that she had asked her companion not to bring any cigarettes to the party, to prevent her from backsliding. When she got there, she was unable to stick to her decision, and left to buy a pack of cigarettes. As she left, she said to her companion: 'And if I ask you not to bring cigarettes the next time we go to a party, don't listen to me.' For another, hypothetical, example see Elster (1984, p. 41).

Consider the analogy with nations. Two opposed countries might engage in mutual strategic interaction. They might also engage in mutual deception by planting false intelligence, including intelligence that if believed would undermine the intelligence operations of the other. The intra-personal analogy to mutual strategic interaction is at least conceivable, but the analogy to mutual deception seems more than far-fetched. Hence if the deceived self decides to counter-attack, it must do so by other means. Perhaps it could persuade the subversive self that its 'altruistic' efforts (Pears 1984, p. 91) are in fact misguided; or, as I said, it could try to contain the damage. This would reestablish the supremacy of the deceived system. Being weak and knowing it is better than being weak unknowingly, although the best is to be without weakness. Again, the place in the hierarchy does not depend on getting one's way. The effort to get rid of self-deception may meet with small success. Yet this would be due to the weakness of the counter-attack, not to any measures taken *in order to* neutralize it. The last claim, of course, would be falsified if the deceiving system's awareness of the deceived system included awareness of the counter-subversive measures and if it remained unaffected by the knowledge that the deceived system did not really want to be deceived. Both of these assumptions are, however, highly speculative, bordering on un-intelligibility.

The distinction between horizontal and vertical divisions of the self has been formulated in the language of meta-preferences. A person may possess several first-order preferences, each of which evaluates the options from a certain point of view (e.g. morality, sympathy, self-interest). This gives rise to a horizontal division of the self. Depending on how the various preferences interact – by aggregation, bargaining or manipulation – choices will be produced that may or may not fall into a consistent pattern. Amartya Sen has suggested that we should also envisage a vertical division, with a ranking (that may only be a partial ordering) of the preferences themselves (Sen 1977). An individual might ask himself: 'Would I rather have (and act upon) preferences R than preferences R'' The outcome of many such pairwise choices will be a ranking of the preferences.

In one sense it is misleading to talk about meta-preferences. The basis for ranking the first-order preferences must itself be a first-order preference about what the person thinks he should do, all things considered. We care about preferences because they produce things we care about – actions and outcomes. I can make no sense of the notion of a meta-ranking not thus anchored in first-order evaluations. Yet in another sense the concept may be useful. If in a given situation I know the choices I ought to make, all things considered, yet find myself unable to stick to my resolutions, I may undertake a process of planned character change. I first decide that I want to become the kind of person who just does the right thing, but then I decide that this is setting my sights too high. My ideal self simply is not to be found in the set of outcomes of feasible character changes. Hence I will have to make a decision about which of the selves in that set I most would like to become. This would involve comparing each possible self with the ideal self, in order to rank the options and make a decision about what I would like to become. Now the foundation for this ranking must be my conception of the ideal self. To ask me to compare the options with one another, with no reference to this bench-mark, would not make sense. Hence one of the preference orderings must be both referee and contestant. It goes without saying that it will always come out on top in the unrestricted set of selves, but if it is not itself in the set of feasible set of selves it can serve to guide the choice between those that are.

Hence the notion of a hierarchy of preferences depends, if I am right, on the notion of an asymmetric distribution of the capacity to have second-order intentions. If my day-time self and my night-time self were both able to behave strategically toward the other, we could not decide which of them to use as a bench-mark. There would be two sets of meta-rankings. However, once we have firmly identified *the* person with one of the selves, on the basis of that self's unique capacity to form higher-order intentions about the other, we can use the preferences of that self to construct *the* meta-ranking of the person.

V. Successive selves

The coherence and identity of a person centrally involves *time*, in at least three ways. First, and most obviously, the individual may become 'a different person' because he changes in some profound way. Derek Parfit (1973) has cited the example of a Russian nobleman who, in his idealist youth, views with horror the prospect of changing into a more cynical and – to him – altogether different self. The example does not work well, however, since in such cases the older, cynical self does not usually disavow the earlier one. Rather he might see the youthful idealism as part of what made him the person he turned into; and he might cite the phrase to the effect that the person who is not radical in his youth is as much a subject for pity as the person who remains radical in his old age. For successive selves in a sharper sense we must look to cases of religious or political conversion, in which there is a relation of mutual disavowal between the pre-conversion and the post-conversion selves. Even in such cases, however, we might decide that the continuity runs deeper than the difference. The communist who turns into a militant anti-communist does remain in touch with his earlier self, in spite of the break; moreover, the fervour of the earlier self may continue to animate the later. My hunch is that in close examination of any actual case we would come to the conclusion that talk of several selves creates more confusion than illumination.

When a person changes, he may regret some of the choices he made before the change. Also, he may find that he does not want to stick to his earlier decisions when they had a scope extending beyond the change. These phenomena – regret and incontinence – may also occur in the absence of any character change. They can stem from inconsistencies within the person's (unchanging) attitude towards time. Consider first weakness of will, in the form of a high discounting of the future. If because of this myopic attitude a person is led to prefer a smaller immediate pleasure over a greater, delayed one, he may well experience regret and desolidarize himself from the choice. Consider next a more complex phenomenon, the person who has to allocate some scarce resource over more than two periods in the future. He may give a disproportionately high weight to the first period, less to the second, even less to third and so on. If the discounting has a non-exponential character, as set out in Ainslie's paper, he will not be able to stick to his first decision when the second period arrives. He will reconsider his choice, so as to give more weight to the second period (relatively to the third) than he originally planned to do (Elster 1984, Ch. II.5). Persons subject to either of these liabilities suffer from lack of integration, but there is no need to talk about distinct selves, except in the Davidson–Pears sense. If the person believes that he ought to do what is best, all things considered, and nevertheless fails to do so on a particular occasion, there must be some split in the mind that prevents the first belief from having the influence it ought to have. But, although temporal inconsistency may involve a reference to a divided self, there is no need to talk about successive selves.

Steedman and Krause draw our attention to a third way in which time matters for identity: by the nested system of memories and anticipation. Pleasures have a life after death as well as a pre-natal life; some linger on in memory and provide continued satisfaction, while others yet unborn offer the pleasures of anticipation. Steedman and Krause offer a novel and valuable distinction between two ways in which future benefits matter in the present. First, the anticipation of future (first-order)[11] benefits may actually add to my pleasure in the present on a par with the memory of earlier experiences. Secondly, the pleasure that in the future I shall derive from those benefits matters to me now, because I view myself as extending over time with more than just momentary interests. The distinction may seem tenuous, but on reflection it is quite robust. I may be the sort of person who 'lives in the present', in the sense of not thinking much about specific past and future experiences. I concentrate all my attention on the matters at hand, enjoying them to the hilt. Yet this is quite compatible with having a prudential concern for my own future ability to enjoy similarly present-centred pleasures. The converse case may seem less plausible. Can we imagine someone who 'lives in the present' in the sense of not saving anything for the future, yet derives much satisfaction from anticipating whatever pleasures he expects to get later on? I believe we can, if we stipulate that the future benefits are non-convertible into present ones. Hence they are not subject to his weakness of will, and he may contemplate their arrival with pleasure untainted by inner struggle. If it were possible to have spring come in December, I might choose to do so, but since it is not, I have the daily satisfaction of seeing the days grow longer and the time for that sudden acceleration of nature approach.

In the absence of the one or the other form for concern about the future, can we plausibly speak of a divided self? First, note that myopia need not be a case of weakness of the will, as pointed out in Section II.

---

[11] If my anticipation also covers the future higher-order pleasures (from memory of earlier first-order pleasures, memory of anticipation etc.) a more complex construction is needed, similar to the one used by Becker (1977, pp. 270–1) in his discussion of interpersonal externalities in the utility functions.

Some people with short time horizons do not wish they had longer ones. If they do, we might want to say that (at any given point in time) they have a divided self; if not, that they suffer from lack of temporal integration. Such people could be so myopic that they do not even perceive that they are involved in an intra-personal, inter-temporal problem of collective action; and a fortiori do not have the motivation to arrive at the cooperative solution. (This involves cognitive myopia, rather than motivational. It is not unreasonable to think that the two often go together, although either may exist without the other.) Secondly, the absence of externalities in the utility functions in the successive periods is also, I believe, better seen as a lack of integration than as a succession of selves. The person who lives in the present, in the first of the two senses distinguished above, would be poorly linked up with his own past actions. He might remember them, but the memory would not be invested with much emotional significance. Yet there is no split in the sense of relatively autonomous entities each promoting its own interest, if need be at the expense of that of others.

The strategic element could be important in many of these cases. Consider first character changes over the life-cycle. The earlier self has two kinds of interests in the future. He cares about the accomplishment of his current plans, and about the kind of person he will turn into later on. In particular, he might – like Parfit's nobleman – be afraid that the later self might frustrate the plans laid by the earlier one. If he has no influence on what he will become, he must then entrust the safeguarding of those earlier plans to another person (his wife in Parfit's story) or to some institutional device for precommitment (as discussed at length by Schelling, 1983). If he can shape his future character, there could be a conflict between the two concerns. He might decide that the future self that would best ensure the realization of his current plans is one that he would not care to become. My current plan may be for my children to lead a happy life. To ensure this I may have to turn myself into a solid wage-earner, with both the income and the sense of responsibility (induced by work) that would be required, yet that person may be very different from the Bohemian character I should really have wanted to become.

Consider next weakness of will in the simple or the complex form (i.e. with exponential or non-exponential time-discounting). This has been the paradigm for writers on strategic manipulation of the self

(Thaler and Shefrin 1981; Winston 1980; Elster 1984, Ch. II). The goal of the manipulation could be to overcome regret-inducing behaviour, arising from time preferences *tout court*, or to prevent incontinence, that is, the inability to stick to past plans that arises out of non-exponential time preferences. Such manipulation has a paradoxical character: it is motivated by the future inability to relate to (what will then be) the future. Since by assumption the person will remain the same, he should be just as unable now to relate to the future as he will be later on. The answer, of course, is that the two situations must be different. The sacrifices of present benefits must be smaller at the time the manipulative scheme is set up than it will be at the time when it comes into operation. Essentially, it costs nothing to tell all my friends that I shall quit smoking on 1 January next year, or to throw away all bottles of whisky save one. Yet these moves may enable me to carry out my decision to quit by ensuring that certain options become unavailable at the time when I might want to choose them.

VI. Parallel selves

In addition to our immediate personal experience we often enjoy the vicarious experience provided by daydreaming, reading novels or writing them. In fanciful exaggeration we may say that the vicarious experience belongs to a parallel self, one that runs its course alongside the main self. In non-fanciful language, of course, the fictional self is embedded in the main self. When I am daydreaming, *I* am daydreaming. Yet the fanciful language can serve the function of pointing to the importance that satisfaction by proxy can take on. Sometimes the consumption or creation of possible worlds comes to dominate the life of the mind at the expense of one's engagement in the actual world. Instead of speaking of parallel selves, we might think of the person as communicating between parallel lives.

Consider first daydreaming. Daydreams come in many varieties, depending on whether their starting-point is in the past or in the future and whether they are constrained to branch off from one's real life. I may wish that I had been a general in Napoleon's army, or were born in the twenty-fifth century, and construct elaborate daydreams to flesh out such wishes. Most daydreams, however, are hooked up with my own life in some way. There are the might-have-beens of my past: if only I had had the wit to reply in kind; if only I had had the courage to ask her to marry me. Although not all the might-have-beens turn into daydreams, some of them do and are frequently updated to keep abreast wth current developments in the real world. Sometimes the central counterfactual element in the daydream is not something I might have done, but what someone else might have done or some event that might have occurred: if only she had said yes; if only I had won the big prize in the lottery. And then there are the daydreams that might still come true, those which branch off from my life at some point in the future. These are especially prominent in youth, when the future is open and the borderline between plans and daydreams is easily blurred.

The basic flaw of daydreams as a source of satisfaction is well characterized by Ainslie: they suffer from a *shortage of scarcity*. With a few exceptions satisfaction and pleasure derive from the relief of tension. (Cp. also the contribution of Schelling below, and the 'opponent-process theory of motivation' to which he refers.) Tension is created by scarcity: of talent, time, knowledge and money. It is because we are not omniscient that the search for truth offers an occasion for pleasure; it is because we are not omnipotent that we find our deepest satisfaction in stretching our limited abilities to the limit. In daydreams there is no scarcity; or if there is, there is nothing we can do about it. We can do anything we want; we do not have to build airplanes since we can just as easily imagine that we are endowed with wings. True, we cannot know everything, but nor can we do anything to increase our knowledge. (We can of course imagine that we know the truth about Fermat's last theorem, but the pleasure derived from this remains shallow as long as we not know what the truth about it is.)

By writing a novel we can overcome these defects. Novels are subject to *constraints* that provide the scarcity lacking in daydreams. First, and most obviously, a novel is essentially finite and complete. When the artist's vision has been externalized and given to the public, he cannot go on adding details; nor can he answer critics by saying that they simply don't know the characters well enough. It is his task – and his constraint – to ensure that the readers know exactly what is needed to understand what is going on. Indeed, there is nothing more to be known about the characters than what appears in the novel itself. If the author thinks he has a private peephole into what his characters do off-stage, he confuses the novel with an unconstrained daydream. Secondly, unlike daydreams, a novel must respect the laws of probability. In daydreams a mere possibility suffices to launch a train of events. One can call upon any coincidence to make things turn out the way one wants. A coincidence in a novel – like the one at the centre of *Middlemarch* – is rightly seen as a sign of authorial self-indulgence.

I argue in my contribution below that in Stendhal's case, the novel served largely as a means of vicarious satisfaction. In *Lucien Leuwen* he even experimented with multiple fictional selves – turning Lucien into the person he had wanted to be in his youth and Leuwen *père* into the character he wanted to become in his mature age. Observe, however, that this is not the same as having multiple plots in a novel. I tend to agree with Schelling when he writes that 'You cannot show two episodes and let each viewer choose.' Yet in *The French Lieutenant's Woman* John Fowles did exactly that, when he left the reader to choose between one ending in which the two main characters are united with one another and one in which they are not. The reason why I find this unsatisfactory is related to the role of constraints in fictional writing. In the beginning of a novel each action, choice or remark is heavily underdetermined by what we already know about the person. Their main purpose is to contribute to our knowledge of his character, that is, to narrow down the set of things that he can say or do at that point. A properly constructed novel ends at the point when the options open to the person are limited to the point of inevitability. Or more precisely: if in the penultimate period of the novel several options are open to a person, given what at that point the reader knows about his character, his final choice should improve our understanding of his character so as to make that choice the only possible one. *The French Lieutenant's Woman* ends before any such point is reached. Other novels sin in the opposite direction, by going on after that point has been reached. This is the case of all the novels whose authors could not resist the temptation to dwell on the bliss of the deserving and the misery of the undeserving. Our uneasy pleasure in reading about these inconsequential details is related to the pleasures of daydreaming; it is gorging oneself in a way that stills no hunger.

What, finally, about the vicarious experience provided by *reading* a novel? The operative constraint here is that of lack of knowledge: we want to see how it all turns out. Hence the twin dangers referred to in the previous paragraph: that of frustration when our tension is not relieved and that of boredom when the narrative goes on after the relief with no new tensions being provided. The author writes under the constraint that he must provide the reader first with the knowledge constraint that sets up the tension and then with the knowledge that is necessary and sufficient to relieve it. If he succeeds, he has created a source of vicarious satisfaction both for himself and for the reader. The author and the reader – 'mon semblable, mon frère' – become truly parallel selves, since they live off the same daydream, the presence of each being a condition for the satisfaction of the other.[12]

VII. The Freudian legacy

Freud left us with a new language for talking about the divided self. On the one hand he introduced the division into conscious, preconscious and unconscious; in addition he proposed a distinction between id, ego and superego. The former is more like a distinction between territories, the latter approaches a distinction between agents. The exegetical and conceptual difficulties of understanding exactly what Freud intended by these notions are enormous. Fortunately, I can restrict myself to problems that impinge on the issues raised in the contributions to this volume. I shall consider two such issues: the relation between the conscious and the preconscious, and the idea that self-control can be a problem as well as a solution.

In our dictionary of mental categories there is room for something that is more than awareness and less than self-consciousness. Awareness is what animals and men enjoy in perception of external objects. When my dog watches me to see if I am going to slip a morsel of food to her, she is certainly aware of me. Self-consciousness is what men enjoy when they turn the mind inwards to watch its own operation. An instance is the effort to remember someone's name by bringing to mind all the circumstances in which one has met him. The intermediate category, which we may call consciousness, is what we possess when relating to external objects not immediately perceptible by the senses. Going back to Alaska from Florida we take a warm overcoat – an

---

[12] For other ways in which constraints are important for artistic creation, see Elster (1983, Ch. II. 7).

action not triggered by anything in the environment of choice. This ability to re-present what is physically absent is probably not an exclusive feature of men, but shared with some animals (Griffin 1984). It is, broadly speaking, what enables men to relate to the future and, if need be, to their future inability to relate to the future (Elster 1984, Ch. I). I am not saying that every form of consciousness is also awareness, and all self-consciousness also consciousness; nor am I denying these propositions. I am only arguing that there is a peculiar state of mind that makes mental representing possible, and that is closely related to what we usually refer to as consciousness.

There is another way of understanding the notion of consciousness. It may be taken to be a state peculiarly transparent to itself, so that a person, when asked if he remembers something of which he was conscious a few moments ago, could never truthfully say 'No'. This is Sartre's 'conscience (de) soi' – a knowledge of what one is doing that does not have the explicitly intentional structure of self-consciousness. This may appear mystical. Consider, however, an example from game theory. The 'common knowledge' condition among the players in a game can be set up by an umpire or experimenter telling all the players, in each other's presence, about the rules of the game. This does not mean that each player must have, with respect to each of the others, an explicit knowledge that 'I know that he knows that . . . I know the rules of the game', since this would involve a completed infinite regress. Yet, for any n, if one asked the player whether he had knowledge of degree n about the other, he would say that he had such knowledge.

Frequently, consciousness in the sense of re-presenting what is absent goes together with consciousness in the sense of pre-intentional transparency. Freud, or some Freudians, may be understood as saying that there can be consciousness in the first sense unaccompanied by consciousness in the second sense. This, if I understand him rightly, is how David Pears (1984, p. 79) interprets and defends Freud's doctrine of the preconscious. On this view, mental representations may exist and do their work, whatever that is, even when the person cannot tell whether he has them. (To assert that they exist but do not do any work when the person does not know that he has them, is not, I believe, to say anything.) The preconscious on this conception is not just a store-house from which mental entities or their precursors can be retrieved when needed. It is itself the centre of a great many mental activities, such as representing, imagining, even choosing.

I feel deeply uncomfortable about this suggestion, but I do not feel my understanding of the problem goes far enough to buttress my uneasiness with arguments. Suffice it to say that the proposal does not appear to involve any logical contradiction (although I am not sure); it may be indispensable to account for certain mental phenomena that would otherwise be inexplicable (although in this domain such backward reasoning will never be conclusive); there could hardly be any sort of direct evidence for it (not even an analogy to the traces left by an electron in a cloud chamber); and it suffers from an almost total lack of structure (neither the *modus operandi* nor the scope of its operation is specified). Perhaps the best way of summarizing my uneasiness is that the preconscious, on this view, becomes detached both from the objective world (since the items in it are only *representations* of that world) and from the subject (since the person does not know whether he has them). Yet they are representations *of* the external world and belong in some sense *to* the subject. I seem to be able to handle either of these paradoxes by itself, but not both of them simultaneously.[13]

The achievement of George Ainslie's work, in this volume and elsewhere (notably Ainslie, 1982), is to make good analytical sense of what appeared to be the irreducibly metaphorical notions of id, ego and superego. The superego is a way of referring to an overly successful solution to the problem of self-control, that is, the problem of curbing the impulsiveness often referred to as the id. As briefly explained above, the central notion in his account of impulse control is that of *bunching of choices*. The other side of this coin, however, is that the self-control may turn into compulsive behaviour and rigid adherence to rules. The guiding principle 'Never suffer a single exception' is first applied to the specific kind of behaviour that one seeks to control, and then generalized and applied across the board. The superego on this view is not internalized parental authority, but an

---

[13] If animals have consciousness in the sense of having representations, they would appear to have it without possessing consciousness in the second sense. As I have defined the latter, it is necessarily accompanied by the potential for self-consciousness, in the sense of being able to relate to one's own (past) consciousness. If we deny self-consciousness to animals, how can we also ascribe to them consciousness in the first sense without getting into similar conceptual uneasiness? The short answer is that I do not know. More elaborate answers, in more speculative directions, might be suggested, but the ground is really too loose to give more than a momentary foothold.

endogenous by-product of strategies for self-control. The anxiety induced by the prospect of breaking a rule does not stem from infantile attitudes towards one's father, but from fear that the whole structure might unravel by a single violation of the rule, indeed of *any* rule. The person can, however, use a stratagem to give himself a break, without breaking down. He can orient himself by a system of *bright lines* or non-manipulable cues, which tell him when an exception is justified, given the circumstances, and when it is precisely the kind of temptation that motivated the rule in the first place. The autonomy of the person (or the strength of the ego) requires *loose bunching*. Bright lines are a form of mental book-keeping; hence the presently discussed loose bunching may not be unrelated to the reasons why the self tends to be only loosely integrated (cp. Section I above). An interaction between cognitive and motivational elements in creating behavioural slack seems plausible, even if the details elude us.

The two sets of issues I have been discussing have something in common. The ego (i.e. the person) is concerned with the future, while the id (the impulses) is guided by short-term pleasure. The id is climbing along a pleasure-gradient, which makes it as liable as other gradient-climbers to fall into the 'local-maximum trap' (Elster 1984, Ch. I; also Staddon 1983). Hence the id does not need any representation of the future. It scans the actual (as distinct from the potential, future, hypothetical, imagined) alternatives, and chooses the first one that will bring an increment of pleasure. To be sure, this is metaphorical language, treating the 'id' as a separate short-term maximizer competing with a long-term maximizer. Non-metaphorically, it amounts to saying that what is present and what is merely re-presented compete for our attention. I do not know whether those who advocate the possibility of preconscious representations believe that these can similarly compete with the actual, and not always lose out.

VIII. Split brain – split mind?

As a result of work on epileptic patients, it has been found that when the connections between the right and left brain hemispheres are severed, two semi-autonomous functional systems emerge.[14] The left

---

[14] The following is largely based on Springer and Deutsch (1981).

hemisphere controls speech, whereas the right is in charge of the visual and spatial processes. At least, this was the formulation that served as a vehicle for most of the earlier research. Later analysis suggests that other distinctions may be more appropriate. The left hemisphere is analytical, the right holistic; the left is based on sequential processing of information, the right on simultaneous processing.

Information comes to the right hemisphere from the left visual field, the left ear and the left hand; conversely information to the left hemisphere comes from the right side. In the normal brain the information is then pooled between the two hemispheres, but in split-brain patients this does not take place (or not in the same way). An answer to a question about a perceptual event will reflect only the information available to the left, speech-producing hemisphere. The patient will not be able to tell the nature of an object only presented to the left visual field. Yet the left hemisphere may express some awareness of that object, since it is aware of bodily reactions produced by the reception of information about the object in the right hemisphere. Thus a patient who was presented with the picture of a nude woman in the left field reacted emotionally to it, and then expressed a verbal explanation of what was going on. 'It is very common for the verbal left hemisphere to try to make sense of what has occurred in testing situations where information is presented to the right hemisphere. As a result, the left brain sometimes comes out with erroneous and often elaborate rationalizations based on partial cues' (Springer and Deutsch 1981, p. 33).

Split-brain is an extreme case of cognitive compartmentalization (cp. Section I), but I hesitate to talk about a divided self. The left and the right hemispheres do not seem to differ in goal or motivation. True, there have been conjectures about the 'egocentricity' of the left hemisphere (Springer and Deutsch, pp. 176–7), but not in a motivational sense. Rather, the idea seems to be that the left hemisphere is unwilling to admit that it may need cognitive assistance from the right. An experiment set up to find evidence for motivational conflict failed to do so (MacKay and MacKay 1982; cp. also Sergent 1983). Here one hemisphere, which could receive verbal stimuli and refer to them by non-verbal means, was exposed to a number. The other, verbal hemisphere would try to guess what the number was. The first hemisphere would then correct the guess by the non-verbal means at its disposal. The experimenters failed, however, when they tried to turn the game into one of conflict rather than cooperation. The two hemispheres refuse to be drawn into conflict. The authors concluded that although the left and the right hand 'were substantially separate at the cognitive level, their priorities gave no evidence of being under the supervision of two independent normative systems.'

Split-brain experiments also may tell us something about the functioning of the normal brain. In particular, it has been suggested that 'Certain aspects of right hemisphere functioning are congruent with the mode of cognition psychoanalysts have termed primary process, the form of thought that Freud originally assigned to the system Ucs (unconscious)'.[15] It has also been suggested that even in the normal brain the verbal hemisphere engages in a good deal of constructive interpretation of behaviour initiated by the non-verbal one.[16] On this view, each person contains several mental systems – emotional, motivational and perceptual.

> Then, as maturation continues, the behaviours that these separate systems emit are monitored by the one system we come to use more and more, namely, the verbal, natural language system. Gradually, a concept of self-control develops so that the verbal self comes to know the impulses for action that arise from the other selves, and it either tries to inhibit these impulses or free them, as the case may be.[17]

Clearly, these conjectures are related to the discussion in Section VII. Conceivably, they might one day create physiological underpinnings for a suitably purified and de-mythologized Freudian theory. For the time being, however, they offer only a loose parallel between two highly speculative hypotheses.

IX. Homo economicus and homo sociologicus

Each of us seems to be split between a private and a public self. The 'economic man' within us strives for personal hedonic satisfaction. He

---

[15] Galin (1974), cited after Springer and Deutsch (1981).
[16] Cp. the partially related problem discussed in Pears (1984), Ch. IX.
[17] Gazzaniga and LeDoux (1978), cited after Springer and Deutsch (1981, p. 199).

regards other people as so many means to his own selfish ends – or as constraints and obstacles to his pursuit of happiness. The 'social man', by contrast, is governed by moral and social norms. He is kept on course by his concern for other people, and by their approval or disapproval of his behaviour. The problem is to understand the relation between these two homunculi that – like the short-term and the long-term interest – constantly vie for our attention.[18] A paradigm case is that of explaining voting behaviour, with regard to which social scientists have manoeuvred themselves into a situation of theoretical schizophrenia. To explain *that* people vote, an appeal to civic duty or similar normative concepts seems inevitable; to explain *how* they vote, the appeal to self-interest is usually deemed sufficient (Barry 1979). It is as if the voter, upon entering the voting booth, shed the social motivations that had carried him there. Surely, this cannot be the right conceptualization – but what is?

Howard Margolis (1982, esp. Ch. 4) has proposed a general theory of altruist behaviour to explain such phenomena. On his theory, an individual such as Smith behaves as if he were made up of two persons. S-Smith and G-Smith, who are concerned with selfish benefits and group benefits respectively. The rule that explains how Smith's income is allocated between selfish and public purposes has two parts. First, the larger the ratio of the marginal utility of public spending to that of private spending, the greater the tendency for Smith to allocate a marginal dollar to G-Smith. Next, the higher the proportion of Smith's income already spent on public purposes, the larger the tendency to allocate the next dollar to S-Smith. Margolis suggests (among other comparisons)[19] that this is related to the way in which the ego mediates between the superego (G-Smith) and the id (S-Smith). The second part of the rule, in particular, corresponds to the idea that a person must know when to give himself a break – when to temper the claims of duty. It also captures our intuitive notion of doing one's *fair share* of contributing to the common good. Suggestive as this proposal is, it does not turn upon any substantive notion of a divided self. Contrary

[18] For extensive discussions of the analogies between prudence (i.e. long-term selfishness) and altruism, see Nagel (1970) and Parfit (1984). Norm-guided behaviour is not, however, the same as altruistic behaviour. For a discussion, see Elster (1985).

[19] In a passage cited in note 1, he also compares the allocation of personal income between selfish and public spending to the allocation of profit between investment at home and overseas investment.

to what Margolis says, I think the most natural way of understanding the allocation rules is in terms of a unitary preference structure. The *person* seems to be firmly in charge.

Some cases, however, suggest a real conflict between the economic and the social self. The former seems to be able to exploit ambiguities in the norms to get its way. Consider again the lawn-mowing example from Section I. An alternative explanation (suggested to me by Amos Tversky) of that behaviour could be that mowing the neighbour's lawn would be incompatible with the man's self-image. He simply does not think of himself as the kind of person who mows other people's lawns for money. Yet one might easily imagine that he would mow the lawn in return for the neighbour's donating $20 to charity, and that this might make him feel justified in withholding a contribution of $20 that *he* would otherwise have made to charity. The situation is materially equivalent to the first, yet under the new description ('mowing for charity') the behaviour is more acceptable than under the first ('mowing for money'). I believe that this kind of normative reframing (Tversky and Kahneman 1981) is very frequent. It is 'as if' the economic man within us tried to manipulate the way in which choice situations are presented and described, so as to induce the social man to take the course of action that the economic man prefers. Analogously, in the conflict between the short-term and the long-term interest, it often looks 'as if' the former tries to persuade the latter that *this* occasion constitutes a genuine exception to the rule. After all, it would be ridiculous not to take a drink when a friend drops by unexpectedly, or when my candidate wins the presidential election, or when . . . (See also Elster 1985).

This is not a question of trade-offs. True, the question of how much it will take to bribe me into violating a norm is a meaningful one (North 1981, Ch. 5). Even if I wouldn't mow my neighbour's lawn for $20, I might do it for $100. If I do it, however, it may be at some cost to my self-respect. The impact of reframing is to make it possible to violate a norm without any cost to myself; in fact the behaviour that formerly appeared norm-violating may now become positively prescribed. Norms of cooperation, in particular, depend for their application on the specification of the reference group, and may yield different prescriptions if that group is redefined. What appears as cooperative behaviour with respect to my fellow union members may no longer do so in the broader perspective of all workers (Olson 1982). The free rider may justify his behaviour to himself by placing it in a perspective that makes it appear as a form of society-wide or long-term cooperation. The pacifist who is asked, 'But who would fight the enemy if everyone acted like you?' may reply, 'If everyone acted like me, there would be no enemy to fight.'

I am not making the cynical point that a person may often be able to justify his behaviour to *others* by invoking norms on an *ad hoc* basis, exploiting the almost endless repertoire of norms to disguise the fact that he is moved by self-interest. My point is that a person must be able to live with his decisions – so he has to justify them to himself. There are constraints on the acceptable justifications. In particular, the need for consistency between the norms that are invoked in different situations may be as important as the consistency between the norm and the self-interest. Yet within these constraints a good deal of redefinition of norms is possible. My suggestion is that in addition to the head-on conflict between self-interest and social norms there is an insidious struggle that is more similar to self-deception and thus more closely related to the multiple self.

X. The 'no-self' theory

If the view that there can be a multiple self is carried to its extreme conclusion, it is more naturally labelled a 'no-self' theory. In the history of thought this view is associated especially with Hume; a more sophisticated and elaborate version is found in Buddhism.[20] Two Neo-Buddhist theories have recently been proposed by Serge-Christophe Kolm (1982) and by Derek Parfit (1984). I shall present a brief summary of Kolm's view, to provide a context for the chapter from his book, excerpted below.[21]

According to Buddhism, the human being at any given moment is made up of various elements (*dharma*), some of which constitute his body and others various mental states. Among the latter we find the belief in an enduring self, which is thought of both as the unchanging substance underlying the changing mental states and as the active centre of decision-making. Although the belief is an illusionary one, it

---

[20] For a good exposition, see Collins (1982).
[21] The following draws on Collins (1982) and on Kolm (1982).

is very difficult to shake it off, since it arises in a very natural, indeed compelling way. Hence Buddhism offers three doctrines with respect to the self. First, it contains a theoretical critique of the notion of an enduring self, together with a constructive analysis of the actual unity and continuity of the person. On Kolm's view, the unity of the person is merely a property of the causal chains that link together the successive mental states, so that an element can be ascribed to a person if it is sufficiently closely related to other elements that have already been imputed to him. Next, Buddhism offers an account of the emergence of the illusionary belief in the self. Among other things, the inherent logical difficulty of treating oneself as fully causally determined leads almost irresistibly to the invention of the notion of a free agent which is an active maker of decisions, not simply the aggregate of causally related mental states. Finally, Buddhism proposes a way of overcoming this spontaneously arising illusion, through study and meditation. The illusion is to be overcome not because it is a bad thing in itself to live under the sway of an illusion, but because this particular illusion generates so much unhappiness.

We should note the difference between a purely intellectual understanding of the non-self doctrine and the psychological or affective acceptance of the theory. The overt fetter of a theoretical belief in the self is of secondary importance compared to the 'selfishness inherent in the affective structure of experience' (Collins 1982, p. 101), indeed, excessive attachment to a theory of non-self is a sign that one has not liberated oneself from it affectively. 'Right view' in itself is simply one 'karmic agent' among others, a mental state causally producing other states of mind and not necessarily increasing peace of mind. For the latter, training and practice are required. There is a parallel here with psychoanalysis and its emphasis on the insufficiency (and sometimes the non-necessity) of *Bewusstwerden* as a condition of *Ichwerden*. There is also a vast difference, stated by Kolm in the final sentence of his book. Freud argued that 'where id was, Ego shall be'. Buddhism takes the further step of saying, 'where Ego was, consciousness shall be'.

Why should the belief in the existence of the self–ego lead to unhappiness? In the Zen version of Buddhism the answer is found in the corrosive effects of the habit of relating everything to self (cp. Elster 1983, Ch. II.2 and Smullyan 1980). If one is constantly thinking about the impression one is making on other people, instead of just getting ahead with the task at hand, one will not make much of an impression on them. Similarly, in order to overcome such problems as stuttering, insomnia or impotence, one must above all avoid an inward-looking or self-conscious attitude. In such cases there is an interference between the goal one has set for oneself and the way in which one is trying to achieve it. The goal is within reach, if only one can forget about it. These are states that are essentially by-products (Elster 1983, Ch. II): they can come about as a result of action, but cannot be brought about deliberately by action. Much of the attractiveness of Buddhism derives from this simple moral point, that happiness tends to elude those who search for it and to fall into the lap of those who concentrate on achieving substantial goals. This view can be stated without reference to any epistemological or ontological doctrine concerning the self.

Kolm, in his contribution below, argues for a different view. The frustration of desires can be eliminated by exploiting the total plasticity of character. Since there is no permanent self opposing or constraining character changes, one may act strategically on the desire and preferences so as to achieve the optimum of happiness, or the minimum of suffering. It may be worth while pointing out that his argument presupposes that frustration is inherently bad, contrary to the view (set out in Section VI above) that some frustration is indispensable for happiness. Kolm quotes Benjamin Franklin to the effect that pleasure is the liberation from suffering, but neglects to draw the conclusion that sustained pleasure therefore requires a steadily renewed suffering or frustration. No doubt the 'egonomical' framework[22] could be extended to incorporate the need for an optimal amount of frustration.

XI. Summary

Barring pathological cases (which I have not discussed here) we ought not to take the notion of 'several selves' very literally. In general, we are dealing with exactly *one* person – neither more nor less. That person may have some cognitive coordination problems, and some motivational conflicts, but it is *his* job to sort them out. They do not

[22] The phrase 'egonomics' was coined in Schelling (1978).

sort themselves out in an inner arena where several homunculi struggle to get the upper hand.

Yet some of the motivational conflicts are so deep-seated and permanent that the language of a divided self almost irresistibly forces itself on us. Although only one *person* is in charge, he is challenged by semi-autonomous strivings that confront him as 'alien powers'.[23] To get his way, he may have to resort to ruse and manipulation. The relationship is essentially asymmetrical: it is that of an intentional person confronting causal forces within himself. There is one possible exception. One of the alien powers may in an almost literal sense try to deceive him, by preventing him from acquiring a belief that would interfere with the desire for short-term gratification. For this to be possible, the subsystem must itself have some minimal degree of rationality and intentionality. Yet the person may take cognizance of his tendency to deceive himself, and counteract it with measures to which the deceiving subsystem has no further reply.

All the cases I have come across are dichotomous or trichotomous (disregarding the general *n*-person case discussed by Steedman and Krause). Dual selves underlie the distinction between myopia and prudence; between economic man and social man; between the left and the right hemispheres; between the day-time person who wants to stay alive and the night-time person who wants to be relieved of suffering and anxiety. The tripartite self is at the core of Freud's anatomy of the mind. Actually, this conception amounts to saying that *the* person tries to mediate between the long-term and the short-term interests, or between the private and the public man. The autonomous individual does not want to identify fully with any of these extreme strivings. He wants to do what *he* thinks is best, all things considered, not to be the slave of his impulses or of the rules and norms he has set for himself.

[23] Marx (1845–6, p. 262). Marx saw a close relation – causally as well as conceptually – between such intra-personal 'reification' of mental powers and the inter-personal 'alienation' of the individual from society.

REFERENCES

Ainslie, G. (1982) 'A behavioral economic approach to the defence mechanisms: Freud's energy theory revisited', *Social Science Information* 21, 735–70.

Barry, B. (1979) *Economists, Sociologists and Democracy*, rev. edn, University of Chicago Press.

Becker, G. (1977) *The Economic Approach to Human Behavior*, Chicago: University of Chicago Press.

Collins, S. (1982) *Selfless Persons*, Cambridge: Cambridge University Press.

Davidson, D. (1980) *Essays on Actions and Events*, Oxford: Oxford University Press.

Elster, J. (1983) *Sour Grapes*, Cambridge: Cambridge University Press.

Elster, J. (1984) *Ulysses and the Sirens*, rev. edn, Cambridge: Cambridge University Press.

Elster, J. (1985) 'Weakness of will and the free-rider problem', *Economics and Philosophy* 1, 231–66.

Frankfurt, H. (1971) 'Freedom of will and the concept of a person', *Journal of Philosophy* 68, 5–20.

Føllesdal, D. (1981) 'Sartre on freedom', in P. A. Schilpp (ed.), *Sartre* (The Library of Living Philosophers), pp. 392–407. La Salle, Ill.: Open Court.

Galin, D. (1974) 'Implications for psychiatry of left and right cerebral specialization', *Archives of General Psychiatry* 1974, 572–83.

Gazzaniga, M. S. and LeDoux, J. E. (1978) *The Integrated Mind*, New York: Plenum Press.

Goldman, A. (1978) 'Epistemics', *Journal of Philosophy* 75, 509–24.

Griffin, D. (1984) *Animal Thinking*, Cambridge, Mass.: Harvard University Press.

Kolm, S.-C. (1982) *Le Bonheur-liberté*, Paris: Presses Universitaires de France.

MacKay, D. M. and MacKay, V. (1982) 'Explicit dialogue between left and right half-systems of split brains', *Nature* 295, 690–1.

Margolis, H. (1982) *Selfishness, Altruism and Rationality*, Cambridge: Cambridge University Press.

Marx, K. (1845–6) *The German Ideology*, in Marx and Engels, *Collected Works*, vol. 5, London: Lawrence and Wishart.

Nagel, T. (1970) *The Possibility of Altruism*, Oxford: Oxford University Press.

Nisbett, R. and Ross, L. (1980) *Human Inference*, Englewood Cliffs, N.J.: Prentice Hall.

North, D. (1981) *Structure and Change in Economic History*, New York: Norton.

Olsen, M. (1982) *The Rise and Decline of Nations*, New Haven: Yale University Press.

Parfit, D. (1973) 'Later selves and moral principles', in A. Montefiore (ed.), *Philosophy and Personal Relations*, pp. 137–69. London: Routledge and Kegan Paul.

Parfit, D. (1984) *Reasons and Persons*, Oxford: Oxford University Press.

Pears, D. (1984) *Motivated Irrationality*, Oxford: Oxford University Press.

Schelling, T. C. (1963) *The Strategy of Conflict*, Cambridge, Mass.: Harvard University Press.

Schelling, T. C. (1978) 'Egonomics, or the art of self-management', *American Economic Review: Papers and Proceedings* 68, 290–4.

Schelling, T. C. (1980) 'The intimate contest for self-command', *The Public Interest* 60, 94–118. Cited after the reprint in Schelling (1984).

Schelling, T. C. (1983) 'Ethics, law, and the exercise of self-command', in S. McMurrin (ed.), *The Tanner Lectures on Human Values IV*, Salt Lake City: University of Utah Press, 43–79. Cited after the reprint in Schelling (1984).

Schelling, T. C. (1984) *Choice and Consequence*, Cambridge, Mass.: Harvard University Press.

Schumpeter, J. (1961) *Capitalism, Socialism and Democracy*, London: Allen and Unwin.

Sen, A. (1977) 'Rational fools', *Philosophy and Public Affairs* 6, 317–44.

Sergent, J. (1983) 'Unified response to bilateral hemispheric stimulation by a split-brain patient', *Nature* 305, 800–2.

Smullyan, R. (1980) *This Book Needs No Title*, Englewood Cliffs, N.J.: Prentice Hall.

Springer, S. and Deutsch, G. (1981) *Left Brain, Right Brain*, San Francisco: Freeman.

Staddon, J. E. R. (1983) *Adaptive Behavior and Learning*, Cambridge: Cambridge University Press.

Thaler, R. (1980) 'Towards a positive theory of consumer behavior', *Journal of Economic Behavior and Organization* 1, 39–60.

Thaler, R. and Shefrin, M. (1981) 'An economic theory of self-control', *Journal of Political Economy* 89, 392–406.

Tversky, A. and Kahneman, D. (1981) 'The framing of decisions and the rationality of choice', *Science* 211, 543–58.

Veyne, P. (1978) *Le Pain et le Cirque,* Paris: Seuil.

Veyne, P. (1983) *Les Grecs ont-ils cru a leurs mythes?* Paris: Seuil.

Winston, G. (1980) 'Addiction and backsliding', *Journal of Economic Behavior and Organization* 1, 295–324.

1. Self-deception and the voter's illusion*

GEORGE A. QUATTRONE AND AMOS TVERSKY

A major problem in the analysis of choice concerns the relationship between actions and outcomes. A common assumption is that actions have a causal effect on outcomes. Some actions, however, may be primarily diagnostic of outcomes in that actions and outcomes may both be consequences of a common antecedent cause. When actions are merely diagnostic of outcomes, rather than causal, the analysis of choice becomes more problematic. The extensive literature on Newcomb's paradox is a case in point. In this chapter, we first discuss the normative problem of causal versus diagnostic contingencies. We then turn from the logical to the psychological analysis, where we argue that decision-makers sometimes fail to distinguish between causal and diagnostic contingencies. We further relate our psychological analysis to the theory of cognitive dissonance and to the concept of self-deception. Next, we describe an experiment in which subjects selected actions that were diagnostic of the outcomes, 'good health and longevity', although it was clear to subjects that the actions would have no causal effect on their state of health. A second experiment is presented to demonstrate that an individual may view his own choices as diagnostic of the choices likely to be made by his like-minded peers. The results of the experiment, which are indicative of what we call the 'voter's illusion', may help explain why some people vote in large elections despite the low probability of casting a decisive ballot. Finally, we discuss further implications and extensions of these ideas.

*This research was supported in part by ONR Grant N00014-79-C-0077. The authors would like to acknowledge the assistance of Jane Boreta, Doug Passaro, and Nellie Yoshida in serving as experimenters. This chapter is adapted from an article that appeared in the *Journal of Personality and Social Psychology*, 40.

The logic of decision

Because the outcome of a decision often depends on past or future states of nature that cannot be known with certainty, it is reasonable for the decision-maker to weigh the possible outcomes of an action by the probability of the states on which they depend. In many situations, the relevant states of nature are independent of one's choice. Despite numerous anecdotes to the contrary, the probability of rain does not depend on whether one has decided to wash one's car. We shall use the conventional notation for conditional probabilities, $P(S/A)$, to refer to the probability of a state, S, given act, A. Thus, the state 'rain' is independent of the act 'car wash' in the sense that $P(S/A) = P(S/\text{not } A)$ $= P(S)$, the marginal (i.e. pre-decisional) probability of rain.

It is not always true that the relevant states of nature are independent of one's choice. In deliberating over whether to stop smoking, for example, the decision-maker must weigh the pleasures of tobacco and the pain of withdrawal against the possibility of premature death. Clearly, the risk of contracting lung cancer (S) is not independent of whether one abstains (A) from smoking in that $P(S/A) < P(S/\text{not } A)$. Because states may not be independent of one's choice, the value of each outcome associated with a particular act should be weighted by the probability of the outcome conditional on selecting the act (Jeffrey 1965).

This conception becomes problematic when it is recognized that acts may be *causal* or *diagnostic* of outcomes with which they are correlated. Consider the historical controversy over how to interpret the correlation between smoking and cancer. It is now widely acknowledged that smoking has a direct causal effect on the etiology of lung cancer. But it has not always been so clear. As late as 1959, R. A. Fisher, the great statistician, argued that the correlation could be attributable to a genetic trait that predisposed the individual towards both smoking and cancer. To Fisher, smoking was diagnostic of lung cancer, not causal, in that smoking was merely a sign that the individual had been born with the pre-cancerous gene. Despite the fact that smoking may have a lower expected desirability than abstaining if the value of the outcomes are weighted by the respective conditional probabilities, Fisher cited his genetic thesis as reason enough for lighting up.

One may certainly object to Fisher's theory about the linkage between smoking and cancer. But if the theory were true, Fisher's decision to continue smoking is defensible. According to this theory one either has or does not have the pre-cancerous gene, and hence one's decision to smoke or not does not facilitate or inhibit the emergence of cancerous cells. True, smokers are more likely to die of cancer than non-smokers. But the correlation is channelled through the presence or absence of a genetic trait beyond the individual's control.

One way to conceptualize the problem is to imagine that the hypothetical pre-cancerous gene exerts its influence on smoking by first producing a yen or an urge to smoke (Jeffrey 1981). The knowledge that one does not have the urge (A^*) or that one does, effectively 'screens off' the correlation between the act of smoking (not-A) and cancer (S), in the sense that $P(S/A \& A^*) = P(S/\text{not } A \& A^*) < P(S/A \& \text{not } A^*) = P(S/\text{not } A \& \text{not } A^*)$. The inequality indicates that among people without the urge and among people with the urge, smoking is independent of cancer. The overall correlation between smoking and cancer is merely a consequence of there being more smokers and pre-cancerous persons among people with the gene-induced urge than among people without the urge. Hence, upon recognizing that one has the urge to smoke, one who subscribes to Fisher's theory ought to light up because, given the urge, cancer is independent of smoking. Most philosophical analyses of the problem (Nozick 1969; Gibbard and Harper 1978; Skyrms 1980; Jeffrey 1981) defend smoking under the above assumptions, but question whether it is always possible to screen off the correlation between action and outcome.

The psychology of choice

We now turn from the logical to the psychological analysis, which is complicated by the fact that causal and diagnostic contingencies are usually confounded in the real world. Suppose undergraduates know that students who attend a review session for the final examination get better grades than students who do not attend. Does the correlation between attendance and grade mean that the review session really helps? Or does it mean that reviews are attended primarily by conscientious students who would do well, session or no? Insofar as there is uncertainty about the causal or diagnostic significance of the action (attendance) with respect to the outcome (grade), it is reasonable for students to entertain the causal hypothesis, play it safe and attend the session. We hypothesize, however, that people would select an action correlated with an auspicious outcome even if they believed that the action is only diagnostic of the outcome and in no way causal. Thus even if students were presented with compelling evidence that review sessions have no causal influence on their examination performance, and they accept the evidence, they might nonetheless be tempted to attend, so long as better grades are associated with attendance than with non-attendance.

This problem is reminiscent of the well-known dilemma faced by Calvinists, who subscribe to divine pre-determination. As drawn in the left-hand side of figure 1, Calvinists believe that there are two kinds of people, the chosen and the not-chosen. Whether one is chosen or not has already been decided by the deity prior to one's birth. There are at least two consequences of the deity's decision. First, the chosen will enter paradise after death, whereas the not-chosen will suffer eternal damnation in hell. Second, the chosen will lead a life of virtue, whereas the not-chosen will lead a life of sin. Calvinists do not know who among them are the chosen. But they know that avarice, lust and sloth are sinful acts correlated with eternal damnation. Conversely, they know that charity, purity and hard work are virtuous acts correlated with eternal post-mortal bliss. Although the acts are not believed to influence one's posthumous fate, most Calvinists conclude that they had better live by the *Book* in that the immediate gratifications of the flesh seem hardly worth an eternity in hell. That Calvinists may confuse diagnostic and causal contingencies is illustrated by the following letter circulated by Baptists in 1770: 'Every soul that comes to

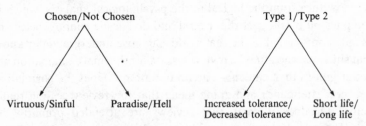

Fig. 1. Illustrated causal structures

Christ to be saved . . . is to be encouraged . . . The coming soul need not fear that he is not elected, for none but such would be willing to come.'

What about the 'urge' or the temptation to sin? Do Calvinists not recognize that temptation itself should screen off the correlation between the virtuousness of one's act and the location of one's life after death? After all, only the not-chosen would even contemplate a dissolute deed. The normative analysis of Fisher's smoking theory would suggest that Calvinists ought to transgress upon experiencing the desire to do so, *ceteris paribus*, for heaven and hell are independent of action conditional on the urge to sin. Contrary to this analysis, we believe that many Calvinists would nonetheless resist the temptation and choose instead the virtuous acts correlated with paradise.

The notion that people may confuse causal and diagnostic contingencies is familiar to social psychologists (see Abelson *et al.* 1968). The theory of cognitive dissonance (Festinger 1957) is an illustrative case. According to this theory, an individual who holds two or more cognitions (i.e., attitudes and beliefs) that are psychologically inconsistent will experience an uncomfortable state of tension, called dissonance. The individual will then be 'driven' to reduce dissonance by changing one or more of the cognitions so that they are no longer inconsistent. For example, suppose a college freshman suffers embarrassment and exerts considerable physical effort as part of an initiation procedure to join a fraternity. Having become a member, he discovers that the organization falls far short of his previous expectations: the food is tasteless, and the parties are dull. The cognition, 'this is a lousy fraternity', can be regarded as psychologically inconsistent with the cognition, 'I incurred costs to enter the fraternity', in the sense that people do not ordinarily expend great effort to attain an undesirable goal. The resulting dissonance can be reduced by re-evaluating the fraternity: 'the food is not really all that bad, and the parties are as good as any on campus'. This hypothesized process can be analysed in terms of the confusion between causal and diagnostic contingencies. It is commonly thought that there is a relationship between the costs one bears to join a group and the overall desirability of the group. The causal impact usually flows from 'desirability' to 'costs'. That is, one is willing to bear costs to enter a group because it is desirable; the group does not become desirable because one bore costs to enter it. Dissonance theory predicts, however, that people may reverse the causal and diagnostic relationships. Thus an individual who, in the absence of bearing costs, would rate two groups as equally desirable would subsequently rate as more desirable the group for which he bore more costs to enter. Hence, the cost one bears comes to influence one's evaluation of the group rather than being merely diagnostic of one's evaluation of the group. The example also illustrates how causal and diagnostic contingencies are confounded in the real world. If we knew only that an individual evaluates highly a group he exerted much effort to join, it is difficult to discern whether he was willing to exert the effort because he had already evaluated the group highly, or whether he evaluated the group highly because of the effort he expended. Finally, dissonance theory does not claim that people must engage in actions that are diagnostic of an inference *in order to* accept the inference. The freshman does not have to act as though the fraternity were desirable to accept the belief that it is. The re-evaluation may be achieved solely through cognitive means. Once the belief is accepted, however, the individual may, according to dissonance theory, act in line with the belief; for example, he may praise the fraternity in public. In contrast, we suspect that these actions may not simply 'follow from' the newly accepted belief. The actions may in part be motivated by the individual's attempt to convince himself that the belief is valid.

Dissonance theory is not inconsistent with the notion that people may select *actions* enabling them to make favourable inferences. The theory allows dissonance to be reduced either through cognitive or behavioural means. What has not been investigated in the social psychological literature are the conditions under which people would be 'taken in' by their own actions. How could actors reasonably make a favourable diagnosis from their behaviour when the behaviour was enacted in order to make the diagnosis? What comfort could a Calvinist derive from a virtuous act if performed while one is tempted to sin? One possibility is that people do not quite recognize that for diagnostic contingencies the urge to act (e.g., to smoke or to sin) screens off the correlation between action and outcome. People may adopt a quasi-behaviouristic doctrine in which actions speak louder than urges and related inner states. This account is consistent with Bem's (1972) theory of self-perception in that inferences about the self are assumed to be based solely on the observation of one's own behaviour and on the external circumstances in which one behaves. It is also possible, however, that a certain degree of self-deception may contribute to the acceptance of the diagnosis implied by one's behaviour. That is, actors may have to avoid admitting to themselves that the behaviour was produced more by the motive to infer an auspicious antecedent cause than by the auspicious antecedent cause itself. Calvinists may deny their temptation to sin and convince themselves that the virtuous act was not selected merely to defend against the inference of not being chosen.

Gur and Sackheim (1979) have characterized self-deception by the following criteria: (a) the individual simultaneously holds two contradictory beliefs, (b) the individual is not aware of holding one of the beliefs and (c) the lack of awareness is motivated. We are arguing that when people select actions to infer an auspicious antecedent cause, then, to accept the inference as valid, they often render themselves unaware of the fact that they selected the action just in order to infer the cause. Unless they deny to themselves that their action was purposefully chosen to make a favourable diagnosis, they may not attribute the action to the target antecedent cause but rather to the motive to infer that cause. This view is compatible with the criteria put forth by Gur and Sackheim. The beliefs, 'I purposefully engaged in the behaviour to make a favourable diagnosis', and 'I did not purposefully engage in the behaviour to make a favourable diagnosis', are clearly contradictory (a), and one's lack of awareness (b) regarding the former belief is motivated by the individual's desire to accept the diagnosis implied by behaviour (c). When people select an action to make a favourable diagnosis, but fail to realize that they purposefully selected the action in order to make the diagnosis, we classify the action and the denial collectively as a form of *deceptive diagnosis*.

Deceptive diagnosis

We now describe an experiment that tested our basic thesis that people select actions diagnostic of favourable outcomes, even if it is clear that the action does not facilitate the outcome. Self-report measures were also included to test the notion that, even if people do engage in the diagnostic behaviour, the favourable diagnosis would be made primarily by subjects who deny that the action was purposefully selected. We chose to investigate these issues in a medical context. Medical examinations consist of tests that are diagnostic or indicative of one's underlying state of health. How one does on the examination does not, in general, affect one's state of health. Rather, it is one's state of health that determines how one does on the examination. If people were given an opportunity, we predict that they would 'cheat' on a medical examination in a direction correlated with desirable outcomes, such as good health and longevity. To test this hypothesis, we constructed an analogue of the Calvinist dilemma in the medical realm. Subjects learned that there were two kinds of hearts, namely, Type 1 and Type 2. Heart type allegedly had two sets of consequences. First, people with Type 1 heart are frequently ill, are prone to heart disease, and have a shorter-than-average life expectancy. People with Type 2 heart enjoy good health, have a low risk of heart disease, and show a longer-than-average life expectancy. Second, heart type was said to determine how exercise would change an individual's tolerance to cold water. Half of our subjects were informed that a Type 1 heart would increase tolerance to cold water after exercise whereas a Type 2 heart would decrease tolerance. The remaining subjects learned that a Type 1 heart would decrease tolerance to cold water after exercise, whereas a Type 2 heart would increase tolerance. We shall refer to these treatments as the Decrease and Increase conditions, respectively, to indicate the change in tolerance associated with good health and longevity. The righthand side of figure 1 illustrates the correlational structure received by subjects in the Decrease condition. All three variables (i.e., heart type, life expectancy and shifts in tolerance) were treated as continuous. For example, subjects in the Increase condition were led to believe that the closer they are to having a Type 2 heart, the more would exercise increase their tolerance and the longer would their life expectancy be.

Subjects first underwent a baseline trial of the cold-pressor pain task (Hilgard *et al.* 1974), which requires them to submerge their forearms into a chest of circulating cold water until they can no longer tolerate it. Subjects then pedalled an exercycle for one minute, which was followed by the information about heart types, life expectancy, and tolerance shifts. Subjects then repeated the cold-pressor task to their tolerance threshold in the presence of a second 'blind' experimenter. Finally, subjects indicated on a questionnaire whether they believed they were Type 1 or Type 2 and whether they had purposefully tried to alter the amount of time they kept their arm in the water on the post-exercise trial. We tested the following three hypotheses:

1. On the post-exercise or 'experimental' trial, subjects would shift their tolerance threshold in the direction correlated with health and longevity: that is, a downward shift in the Decrease condition and an upward shift in the Increase condition. The prediction for the Increase condition is especially noteworthy because it implies that people will incur painful consequences of their action so long as the action were diagnostic of an outcome more important than transient pain.

2. By and large, subjects will deny that they purposefully tried to shift their tolerance on the post-exercise trial.

3. Those subjects who do admit that they had purposefully tried to shift their tolerance would be less likely to infer that they had the preferred Type 2 heart than would subjects who deny the attempt to shift.

Procedure

The subjects were 38 undergraduates at Stanford University. They arrived for an experiment on the 'psychological and medical aspects of athletics'. The experimental room was on the physiological floor of the psychology building where animals, chemicals and electronic equipment are readily visible. The location was selected to establish credibility for our alleged interest in cardiovascular matters. A female experimenter, wearing a white lab coat, told subjects that the purpose of the study was to examine the effects of rapid changes in temperature on heart rate after exercise. The research question was allegedly inspired by wondering what were the coronary implications of athletes' jumping into a cold shower after working out on a hot day. Subjects were given an overview of the entire experimental procedure. The cold-pressor task was said to provide the necessary 'change in temperature', pulse-readings to provide the measures of 'heart rate', and pedalling an exercycle to provide the 'exercise'. Subjects understood that they would undergo two trials of the cold-pressor task, each followed by a pulse-reading, and separated from each other by a minute of exercycling. Thus the first trial would provide a baseline measure of heart rate in response to temperature change, which could then be compared to heart rate in response to temperature change following exercise. After subjects understood the procedure and were forewarned of the discomfort associated with the cold-pressor task, they were asked to express their informed consent. All subjects consented.

The baseline trial of the cold-pressor was administered after subjects had given their consent. The apparatus consisted of a picnic chest, partitioned in the middle and filled with water. Ice cubes were placed in one side of the partition, and a motor circulated the water to maintain its temperature at about 35°F. Subjects immersed their bare hands and forearms into the water. After every five seconds they reported a number from one to ten to express their discomfort. The number ten was taken to mean that point at which subjects would rather not tolerate the cold any longer. When subjects reached ten, they were asked to remove their arm from the chest. Subjects reported their numbers in response to a letter called out by the experimenter. Subjects heard 'A' after five seconds, 'B' after ten seconds, 'C' after fifteen seconds and so on. This procedure was used to help subjects to recall how long they tolerated the water on the baseline trial thus providing them with a target for the experimental trial. Subjects then had their pulse taken and pedalled an exercycle vigorously for one minute.

A brief 'rest period' was inserted between the exercycling and the experimental cold-pressor trial. This interval gave the experimenter the opportunity to present the correlational structure discussed previously. To prevent subjects from discovering the true purpose of the study, the crucial information was embedded in a mini-lecture on psychophysics. Subjects learned that the cold-pressor was used to study the psychophysics of pain. Psychophysics was defined as the attempt to relate mathematically the perception of a stimulus to the physical properties of a stimulus. Subjects were shown a curve on a blackboard that related time of immersion in cold water to subjective discomfort (i.e., numbers from one to ten). The curve depicted the typical relationship and it was said to be based on data averaged over many people. Individual differences were said to exist, illustrated by showing two curves that reached ten at different rates. Skin type was said to be one factor that distinguished between people with high or low tolerance to cold water. Heart type was said to be another factor.

Subjects learned that people could be characterized as having either one of two cardiovascular complexes, referred to as Type 1 and Type 2 hearts. Subjects viewed a histogram, on a glossy photograph, which showed that longer life expectancies were associated with increasing degrees of Type 2 hearts and that shorter life expectancies were associated with increasing degrees of Type 1 hearts. Allegedly, some investigators had suggested that Type 1 subjects do not differ from Type 2 subjects in tolerance on the pre-exercise trial. However, exercise supposedly may create a difference between the two types. Subjects were then randomly assigned to either the Decrease or Increase described earlier. The information was conveyed verbally and displayed in a histogram.

A second female experimenter administered the experimental cold-pressor trial. To guard against experimenter bias, she was blind to subjects' condition and performance on the baseline trial. We also tried to reduce the likelihood that subjects would show self-presentational shifts in tolerance to impress the experimenter that they were healthy. First, it was made clear to subjects that there was a lot of variability within Types 1 and 2 on both trials. Thus, the second experimenter could not infer from the length of the second trial subjects' likely type. Only shifts between trials would be telling. Second, subjects were assured that the first experimenter would be kept ignorant of their performance on the second trial and that the second experimenter would be kept ignorant of their performance on the baseline trial. Thus, neither experimenter would have the data required to infer subjects' likely type. Finally, the experimenter who administered the post-experimental trial was presented as a secretary, wearing ordinary clothing, employed here simply to administer the trial. Thus her appearance and behaviour were designed to make it seem as though she knew nothing of the study's hypotheses, description or rationale. After the second cold-pressor trial, subjects completed a brief questionnaire. They were asked to infer whether they were Type 1 or 2, and they checked either 'Yes' or 'No' to the question, 'Did you purposefully try to alter the amount of time you kept your hand in the water after exercise?' Finally, subjects were thoroughly debriefed of all deception and sworn to secrecy. Prior to the debriefing, no subject could articulate the hypotheses when probed.

Table 1. *Mean time of immersion in seconds*

Condition	Baseline	Trial Experimental	Change
Decrease	44.74	37.11	−7.63
Increase	34.21	46.05	+11.84

Results

The number of seconds during which subjects kept their arms in the cold water was recorded after each of the two trials. The cell means are shown in table 1. In line with our first hypothesis, subjects in the Decrease condition showed significantly less tolerance on the experimental trial than on the baseline trial, $F(1,36) = 9.41, p < .005$, whereas subjects in the Increase condition showed significantly more tolerance, $F(1,36) = 23.25, p < .001$.

Of the 38 subjects tested, 27 showed the predicted shift (13 of 19 in the Decrease condition and 14 of 19 in the Increase condition), and 11 did not, $p < .01$ by the sign test. Five subjects in each condition showed no shift, whereas one subject in the Decrease condition, a 'suicidal type', showed a shift opposite from prediction.

Only 9 of our 38 subjects indicated on the anonymous questionnaire that they had purposefully tried to change the amount of time they held their hand in the water after exercise. In line with our second hypothesis, this number was smaller than the number (i.e., 29) who indicated no attempt to shift, $p < .005$ by sign test. The tendency to deny or to admit an attempt to shift could not be attributed to actual differences in behaviour. That is, the percentage of subjects who did shift as predicted was no greater among subjects who indicated that they tried to shift (67%) than it was among subjects who indicated that they did not try to shift (72%). Table 2 shows the mean changes in tolerance in the Decrease and Increase conditions both for the group of subjects who indicated that they did try to shift ('non-deniers') and for the group who indicated that they did not try to shift ('deniers'). The predicted difference between conditions was significant within each group of subjects, and no interaction between condition and subjects' group was observed, $F(1,34) < 1$.

We have shown that a majority of subjects show the hypothesized shift and that a majority deny that they attempted to shift. Moreover,

Table 2. *Mean time in tolerance*

	Subjects' self-reported group	
Condition	Non-Deniers	Deniers
Decrease	−5.00	−8.13
Increase	+19.11	+8.08
Difference	24.17	16.21
$F(1,34)$	11.54	18.61
p	.005	.001

the deniers did not differ from the non-deniers in the degree to which their behaviour was diagnostic of having a Type 2 heart. In line with our third hypothesis, however, the two groups of subjects *did* differ in their acceptance of the diagnosis implied by their behaviour. Only two of the nine non-deniers (or 22%) inferred having a Type 2 heart, whereas 20 of the 29 deniers (or 69%) inferred a Type 2 heart, $p < .05$.

To summarize, the preceding experiment employed a procedure that resembles a medical examination. Subjects believed that a directional change in tolerance to cold water correlated with their state of health and expected lifespan. It should have been clear to subjects that shifts in tolerance would have no *causal* impact on their life expectancy. Shifts would be merely *diagnostic* of their life expectancy in that both shifts and life expectancy were affected by an individual's heart type. As predicted, subjects 'cheated' on this medical examination in a direction that correlated with having a robust heart and long expected life. Subjects who believed that longevity was associated with an exercise-induced decrease in tolerance removed their arm from near-freezing water sooner after exercise than before exercise. Subjects who believed that longevity was associated with an exercise-induced increase in tolerance removed their arm from the water later after exercise than before exercise. The latter result indicated that people are willing to bear painful behavioural consequences so long as the behaviour is a sign, though not a cause, of good health and long life.

As hypothesized, a majority of subjects indicated that they had not purposefully tried to alter the amount of time they kept their hand in the cold. Moreover, the few subjects who indicated that they did try to shift were no more likely to show the predicted shift than were the many subjects who indicated no attempt to shift. In the post-experimental interview, the first experimenter asked subjects who shifted why they had done so. Subjects in the Decrease condition would typically say something like, 'The water felt a lot colder', whereas subjects in the Increase condition would say something like, 'The water just didn't feel so cold anymore'. By themselves, these data may signify only that subjects were reluctant to admit to the experimenter that they had 'falsified' their scores. The self-presentational account appears less plausible, however, when we consider these data in conjunction with subjects' private inferences as to whether they were Type 1 or Type 2. A majority of the subjects who indicated on the anonymous questionnaire that they tried to shift inferred that they were Type 1, fated to a life of illness. But the majority of subjects who indicated no attempt to shift inferred that they were Type 2. These inferential differences were obtained despite there being no behavioural differences between the deniers and non-deniers. The data therefore suggest that a majority of subjects may have been reluctant to admit to *themselves* that they acted with a target inference in mind. Subjects probably sensed the dubious legitimacy of an inference based on behaviour that was motivated by the desire to make the inference. Denying the ulterior motive makes it easier for subjects to make the comforting diagnosis. Conversely, the difficulty of denying one's intentions may help explain the limited success of behavioural therapies. Clients are trained to act assertively, but they do not feel like assertive people because they know that the behaviour is a deliberate attempt to create an assertive image and is thus an invalid indicator.[1] To be sure, self-deception and denial are not matters of all-or-none. Deceptive diagnosis may come in finer gradations than would be apparent from dichotomous reports. Even subjects who indicated no attempt to shift may have harboured a lingering doubt to the contrary.

The voter's illusion

The idea that people may select an action to make a favourable self-diagnosis is not new. The first experiment went beyond earlier treatments of the problem by demonstrating that self-deception may contribute to accepting the diagnosis implied by behaviour. The

---

[1] We are indebted to an anonymous reviewer for bringing this point to our attention.

second experiment extends our analysis of the problem further by testing the hypothesis that people would select actions correlated with auspicious outcomes, even if the actions do not directly involve inferences about oneself. For example, an individual may regard his or her own decisions as diagnostic of the decisions likely to be made by other 'like-minded' persons. If the individual recognizes that beneficial outcomes would ensue if very many like-minded persons select a particular alternative, then the individual may select that alternative, even if the choice is costly, not witnessed by others and not likely by itself to affect the final outcome. In these circumstances, the choice is made to 'induce' others who think and act like oneself to do the same, rather than to make comforting diagnoses about one's own attributes. The following analysis of voting is a case in point.

Political scientists have long noted the paradoxical nature of an individual's voting in large national elections. A single vote is highly unlikely to be decisive, and the time and effort required to register and vote can be considerable. To understand voting in terms of rational choice, political scientists have maintained that an individual may derive from voting other benefits than just the prospect of casting the decisive ballot (cp. Riker and Ordeshook 1968). These additional benefits may include fulfilling one's duty as a citizen, participating in a common social ritual and signalling to others that voting is essential for the survival of democracy. To these rational *causal* consequences of voting, we suggest adding a less rational *diagnostic* aspect. People may reason that, within the electorate, there are citizens whose political orientation is similar to theirs (i.e., like-minded persons) as well as citizens whose political orientation is dissimilar (i.e., unlike-minded persons). The political dichotomy may be based on a single important issue, like abortion, or on an entire ideology, like liberalism/conservatism. Two sets of consequences may follow from political orientation. First, like-minded persons would prefer one line of candidates, whereas unlike-minded persons would prefer the opposing line. Second, political orientation may also affect the likelihood of voting. There are three relevant possibilities to consider: like-minded persons may vote in larger numbers than do unlike-minded persons; unlike-minded persons may vote in larger numbers than do like-minded persons; or there may be no relationship between political orientation and likelihood of voting. One may not know which of these three states of the world will be in effect in the upcoming election. But one may reason that if one votes, then one's politically like-minded peers, who think and act like oneself, will also vote. Conversely, if one abstains, then one's like-minded peers will also abstain. Because the preferred candidates could defeat the opposition only if like-minded citizens vote in larger numbers than do unlike-minded citizens, the individual may conclude that he or she had better vote. That is, an individual may regard his or her *single* vote as diagnostic of *millions* of votes, and hence as a sign that the preferred candidates will emerge victorious. This analysis of voting can be likened to a Prisoner's Dilemma game played by identical twins, which is a variant of the well-known Newcomb's paradox (Nozick 1969). The twins reason that each will eventually select the same option. Therefore, each twin should select the dominated cooperative response to 'induce' the other to do the same.

To explore the plausibility of 'diagnostic voting', we created a political scenario about an imaginary country named Delta, whose electorate consisted of 4 million supporters of Party A, 4 million supporters of Party B and 4 million non-aligned voters. Subjects were asked to imagine that they support Party A, and that they wonder whether it is worthwhile to vote in the upcoming election. They were presented with one of two theories about who would determine the margin of victory in the election. Both theories maintained that the victorious party would win by a margin of 200,000 to 400,000 votes. But according to the 'Non-Aligned Voters Theory', party supporters will vote in roughly equal numbers; hence the margin of victory will be determined by the non-aligned voters, who will either swing disproportionately for Party A or for Party B depending on which group of political experts one consulted. In contrast, the Party Supporters Theory held that non-aligned voters will split their vote equally between the two parties. The margin of victory would therefore depend on which of the two parties voted in greater numbers. That is, supporters of one party will be more likely to vote than supporters of the other party, although the political experts did not agree as to which party it would be.

Note that the Party Supporters Theory holds that there will be a correlation between political orientation and vote turnout. That is, either the supporters of Party A will vote in greater numbers than the

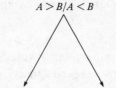

$A > B/A < B$

I vote/I abstain   Party A wins/Party B wins

Fig. 2. Voting decisions faced by subjects in the party supporters' condition

supporters of Party B (i.e., $A > B$) or vice-versa (i.e., $A < B$). In contrast, the Non-aligned Voters Theory holds that there will be no correlation ($A = B$). The correlational structure expected to be generated by subjects in the Party Supporters condition is shown in figure 2. Thus although the causal consequences of voting were held constant across the two theories, only subjects who receive the Party Supporters Theory could regard their decision to vote or to abstain as diagnostic of the decision reached by the other supporters of Party A. Because one's decision to vote would be diagnostic of a favourable electoral outcome only for subjects exposed to the Party Supporters Theory, these subjects should show a greater willingness to vote than should subjects who receive the Non-aligned Voters Theory. To test these hypotheses, we asked subjects a number of questions after they had read the respective theory, four of which assessed conditional probabilities. Assuming the theory were true, the subjects were asked how likely is it that the supporters of Party A will vote in greater numbers than the supporters of Party B (i.e., $A > B$) given that the subject votes (i.e., V) and given that the subject abstains. The next two questions were similar in that the subject now estimated the probability of Party A's defeating Party B conditional on the subject's voting or abstaining. Finally, subjects were asked whether they would vote, assuming the theory were true and voting were costly. We made the following predictions:

1. The differences in inferred probabilities conditional on voting and abstaining will be greater among subjects who receive the Party Supporters Theory than among those who receive the Non-aligned Voters Theory. That is $P(A > B/V) - P(A > B/\text{not } V)$ will be greater in the former condition than in the latter condition, and this difference will hold for '$A > B$' as well as for 'Party A defeats Party B'.

2. Subjects who receive the Party Supporters Theory will indicate a

greater willingness to vote than will subjects who receive the Non-aligned Voters Theory.

3. The greater the difference in inferred probabilities conditional on voting and abstaining, the greater the willingness to vote. That is, the more a subject believes that his or her voting is diagnostic of what other supporters of Party A would do, the more willing is the subject to vote.

Procedure

The subjects were 315 Stanford undergraduate volunteers. The diagnostic voting problem was included in a questionnaire that subjects completed in their dormitories. It presented the information given in the introduction to this experiment in greater detail. Subjects were asked to imagine themselves citizens of the nation, Delta, which was said to have two major opposing parties. Party A favours peace and prosperity. Party B favours offensive warfare. Subjects imagined they were supporters of Party A, which consists of politically like-minded persons. Delta was about to hold an election with the presidency and other important offices being contested. A recent poll showed that 4 million eligible voters supported Party A, 4 million supported Party B and 4 million were not aligned with either party. Subjects imagined that they were deciding whether to vote, for registering to vote in Delta is costly in time and effort. They could not ask others if they would vote, because it is considered impolite in Delta to inquire into the voting intentions of others. To facilitate the decision, they were to consult the prevailing theory about the sort of voters that determine the margin of victory for the winning party. The proponents of the theory were said to be expert political analysts.

Subjects who received the Party Supporters Theory learned that the non-aligned voters would split their votes equally between the two parties. The outcome of the election would be due to the fact that the supporters of Party A will differ from the supporters of Party B in how involved they become in the election. Half of the experts believed that Party A supporters would become more involved than Party B supporters and half believed that Party B supporters would become more involved than Party A supporters. All experts agreed that the party whose supporters became more involved would win by a margin of

200,000 to 400,000 votes. The Non-aligned Voters Theory informed the remaining subjects that Party *A* and Party *B* supporters will vote in equal numbers. But the majority of the non-aligned voters will side with one unspecified party (the experts were split as to which party it would be), and that party will win by a margin of 200,000 to 400,000 votes.

Having read the theory, subjects responded to six questions. The first four questions assessed the conditional probabilities hypothesized in part to motivate the vote: (1) if you vote, how likely is it that the other supporters of Party *A* will vote in larger numbers than the supporters of Party *B*? (2) If you abstain, how likely is it that the other supporters of Party *A* will vote in larger numbers than the supporters of Party *B*? (3) If you vote, how likely is it that Party *A* will defeat Party *B*? And (4), if you abstain, how likely is it that Party *A* will defeat Party *B*? Responses were made on 9-point scales labelled in the middle and at the endpoints. On a similar scale, subjects were asked, 'How likely are you to vote if the theory were true and voting in Delta were costly?' and, finally, subjects checked 'yes' or 'no' to the question, 'Would you vote if the theory were true and voting in Delta were costly?'

Results

Each subject was asked to estimate the likelihood that Party *A* would vote in larger numbers than Party *B* if the subject voted and if the subject abstained. The subject was also asked the likelihood that Party *A* would defeat Party *B* conditional on the subjects' voting and abstaining. The cell means are shown in table 3, and data relevant to the predictions are found in the row labelled 'difference'. As expected, the differences in inferred likelihoods conditional on voting and abstaining were significantly greater among subjects in the Party Supporters condition than among subjects in the Non-aligned Voters condition, both for the question concerning whether Party *A* would vote in greater numbers than Party *B*, $F(1,313) = 35.79, p < .001$, and for the question concerning whether Party *A* would defeat Party *B*, $F(1,313) = 40.18, p < .001$.

The difference between conditions in the assumed diagnostic significance of voting translated into differences between conditions in assumed voting intentions. Subjects in the Non-aligned Voters condi-

Table 3. *The inferred likelihood of states given subject's decision*

Condition	Subject's decision	States	
		Party A votes in greater numbers than Party B	Party A defeats Party B
Party supporters theory	vote	5.81	6.06
	abstain	4.13	4.09
	difference	1.68	1.97
Non-aligned voters theory	vote	4.20	5.12
	abstain	3.87	4.60
	difference	0.33	0.52

tion assumed that they would be less willing to vote (M = 6.43) than did subjects in the Party Supporters condition (M = 7.17), $F(1,313) = 7.85, p < .05$. In a like manner, a greater percentage of subjects in the former condition (16%) than in the latter (7%) indicated that they would not vote, $p < .05$. Evidence for the hypothesized linkage between the inferred diagnostic significance of voting and willingness to vote was most directly demonstrated through correlational measures. In the Party Supporters condition, subjects were more willing to vote the more they believed that their decision to vote or to abstain was diagnostic of (a) whether Party A would vote in greater numbers than Party B (i.e., $P(A > B/V) - P(A > B/\text{not } V))$, $r = .27, p < .001$ and (b) whether Party A would defeat Party B (i.e., $P(A$ defeats $B/V) - P(A$ defeats $B/\text{not } V))$, $r = .32, p < .001$. In the Non-aligned Voters condition, the correlations were non-significantly smaller, $r = .07$, n.s. and $r = .17, p < .01$, respectively, perhaps because of the smaller variance in the conditional probability differences.

Discussion

From the perspective of the individual citizen, voting is both causal and diagnostic with respect to a desired electoral outcome. Causally, a single vote may create or break a tie, and the citizen may communicate with like-minded peers, persuading them also to vote. Diagnostically, one's decision to vote or to abstain is an indicator that others who think and act like oneself are likely to make the same decision. The Party Supporters and Non-aligned Voters theories were equivalent in the causal significance of voting. But subjects perceived the Party Supporters Theory as having more diagnostic significance than the Non-aligned Voters Theory. As a consequence, they indicated a greater willingness to vote given the validity of the former theory than given the validity of the latter. These results obtained despite the margin of victory's being kept at from 200,000 to 400,000 votes for both theories.

One could identify additional circumstances, analogous to voting, in which collective action dwarfs the causal significance of a single individual's decision. The outcomes of most wars would not have changed had one fewer draftee been inducted, and the success or failure of many telethons do not hinge on the contributions of a single viewer. The paradox is that if each citizen, draftee or viewer abstains from making his or her paltry contribution upon acknowledging its relative insignificance, then the outcomes would be dramatically affected. Indeed, the moral imperatives to vote, to fight and to help the disabled draws its strength from the argument, 'If you believe that your vote/fighting/contribution doesn't help, then consider what would happen if *everyone* felt that way'. The argument is compelling. Nonetheless, just how *does* an individual's private decision materially affect the decision reached by countless other people?

To summarize, actions may be causal or diagnostic of outcomes with which they are correlated. The normative analysis of choice maintains that, in the evaluation of alternative actions, an outcome ought to be weighted by its probability conditional on selecting the actions only if the actions have a causal effect on the outcome. We have hypothesized, however, that people may weigh an outcome by its subjective conditional probability, even though the alternative actions may be merely diagnostic of the outcome. That is, if both action and outcome are believed to be consequences of a common antecedent cause, people may reason that by selecting the action they have increased the probability of the desirable outcome. Thus, in the first experiment, subjects selected actions that correlated with longevity despite their recognition that the actions would not affect their state of health. The actions, which were directional changes in tolerance to cold water, were mere signs that one possessed the sort of heart that would endure for longer than the normal span of years. The experiment further showed that the comforting diagnosis was accepted primarily by subjects who denied that they had purposefully tried to alter their tolerance to the cold. A certain degree of self-deception was probably involved, for otherwise the action may not have been attributed to the auspicious antecedent cause but rather to the motive to infer that cause. The second experiment demonstrated that people may make decisions diagnostic not only of their own attributes but of the decisions likely to be made by their like-minded peers. The experiment may shed light on why some people may vote in spite of the low probability of casting a decisive ballot.

We suspect that the assumed physiological mechanism of pain and heart responses may have facilitated self-deception in the first experiment. Most people believe that such responses are not under an individual's voluntary control. This widespread belief makes it very easy to deny to oneself that the action was deliberately enacted to make a cheerful diagnosis, for how does one intentionally 'pull the strings'. That self-deception may occur more often and be more successful for actions (incorrectly) believed to be uncontrollable than controllable is an interesting question for further research. The possibility of a 'motivational placebo effect', in which the desire to have one's tolerance shifted produces actual changes in physiological tolerance thresholds, seems worth exploring.

We have argued that people often select *actions* to make favourable diagnoses. But favourable diagnoses may be reached also by varying the *circumstances* under which an action is performed. Suppose subjects in the first experiment were required to keep their arm in the cold as long on the second trial as on the first, but they were allowed to adjust the temperature of the water on the second trial. Then subjects who learned that longevity was associated with an exercise-induced increase or decrease in tolerance may have, respectively, lowered or raised the water's temperature on the second trial. That is, by making the water temperature either colder or hotter, they could still infer an increase or a decrease in tolerance without altering the time of immersion. This point is reminiscent of the self-handicapping strategies discussed by Jones and Berglas (1978). These authors have argued that people may alter the circumstances of diagnostic performance to protect the belief that they are basically competent. For example, by drinking or taking drugs, any level of intellectual performance would not destroy the belief that one is basically bright, for even failure could be attributed to the debilitating effects of alcohol.

Finally, subsequent research should explicitly manipulate whether people believe an action to be causal or diagnostic of a favourable outcome. Intuitively, it appears as though the action would be chosen more often by subjects with a causal theory than by subjects with a diagnostic theory. But ironically, the intuition may not always be valid.[2] Compare the Catholic to the Calvinist. Both believe that one's conduct on earth (virtuous or sinful) is correlated with one's post-mortal fate (paradise or hell). But the Catholic subscribes to a causal theory in which the location of one's soul after death is a direct consequence of how one led one's life on earth. In contrast, the Calvinist champions a diagnostic theory in which earthly conduct and post-mortal fate are both consequences of the deity's prior decision. Although Catholics believe they can influence the location of their life after death, whereas Calvinists believe they cannot, Calvinists may be even more motivated than Catholics to select the virtuous acts correlated with paradise. To the Calvinist, even a single sinful deed is evidence enough that he or she is not among the chosen. To the Catholic, it is more a matter of one's total good and bad deeds that determines heaven or hell. And besides, there is always confession.

[2] We wish to thank Lee Ross for this idea.

REFERENCES

Abelson, R. P., Aronson, E., McGuire, W. J., Newcomb, T. M., Rosenberg, M. J., and Tannenbaum, P. H. (eds.) (1968) *Theories of Cognitive Consistency: A Source-book*, Chicago: Rand McNally.

Bem, D. J. (1972) 'Self-perception theory', in L. Berkowitz (ed.), *Advances in Experimental Social Psychology*, Vol. 6, New York: Academic Press.

Festinger, L. (1957) *A Theory of Cognitive Dissonance*, Evanston, Ill.: Row, Peterson.

Fisher, R. A. (1959) *Smoking*, London: Oliver and Boyd.

Gibbard, A., and Harper, W. L. (1978) 'Counterfactuals and two kinds of expected utility', in C. A. Hooker, J. J. Leach, and E. F. McClennan (eds.), *Foundations and Applications of Decision Theory*, Vol. 1, Dordrecht, Holland: D. Reidel Publishing Co.

Gur, R. C., and Sackheim, H. A. (1979) 'Self-deception: a concept in search of a phenomenon', *Journal of Personality and Social Psychology* 37, 147–69.

Hilgard, E. R., Ruch, J. C., Lange, A. F., Lenox, J. R., Morgan, A. H., and Sachs, L. B. (1974) 'The psychophysics of cold pressor pain and its modification through hypnotic suggestion', *American Journal of Psychology* 87, 17–31.

Jeffrey, R. (1965) *The Logic of Decision*, New York: McGraw-Hill.

Jeffrey, R. (1981) 'The logic of decision defended', *Synthese* 48, 473–92.

Jones, E. E., and Berglas, S. C. (1978) 'Control of attributions about the self through self-handicapping strategies: the appeal of alcohol and the role of underachievement', *Personality and Social Psychology Bulletin* 4, 200–6.

Nozick, R. (1969) 'Newcomb's problem and two principles of choice', in N. Racher (ed.), *Essays in Honor of Carl G. Hempel.* Dordrecht, Holland: D. Reidel Publishing Co.

Riker, W. H., and Ordeshook, P. C. (1968) 'A theory of the calculus of voting', *American Political Science Review* 62, 25–42.

Skyrms, B. (1980) *'Causal Necessity'*, New Haven, Conn: Yale University Press.

2. The goals and strategies of self-deception

DAVID PEARS

I. Introduction

Philosophers are always struck by the paradox of self-deception. How can anyone persuade himself that *p* and yet all the time maintain his original belief that *not-p*, as the word 'deception' seems to require? It is, however, doubtful if this paradox deserves the space that is usually assigned to it. True, it identifies one point at which self-deception cannot be quite like the deception of others, but it is not the only point of dissimilarity and some of the others are at least of equal interest. Nevertheless, it may turn out that, when we have added up all the dissimilarities, we shall find that they are outweighed by the similarities, so that the word 'self-deception' gets away with enough of its surface connotation, though not, of course, with all of it.

When we encounter the paradox of self-deception, it is probably better not to meet it head-on, but to ask whether it really besets all the different types of case that we readily diagnose as self-deception in real life and in literature. This would be a good question to ask even if current dissolutions of the paradox were obviously successful, because a remedy may be right without always being needed. In fact many of the common remedies in this case are desperate ones. Either self-deception is analysed in a way that eliminates belief, or, at least, puts too much emphasis on activities other than belief-formation (but that sacrifices the patient), or else the theory is that self-deception is necessarily hidden from the subject (but that is evidently not true). There is more than one reason for trying to manoeuvre on a broader front.

One way of breaking out would be to consider the more general paradox of irrational belief-formation. It is irrational to form a belief that is not supported by one's evidence, and even more irrational to form one that goes against it. Here we can arrange the mistakes on a scale of increasing badness. It is a mistake to believe p firmly when the evidence is equally distributed between p and $not\text{-}p$, a worse mistake to believe p in the teeth of inductive evidence for $not\text{-}p$, and an even worse mistake when logical or mathematical necessity are defied. Now the most extreme form of this last mistake is to believe both p and $not\text{-}p$, which is what is required by the full surface connotation of the word 'self-deception'. So we may identify the familiar paradox of self-deception with the most extreme form of the paradox of irrationality. Then as we move down the scale of the paradox of irrationality we shall be able to identify milder forms of the paradox of self-deception with less extreme forms of the paradox of irrationality. For a person may be deceiving himself if he gets too high a total when he is adding up his bank deposits, or – one step further down the scale – if he disbelieves bad news in a telegram from a reliable source. It is not so clear that self-deception can occur at the bottom of the scale when someone bases his firm belief that p on evidence equally distributed between p and $not\text{-}p$. However, the other two cases certainly may be examples of self-deception (they are likely to be, if they are not caused by stupidity, bad luck, etc.) and that suggests that there are other forms of the paradox of self-deception which are at least as interesting as the familiar one.

In fact, they are more interesting, but, before we explore them, two caveats are needed.

First, it would be an exaggeration to say that all self-deceptive belief-formation goes against premises already installed in the subject's mind. For self-deception about one's own feelings, valuations and intentions is a conspicuous exception to this generalization. True, the subject can use the evidence of his own behaviour to check such things, but his primary source of information is their immediate self-monitoring. This makes it a little odd to count such phenomena as examples of self-deception. Self-deception does not cover wishful misperception of things in the external world and so it is arguable that it ought not to cover wishful mis-monitoring of feelings and suchlike. However, these cases certainly do fall within its extension, and the explanation of this fact may be that the subject too can use behavioural evidence to check the self-monitoring of his feelings; or perhaps it is that in these cases the objects themselves are internal, like the premises in cases of the other kind. Anyway, these are the examples of self-deception that people think of first, and they block the facile generalization that all self-deception operates against premises already in the subject's mind.

The second caveat is that there is a price to be paid for extending the paradox of self-deception down the scale of the paradox of irrationality. The extension starts with the discovery that a self-deceiver who persuades himself that p does not have to believe *not-p*. When this is accepted, as it must be, a gap begins to open up between self-deception and the deception of others. If A had, and was able to evaluate premises that made p logically or mathematically impossible, and yet he told B that p, we would probably say that he had deceived B, but the case is less clear when A only has, and is able to evaluate inductive evidence against p. Even in this case he has deceived B in an indirect way about his evidence, but it is not clear that he has deceived him about what he actually told him, unless he himself has formed the belief that *not-p*. If this were the only divergence between self-deception and the deception of others, we might make an adjustment to the concept of self-deception in order to get rid of it. In fact, as we shall soon see, there are other divergences.

What makes this realistic extension of the paradox of self-deception interesting is that it introduces latitude into the situation confronting the subject. At the top of the scale logic and mathematics, so far as he understands them, give him no latitude to argue irrationally, because he simply contradicts himself if he draws an irrational conclusion. But lower down the scale he can argue irrationally without contradicting himself (a fact exploited by Donald Davidson in his explanation of *akrasia*),[1] and so, as far as this aspect of irrationality goes, he may be aware of what he is doing. For example, he is aware that his disbelief in the bad news goes against the evidence of the telegram, but he knows that his disbelief may still be correct, and so this discrepancy does not force him to conceal from himself what he is doing. True, the irrationality of the argument would not be the only reason for concealment. The fact that the conclusion is produced by a wish is also discrediting and that provides another, independent reason for concealment. No doubt, this is part of the explanation of the fact that self-deception covers up its own operations more often than it really needs

[1] D. Davidson (1980) *Essays on Actions and Events*, Ch. 2, Oxford: Oxford University Press.

to. But even if latitude is not the only factor at work here, it is certainly a necessary condition of open self-deception.

In this paper I shall try to do three things. First, I shall say something about the motives and strategies of self-deception: then I shall examine cases of self-deception in which the subject's premises allow latitude; and finally I shall try to establish what happens in non-latitude cases.

II. Motives and strategies

This is a large subject and all that I shall do is to organize the raw material by drawing a few broad distinctions. I shall resist the temptation to choose elaborate examples of self-deception, because the essential structures of different kinds of case are easily lost among the details. Real life is, of course, complex and the philosopher's self-deceiver who persuades himself that p is a simplification. However, it is a good idea to start with simple structures that can be clearly understood and to add the encrustation of detail later.

Whatever may be thought of self-deception, nobody doubts that wishes do sometimes bias rational thought-processes. But why do they bias them? Truth seems to be an overriding goal and it is surely obvious that rationality gives us our best chance of attaining it.

There is an important distinction between two different ways in which the biasing may be motivated. It may be done with a view to an action, or it may be done for some other end. It is difficult to bring the greater variety of motives of the second kind under a single positive heading and a common example must suffice. People often rewrite their own past histories to reduce the gap between their actual lives and their preferred images of them.

When someone deceives himself from the first motive, the biasing is part of the larger process of self-deceptive *akrasia*. For example, he persuades himself, against the weight of his evidence, that smoking is not harmful, in order for him to make it easier for him to go on smoking.[2] A very similar piece of self-deception may issue from the second motive. Suppose that a smoker knows that he is damaging his health and after a long struggle gives up the habit. Then his desire to appear rational to himself may cause him to persuade himself that right

---

[2] D. Davidson describes a special type of self-deceptive *akrasia* in which it is the agent's outright value-judgment that is biased. See note 1, above.

up to the point at which he gave up smoking he was unaware of its damaging effect. Or perhaps he is still smoking and persuades himself that it is not damaging partly from this motive. Here the content of the self-deceptively formed belief is exactly the same as it was in the case of *akrasia*, but the motive is a different one.[3]

It is an important fact that self-deception always needs a further goal to override the usual goal, truth or, at least, rationality, which gives us the best chance of attaining truth. This is another point of dissimilarity between self-deception and the deception of others. For the desire to give others the best chance of attaining the truth is not universal and so it is possible to deceive someone else with no further end in view.

This difference is connected with an important fact about the motivation of self-deception. Suppose that we distinguish two parts or systems in the self-deceiver, the subject and the object of deception, S and O (the nature of the division and the reasons for making it in certain cases will be discussed in Section IV). Then S is well disposed towards O. No doubt, the altruism is often misguided, but it is always operating, because S always does something for O. Perhaps it gratifies O's desire for a comforting self-image, or perhaps it facilitates O's *akrasia*. Either way, it is a desire of O's that is indulged, even if O is going to regret the long-term consequences.

It may be objected that there is no reason why S should care about O's chances of attaining the truth and so S could deceive O for no further motive and certainly would not need an altruistic motive. When we split the self-deceiver up into S and O, we lose the right to argue that the truth-seeking motive always needs another motive to override it, because it is truth for O and not for S, and we also lose the right to argue that the other motive would have to be an altruistic one.

However, though S need not have cared about O's chances of attaining the truth, and need not have allowed that consideration to be overridden only by another altruistic consideration, the fact is that S is motivated in this way and it is an understandable fact. For the wish to form the irrational belief, *p* becomes the nucleus of S because it belongs to O.[4] This wish is resisted by O and it then sets off on its own

---

[3] The motive is to reduce cognitive dissonance. Cp. E. Aronson (1972) *The Social Animal*, Ch. 4. San Francisco.

[4] This explanation needs to be formulated more precisely. See p. 74. S's wish is the wish that O should believe *p*, and O's wish is normally the wish that *p* were true and that it, O, should believe *p*. However, in self-deception S's strategy is guided only by the wish

like a child who feels that insufficient attention has been paid to his contribution to the deliberations of the family. It is, of course, difficult to give an adequate account of this secession and I shall try to do that in Section IV. The point that I am making now is that the altruism of S is a fact and that it is explained by the origin of S. There is a fairly good analogy to it in the physical mechanism for blocking prolonged, intense pain: once the message about severe damage has been received, continuous stimulation at a high intensity would be counter-productive. Self-deception is a more extreme case because it is the message that is suppressed and not the medium. However, even that is sometimes understandable. For people sometimes openly decide that it would be expedient not to know the truth, in spite of the fact that the evasion violates some principle of rationality. If that kind of open decision is understandable, it is certainly possible to understand that the wish should set off on its own to carry out the same project surreptitiously.

It is worth considering some examples of open evasion. There is always a strategy in such cases and it is possible that a classification of the strategies will throw some light on the operations of surreptitious self-deception. It is extremely important that, though the subsystem, S, is more limited than the main system, O, it is from its own internal standpoint equally rational. It is, therefore, essential to understand its modes of operation (and the same applies to the subsystems by which *akrasia* is sometimes produced).

One strategy is to seek evidence always where it is likely to support what one wants to believe and never where it is likely to go the other way. This violates the rational principle that relevant evidence should be maximized and that it should be collected in fair samples. However, it is easy to think of situations in which a person might actually judge it better to violate these principles. For example, he might calculate that, if he avoided situations that could yield confirmation of his suspicion that an employee was dishonest, and if he continued to show trust in him, that might help to put him back, or at least to keep him on the narrow path of scrupulousness. Parents sometimes use this strategy with children.

for the second conjunct because it has reason to believe that the wish for the first conjunct is unfulfillable. (Cp. Freud on the pleasure principle and the reality principle.) However, the eventual belief is, of course, the belief that p is true.

These are cases of openly calculated self-deception, but it is evident that the same strategy is often used in surreptitious cases. It is a strategy that filters input of evidence and that is much easier to do than to form beliefs that run counter to evidence already in the mind. That is why open self-deception uses this strategy so often. Incidentally, it is also a strategy that shows up a further difference between self-deception and the deception of others: steering someone else away from evidence for *not-p* is not quite positive enough to count as deceiving him that *p*.

There is another common strategy of open self-deception that operates through output. If someone acts as if he believed *p*, that is likely to help him to believe it. The behaviour of the employer in the example just now illustrated this strategy too. Presumably, it works through rationalization,[5] and also through what might be called 'investment' – the longer the make-believe continues, the worse the consequences if *p* is in fact false and so the stronger the motive to believe *p*. This strategy provides some support for existentialist analyses of self-deception, like Fingarette's.[6] It is interesting that what happens in a case of this kind may be quite like what happens in a case of self-deceptive *akrasia*. When this is so, the only difference is that in this kind of case the goal is the formation of the belief, whereas in self-deceptive *akrasia* it is the action itself.

A simple principle of division suggests that the only remaining strategy is to operate on the contents of the mind. This seems to be right. Motivated misperception does not count as self-deception and the only remaining way of deceiving oneself is to operate on what is already in the mind. Either self-deception will work on feelings, valuations or intentions before they monitor themselves accurately, or else it will attack the subject's reasoning from premises already in his mind.

It seems that this strategy cannot be planned in advance even in cases of open self-deception. For there is nothing that a deliberate self-deceiver could do in order to implement such a plan, nothing for his will to latch on to. He may begin to think that his evidence suggests *p*, but that is not something that he tells himself, as he might pass

---

[5] Cp. the smoker who rationalized his behaviour, but, of course, he did not smoke in order to persuade himself that it is harmless to smoke.

[6] H. Fingarette (1969) *Self-Deception*, London.

information to someone else whom he was deceiving. Nor is there any other step that he could take in this kind of case. If the self-deception is open, he will be aware that a wish is biasing his thoughts, like the recipient of the telegram, but that does not show that there is anything that he is doing.

If this is how things go when self-deception is open, presumably they will go in the same way when it is surreptitious. In both kinds of case this strategy must dispense with any stepwise plan. The wish, operating from the subsystem, S, will directly attack the thought-processes of the main system, O. It might, therefore, be argued that these cases ought to be classified as mere wishful thinking rather than self-deception, because the deception of others always requires the deceiver to do something. But that would go against the natural intuition that these are paradigm cases of self-deception. So it is better not to make any adjustment to the concept of self-deception at this point, but to register yet another difference between it and the concept of other-deception.

III. Cases of latitude

When a person's evidence is inductive, latitude allows him to deceive himself openly and this provides a solution to the less extreme form of the paradox of irrationality with which the paradox of self-deception may be identified in such cases. That does not mean that open self-deception is common. It is not, but its possibility in cases of latitude is enough to dispel that form of the paradox of self-deception.

The reason why open self-deception is rare even when there is latitude is that a belief is discredited when it is acknowledged to have been caused by a wish. It is more common for a person to form a belief against the weight of inductive evidence because he trusts an intuition, which he may regard as the reliable processing of half-noticed clues. Consequently, when there is no intuition his belief will be more stable if he can represent its origin to himself in that way. But open self-deception requires him to be aware not only of the irrationality of his belief but also of its origin, and wishes, unlike intuitions, have no tendency to produce true, or even probable, beliefs. Consequently, we would not expect the recipient of the telegram to maintain his disbelief in the bad news once he realized its cause.

The instability of open self-deception is notorious and its source is, in a general way, obvious. In cases of latitude the manufactured belief is not only improbable in relation to the evidence but also carries the stigma of an inappropriate cause. However, the details are not so obvious and it is worth dwelling on them.

One way of collecting a fuller explanation is to ask why *akrasia* is more stable than open self-deception. I do not mean to ask why *akrasia* lasts longer – it does not last longer. The point on which I want to focus is that *akrasia* is less likely to disintegrate as soon as the subject realizes exactly what he is doing. The question is why it is in this sense more stable than open self-deception.

Part of the answer is that in cases of open *akrasia* the agent knows that a desire is rebelling against his value-judgment and a desire is not a generally inappropriate cause for an action. True, the action is irrational in relation to his deliberation culminating in the value-judgment, but causation by a rebellious desire is not discredited simply because it is causation by a desire. That yields a contrast with the inappropriate causation of the belief in a case of self-deception and so it provides a fuller explanation of the instability of self-deception when it is open.

There is, however, another, underlying, difference between the two phenomena. In cases where *akrasia* is a possibility, there is a conflict, resolved by the agent's value-judgment but still potentially explosive and, at best, dormant behind his will. Now it is his will that sets the standard to which his actions should conform. In self-deception this direction of fit is reversed and it is the world that sets the standard to which a person's beliefs should conform. This reversal is important, because there is no conflict in the world, and so, when a belief is formed, no conflict latent behind the thing that sets the standard of match. There may of course be some conflict in the person's evidence about the world and his judgment may be baffled. But so long as he has no wish operating against his desire to attain the truth, his judgment will automatically home on to what seems to him to be the truth. Consequently, if some secondary property of a weak piece of evidence, such as its salience, causes it to prevail, he will automatically correct the fault as soon as he becomes aware of it.

Things go very differently in open *akrasia*. If a desire has some secondary property, such as intensity, which causes it to prevail in spite of its earlier defeat in deliberation, there is not the same automatic tendency to correct the fault as soon as it begins to be apparent. This is because the conflict in this case lies behind the will, which sets the standard of match. If the will also carried an onus of match, it might automatically home on to something – perhaps, apparent value – in the way in which judgment automatically homes on to apparent truth, and any deviations would be corrected as soon as they were noticed. But the will does not carry an inescapable onus of match with apparent value, and so in cases of open *akrasia*, when the conflict erupts behind the will, it simply distorts the thing that sets the standard of match.

When this point is added to the previous one, we get a deeper explanation of the greater instability of open self-deception. The first point was that wishes are not appropriate causes for beliefs, and to this we can now add that the dedication of judgment in its pursuit of truth is greater than the dedication of the will in its pursuit of value. The two points are connected. For the will is less dedicated because it has potentially rebellious desires behind it, and desires are able to occupy that position because they are appropriate causes for actions; whereas judgment is more dedicated because it is never distorted by any rebels in its own retinue and any desire that opposes it necessarily belongs to a different camp. However, the two points are not identical, because it is one thing to specify the appropriate causes of beliefs and actions and another thing to describe the line-up of the opposed forces in the two contrasting cases of conflict.

IV. Non-latitude cases

When there is no latitude, the paradox of self-deception is more difficult to deal with, because it is identifiable with one of the more extreme forms of the paradox of irrationality. It is no good suggesting that we ignore the surface connotation of the verb 'to deceive', because the source of the trouble lies deeper, in the actual structure of the self-deceiver's thought-processes.

There are two kinds of case that present this problem. If the subject accepts the wishful mismonitoring of his feelings or valuations or intentions, it seems that he cannot do so consciously, because that would require him to be aware that *not-p*, while accepting the belief that *p*. The other possibility is that a logically valid argument or a mathematically correct computation may leave him no latitude to form the belief that p, and so, if he does form it, it seems that his defiance of logical or mathematical necessity cannot be conscious. If he thinks that he sees his mistake, he cannot persist in it, unless he hopes that further checking will show that it is not really a mistake. So if he does persist in believing that his bank balance adds up to the total that he wants, when in fact it does not, the only possible explanation seems to be that he is not conscious that he is violating mathematical necessity.

Apparently, the absence of latitude forces us to adopt an explanation which also applies to most cases of self-deception with latitude. For the fact that a belief is caused by a wish is discrediting and so, even when there is latitude, self-deception tends to cover up its own operations. The importance of non-latitude cases does not lie in their connection with the surface connotation of the name 'self-deception'. They are important because they are test cases of the paradox of irrationality which firmly establish a theory that is then found to have a much wider application.

But what exactly is the theory? What constitutes the identity of the deceiving subject, S, and the identity of the object of deception, O? And how are they related to one another? At first sight, it seems that the distinction between them must be based squarely on the line dividing consciousness from unconsciousness. From the problem that the dichotomy of the mind has to solve is formulated in a way that seems to make that solution, such as it is, almost inevitable. 'When there is no latitude, how can anyone consciously persist in an irrational belief?' It is difficult to avoid the conclusion that he must be unconscious of its irrationality, and similarly that in many cases where there is latitude he must be unconscious of the fact that his belief is caused by a wish. This was Freud's main idea and it seems that it must be a large part of the truth.

However, it suffers from two defects. First, it is not wholly true, because the line dividing S from O does not exactly coincide with the line dividing consciousness from unconsciousness. Secondly, it is not the whole truth, because it does not explain the genesis of S or the rationality of its operations.

The theory has to explain how and why anyone forms the belief that p when his premises allow him no latitude to form it, or when it goes against the natural self-monitoring of his own states of mind or feeling. Now O is the tolerably rational system of interacting desires and beliefs that maintains its diachronic identity through inner stability and memory and occupies the hot seat between perceptual input and behavioural output. So the question is being asked about O.

The first defect of the proposed explanation is easily seen. Let q be the proposition that, given the person's premises, it would be irrational for him to believe p, and let us suppose that there is no latitude in the case and that he does not lack intellectual competence, so that the belief that q will be in his repertoire. Then the idea is that the main system, O, is consciousness and that O's formation of the belief that p shows that q cannot belong to O. It must, therefore, belong to the subsystem, S, which is the unconscious. This is a plausible theory, but it is vulnerable to the objection that consciousness of a belief is neither a causally necessary nor a causally sufficient condition of the belief's successful intervention. The belief that q might be unconscious or, at least, preconscious (that too would put it in S) and yet it might succeed in stopping the formation of the belief that p and, conversely, it might fail to stop it in spite of being conscious.

The first of these two criticisms needs no reinforcement, because the interventions that it describes are common and well known, but the second might seem a little weak. How, it might be asked, could the belief that q have failed to stop the formation of the belief that p in a person who held it consciously? But there is an answer to this: he may not have put it together with his premises. It is even possible to believe *not-p* consciously and to believe p consciously, provided that they are held apart. What is impossible is to put the two together and to believe their conjunction consciously.

If this is accepted, the two criticisms add up to a formidable objection to the theory that the line dividing S from O is the line dividing what is not conscious from what is conscious. It is no good protesting that the objection is captious because it hammers a theory for breaking down in a few exceptional cases. That is not the situation here. For however much truth there may be in this theory, its breakdowns are very common. It follows that, whatever the importance of consciousness, there must be another factor at work and it is possible that the line dividing S from O ought to be based on that other factor.

The obvious candidate is functional insulation. S may be distinguished from O simply by its containing elements that do not interact with all of O's elements. If self-deception in cases without latitude can be explained in this way, it may then be possible to do justice to the claim of consciousness by treating lack of consciousness as a special case of functional insulation.

Before this suggestion is developed in detail, it has to meet a general objection. How, it may be asked, can a theory of this kind achieve any explanatory power? Its task is to explain the formation of the irrational belief that p in a case without latitude in spite of the fact that q, the belief that it is a case of non-latitude irrationality, is in the person's repertoire. The explanation offered is that q is functionally insulated, but the objection to this is that it is just a technical way of restating the fact to be explained. Nor is anything gained by treating functional insulation as the criterion of belonging to the sub-system S. For if that move is made, the statement that O formed the belief that p because the belief that q belonged to S is only a thinly disguised tautology.

The answer to this objection is to make the criterion of belonging to S a special type of functional insulation. What we have to require is not just that the belief that q should fail to intervene to stop the formation of the belief that p – that might be a failure to exploit the known implications of q as a result of some intellectual fault – but, rather, that the insulation should be produced by the wish to believe p. To put the point in Freud's way, the insulation of q in S must be dynamic. Then it will no longer be tautological to say that O formed the belief that p because the belief that q was confined to S. On the contrary, another possible explanation will be excluded, namely intellectual in-competence.

The second defect in the theory that O contains what is conscious and S what is not conscious is that it neither explains the genesis of S nor the rationality of its operations. No doubt these deficiencies could be made good if there were nothing else wrong with the theory. However, its first defect is irremediable and so the necessary sup-plements will now be added to the rival, functional theory.

The construction of the functional theory presents us with a choice. The criterion for ascribing an element to S is its wishful insulation from O, but there are two degrees of insulation and it is necessary to choose between them. The first degree is simply the obstruction of interven-tion which occurs when q fails to stop the formation of the belief that p. This degree of insulation is present in cases of self-deception with latitude. For example, the belief that it is irrational to reject the evidence of the telegram does not stop the formation of the belief that all is well, and the whole performance may be conscious, because there is latitude in this case. The second degree of insulation is stronger and it is present only in cases where there is no latitude. The belief that q is strongly insulated from the conjunction of O's premises and wishful conclusion when it cannot even be combined with them consciously. For example, if q is the proposition that r entails not-p, it cannot be combined consciously with the conjunction 'r and p'. Let us call this strong degree of insulation 'non-combinability' and the other, weaker degree 'non-intervention'.

Davidson observes that, when we assign an element to a separate sub-system, it is the principle of rationality that forces us to compromise the unity of the person. When the relation between certain elements in a single, unified system would be too irrational to be credible, we mark off a subsystem, which rids the main system of the troublesome elements and combines them in a way that is internally rational. However, this move must not be made too often, because if we mark off too many subsystems, we may lose the basis for any ascriptions of rationality.[7]

So when we choose the criterion for assigning an element to a subsystem, we have to strike a balance. One possibility is to use the stronger of the two degrees of insulation, non-combinability, and that is the line that will be followed in the remainder of this paper. There is, of course, no right or wrong about the choice between the two functional criteria for drawing the line between S and O. It is a choice governed by a rather vague judgment of the level of rationality attained by the average man. If irrational belief formation is common in cases that allow latitude and if these performances may even be conscious, it is perhaps unnecessary to split the person into two systems in order to explain them.

Suppose, then, that the belief that q is assigned to the subsystem, S, on the ground that it is not combinable with other beliefs in the main system, O. Now the genesis of S has to be wishful and this requirement is met in a very simple way: the wish produces the irrational belief that

---

[7] D. Davidson (1982) 'Paradoxes of irrationality', Ernest Jones Memorial Lecture, reprinted in R. A. Wollheim and J. Hopkins (eds.), *Philosophical Essays on Freud*, 2nd edn, Cambridge: Cambridge University Press, and in this volume.

p in O and it is with the conjunction of p and O's premises that q is uncombinable. For example, O's premises might be his beliefs about the figures to be added up and p might be his final wishfully exaggerated total and q would specify the correct way of doing the computation.

So far, the construction of S has been fairly straightforward, but a complication has to be added at this point. Non-combinability is, strictly speaking, the criterion not of belonging to S but of belonging to S and not O. The addition is not redundant, because some elements will belong to O as well as to S and the two systems should be pictured as overlapping circles.

The first step in setting up the two systems is to identify some elements that belong to O whether they also belong to S or not. This is easily done, because O is placed between input and output in the ordinary, mainly conscious life of the person. Then, with these elements as base, non-combinability will put certain elements in S but not O. These may be called 'the founder-members' of S and they will belong to the non-overlapping part of its circle. They will have as their opposite numbers elements which, by the same criteria, non-combinability, cannot belong to S and so, if they belong to the person at all, must be assigned to the non-overlapping part of the circle representing O. It is essential to remember that S too is internally rational[8] and so is just as exclusive a club as O.

The next step might be to add further members to S, placed in the overlap of the two circles, and to explain the principles governing their selection. However, before that is done, something needs to be said about the most important of the elements belonging to O but not S, namely the belief that p.

Assume that O's set of premises, E, also belongs to S (the reason for this assumption will become clear in a moment). Now q belongs to S. It follows that p cannot belong to S, because it is q's opposite number. It is, therefore, a bit misleading to say that S produces the belief that p. Strictly speaking, S produces the belief that p in O.

Sartre's main criticism of Freud misses this point.[9] He argues that Freud has to explain how the self-deceiver can form the belief that p

---

[8] A point emphasized by Davidson. See note 7 above.
[9] Sartre (1943) *L'Etre et le Néant*, tr. Hazel Barnes, *Being and Nothingness*, London, pp. 49ff.

while still believing *not-p*, and that his explanation, which is that the belief that *not-p* is repressed in the unconscious, will not work, because the same conflict between the two incompatible beliefs will then break out in the unconscious. Never mind that Sartre is discussing the simple paradox of self-deception rather than the graduated paradoxes of irrationality, or that he is supposing that O is consciousness and S the unconscious. The basis of his criticism is the structural assumption that S must produce the belief that *p* in itself. But that is not necessary and so it is no criticism of the theory of insulated systems that, if it happened, the uncombinable would be combined. However, Sartre may have a limited point against Freud: the unconscious, in Freud's theory, does not obey the principles of rationality and maybe he does not make it sufficiently clear that the preconscious is internally rational, as it surely must be in these limited operations.

Let us now return to the task of adding further members to S. These will belong to O as well as S and so their place will be in the overlap of the two circles. But what will they be? There are two principles governing their selection. One is that enough elements must be included in S to make it internally rational and the other is that any elements that would deprive it of its internal rationality must be excluded.

The first principle requires the inclusion of the wish to believe *p*, which is the force that produces the secession of S and motivates all its operations. The point just made against Sartre is that this wish is more accurately described as 'the wish that O should believe *p*'. It is, of course, shared by O because, unlike many of the wishes in Freud's case histories, it is not reprehensible (only its operation is reprehensible) and O finds the usual, briefer description of it sufficient.

There are also other elements that the first principle requires us to include in S. We must include O's premises, because S needs a reason for undertaking the task of producing the belief that *p* in O, and, though the belief that O has the premises would be sufficient, it is hard to see why S should acquire this belief without the premises themselves. The performance of the task will then require further beliefs in S. The complexity of the strategy that is adopted will determine how many more are involved. If it is the sustained strategy of avoiding situations likely to contain evidence for *not-p*, a lot more beliefs will have to be included in S.

If the first principle gives S its internal rationality, the second principle preserves it by excluding any element that is uncombinable with its existing elements. The most important element to be excluded is the one already noted, the belief that p. The need to exclude such elements from S is neglected in many theories because it is natural to adopt the stance of daily life and to view the whole scene from the high ground of O. This encourages the erroneous assumption that it is only O that needs to be preserved from irrationality in cases of self-deception without latitude and that S does not have the same need.

At this point we can get a clearer view of the first defect of the theory that the line dividing O from S is the line dividing what is conscious and what is not conscious. We have just seen that the preconscious too has to be internally rational and this theory would have to explain the exclusion of an element from the preconscious by saying that it is not an object of the consciousness that is internal to the preconscious. One difficulty about this is that no such consciousness has been introduced in the theory and there is no empirical basis for introducing it.[10] If the preconscious took over the person's voice and spoke to us like a dissociated personality, the internal consciousness of the preconscious would begin to acquire the same kind of basis as the ordinary consciousness of O.[11] However, this does not happen, and so the hypothesis lacks any empirical basis.

Perhaps this is not too damaging in an area where so much is inferential. But there is a second, more serious difficulty. Even if the hypothesis did acquire an empirical basis, it would still be inadequate. This is easily seen. Suppose that the preconscious did take over the person's voice and did speak to us like a dissociated personality. We would then have direct access to two centres of consciousness in a single person, C_1 and C_2, and from what the person said in his two different phases we could tell which elements belonged to which. Of course, we would have to be able to distinguish the two phases from one another, perhaps by noticing that there were no memory-links between them but ramified memory-links between the elements within each of them. Now consider what would happen when we questioned

---

[10] Freud makes this point about the unconscious. See R. A. Wollheim (1971) *Freud*, London, p. 166. Cp. T. Nagel (1974), 'Freud's anthropomorphism', in R. A. Wollheim (ed.), *Freud*, New York, p. 16.

[11] See M. R. Haight (1980), *A Study of Self-Deception*, Ch. 4, Brighton: Harvester.

this person. One possibility is that, whenever we found an element which had to be assigned to the person as a whole, but which by the criterion of the uncombinability could not be assigned to C_1, it would turn up in C_2, and vice versa. However, there is no guarantee that our results would come in this convenient form and, if they did not, we would have to provide each centre of consciousness with a subsystem split off from it by the criterion of uncombinability. The same thing might happen if we used the weaker functional criterion, non-intervention. In general, any centre of consciousness is subject to whatever principle of rationality we impose and may be split into two systems by it.

This point is simply a dramatization of the first defect of the theory that identifies O with consciousness and S with the preconscious. If both systems have to be rational in the end, the best policy is to use rationality as the original criterion for setting them up and to hope that the line running between them will more or less coincide with the line between consciousness and the preconscious (without postulating any internal consciousness). In fact, the coincidence is far from perfect, but it is fairly good and that, no doubt, accounts for the plausibility of theories like Freud's.

In any case, it is necessary to treat lack of consciousness as a special kind of functional insulation. This too is easily seen. It was pointed out earlier that O will often be unaware of the operation of the wish that it should believe p. It will also often be unaware of the existence of the belief that q in the repertoire of the person as a whole. We may express these points by saying that these items often produce no representations of themselves in O. It is immediately obvious that we can, and should, ask which elements produce representations of themselves in S. For example, in a sustained piece of self-deception S would need information about the progress of its campaign and this information may be regarded as a set of representations in S of elements in O. The point has been made before, but it needs emphasizing because we are so susceptible to the mistaken assumption that information implies consciousness.

The theory of systems sketched in this paper is based on a strong criterion of functional insulation. It differs from Freudian theory in many ways, some of which need special mention. First, there is a point about the scope of the two theories: the problem that the theory of insulated systems is designed to solve is a limited problem about self-deception, especially self-deception without latitude, whereas Freud's theory of the unconscious covers a much wider field. The suggested solution to the problem of self-deception, that it is practised on the main system, O, by the subsystem, S, is closer to Freud's theory of the preconscious than to his theory of the unconscious. Of course, S is not identified with the preconscious, but it is like it in more than one way. S is a small, temporary system, like a camp set up for the duration of a particular campaign and then abandoned, and the force that splits it off from O is an ordinary wish, which is far less strong than the forces that maintain the division between the unconscious and consciousness in Freud's theory. The wish is often not reprehensible in itself and so both it and its representations can belong to O as well as S.[12] Finally, most important of all, S, unlike Freud's unconsciousness, is subject to the requirements of rationality.

[12] Freud makes use of the distinction between lack of awareness of a wish and the much more common lack of awareness of its operation both when he is explaining slips of the tongue (1916–17, XV, pp. 64–5) and when he is explaining obsessional symptoms (XVI, pp. 282–3).

3. Deception and division

DONALD DAVIDSON

Self-deception is usually no great problem for its practitioner; on the contrary, it typically relieves a person of some of the burden of painful thoughts, the causes of which are beyond his or her control. But self-deception is a problem for philosophical psychology. For in thinking about self-deception, as in thinking about other forms of irrationality, we find ourselves tempted by opposing thoughts. On the one hand, it is not clear that there is a genuine case of irrationality unless an inconsistency in the thought of the agent can be identified, something that is inconsistent by the standards of the agent himself. On the other hand, when we try to explain in any detail how the agent can have come to be in this state, we find ourselves inventing some form of rationalization that we can attribute to the self-deceiver, thus diluting the imputed inconsistency. Self-deception is notoriously troublesome, since in some of its manifestations it seems to require us not only to say that someone believes both a certain proposition and its negation, but also to hold that the one belief sustains the other.

Consider these four statements:

(1) D believes that he is bald.
(2) D believes that he is not bald.
(3) D believes that (he is bald and he is not bald).
(4) D does not believe that he is bald.

In the sort of self-deception that I shall discuss, a belief like that reported in (1) is a causal condition of a belief which contradicts it, such as (2). It is tempting, of course, to suppose that (2) entails (4), but if we allow this, we will contradict ourselves. In the attempt to give a consistent description of D's inconsistent frame of mind, we might then say that since D both believes that he is not bald and believes that

79

he is bald (which is why (4) is false) he must then believe that he is bald and not bald, as (3) states. This step also must be resisted: nothing a person could say or do would count as good enough grounds for the attribution of a straightforwardly and obviously contradictory belief, just as nothing could sustain an interpretation of a sincerely and literally asserted sentence as a sentence that was true if and only if D was both bald and not bald, though the words uttered may have been 'D is and is not bald.' It is possible to believe each of two statements without believing the conjunction of the two.

We have the task, then, of explaining how someone can have beliefs like (1) and (2) without his putting (1) and (2) together, even though he believes (2) *because* he believes (1).

The problem may be generalized in the following way. Probably it seldom happens that a person is *certain* that some proposition is true and also certain that the negation is true. A more common situation would be that the sum of the evidence available to the agent points to the truth of some proposition, which inclines the agent to believe it (make him treat it as more likely to be true than not). This inclination (high subjective probability) causes him, in ways to be discussed, to seek, favour or emphasize the evidence for the falsity of the proposition, or to disregard the evidence for its truth. The agent then is more inclined than not to believe the negation of the original proposition, even though the totality of the evidence available to him does not support this attitude. (The phrase 'inclined to believe' is too anodyne for some of the states of mind I want it to describe; perhaps one can say the agent believes the proposition is false, but is not quite certain of this.)

This characterization of self-deception makes it similar in an important way to weakness of the will. Weakness of the will is a matter of acting intentionally (or forming an intention to act) on the basis of less than all the reasons one recognizes as relevant. A weak-willed action occurs in a context of conflict; the akratic agent has what he takes to be reasons both for and against a course of action. He judges, on the basis of all his reasons, that one course of action is best, yet opts for another; he has acted 'contrary to his own best judgment'.[1] In one sense, it is easy to say why he acted as he did, since he had reasons for his action.

[1] I discuss weakness of the will in Essay 2 of *Essays on Actions and Events* (1980), Oxford: Oxford University Press.

But this explanation leaves aside the element of irrationality; it does not explain why the agent went against his own best judgment.

An act that reveals weakness of the will sins against the normative principle that one should not intentionally perform an action when one judges on the basis of what one deems to be all the available considerations that an alternative and accessible course of action would be better.[2] This principle, which I call the Principle of Continence, enjoins a fundamental kind of consistency in thought, intention, evaluation and action. An agent who acts in accordance with this principle has the virtue of continence. It is not clear whether a person could fail to recognize the norm of continence; this is an issue to which I shall turn presently. In any case, it is clear that there are many people who accept the norm but fail from time to time to act in accordance with it. In such cases, not only do agents fail to conform their actions to their own principles, but they also fail to reason as they think they should. For their intentional action shows they have set a higher value on the act they perform than their principles and their reasons say they should.

Self-deception and weakness of the will often reinforce one another, but they are not the same thing. This may be seen from the fact that the outcome of weakness of the will is an intention, or an intentional action, while the outcome of self-deception is a belief. The former consists of or essentially involves a faultily reached evaluative attitude, the latter of a faultily reached cognitive attitude.

Weakness of the will is analogous to a certain cognitive error, which I shall call *weakness of the warrant*. Weakness of the warrant can occur only when a person has evidence both for and against a hypothesis; the person judges that relative to all the evidence available to him, the hypothesis is more probable than not; yet he does not accept the hypothesis (or the strength of his belief in the hypothesis is less than the strength of his belief in the negation of the hypothesis). The normative principle against which such a person has sinned is what Hempel and Carnap have called *the requirement of total evidence for inductive reasoning*: when we are deciding among a set of mutually exclusive hypotheses, this requirement enjoins us to give credence to

---

[2] What considerations are 'available' to the agent? Does this include only information he has, or does it also embrace information he could (if he knew this?) obtain? In this essay I must leave most of these questions open.

the hypothesis most highly supported by all available relevant evidence.[3] Weakness of the warrant obviously has the same logical structure (or, better, illogical structure) as weakness of the will; the former involves an irrational belief in the face of conflicting evidence, the latter an irrational intention (and perhaps also action) in the face of conflicting values. The existence of conflict is a necessary condition of both forms of irrationality, and may in some cases be a cause of the lapse; but there is nothing about conflict of these kinds that necessarily requires or reveals a failure of reason.

Weakness of the warrant is not a matter simply of overlooking evidence one has (though 'purposeful' overlooking may be another matter, and one that is relevant to self-deception), nor is it a matter of not appreciating the fact that things one knows or believes constitute evidence for or against a hypothesis. Taken at face value, the following story does not show me to have been self-deceived. A companion and I were spying on the animals in the Amboseli National Park in Kenya. Self-guided we did not find a cheetah, so we hired an official guide for a morning. After returning the guide to Park Headquarters, I spoke along these lines to my companion: 'Too bad we didn't find a cheetah; that's the only large animal we've missed. Say, didn't that guide have an oddly high-pitched voice? And do you think it is common for a man in these parts to be named "Helen"? I suppose that was the official uniform, but it seems strange he was wearing a skirt.' My companion: 'He was a she.' My original assumption was stereotyped and stupid, but unless I considered the hypothesis that the guide was a woman and rejected it in spite of the evidence, this was not a simple case of self-deception. Others may think of deeper explanations for my stubborn assumption that our guide was a man.

Suppose that (whatever the truth may be) I did consider the possibility that the guide was a woman, and rejected that hypothesis despite the overwhelming evidence I had to the contrary. Would this necessarily show I was irrational? It is hard to say unless we are able to make a strong distinction between lacking certain standards of reasoning and failing to apply them. Suppose, for example, that though I had the evidence, I failed to recognize what it was evidence for? Surely this *can* happen. How likely an explanation it is depends on the exact

[3] See Carl Hempel (1965) *Aspects of Scientific Explanation*, New York: Free Press, pp. 397–403.

circumstances. So let us insist that there is no failure of inductive reasoning unless the evidence is taken to be evidence. And could it not happen that though the evidence was taken to be evidence, the fact that the totality of evidence made some hypothesis overwhelmingly probable was not appreciated? This too could happen, however unlikely it might be in a particular case. There are endless further questions that the tortoise can ask Achilles along these lines (there being as many gaps that unhappy reasoning may fail to close as happy reasoning must). So without trying to specify all the conditions that make for an absolutely clear case of weakness of the warrant, I want to raise one more question. Must someone accept the requirement of total evidence for inductive reasoning before his or her failure to act in accordance with the requirement demonstrates irrationality? Several issues are embedded in this question.

We should not demand of someone who accepts it that he or she always reasons or thinks in accordance with the requirement, otherwise a real inconsistency, an inner inconsistency, of this kind would be impossible. On the other hand, it would not make sense to suppose that someone could accept the principle and seldom or never think in accordance with it; at least part of what it is to accept such a principle is to manifest the principle in thinking and reasoning. If we grant, then, as I think we must, that for a person to 'accept' or have a principle like the requirement of total evidence mainly consists in that person's pattern of thoughts being in accordance with the principle, it makes sense to imagine that a person has the principle without being aware of it or able to articulate it. But we might want to add to the obvious subjunctive conditional ('a person accepts the requirement of total evidence for inductive reasoning only if that person is disposed in the appropriate circumstances to conform to it') some further condition or conditions, for example that conformity is more likely when there is more time for thought, less associated emotional investment in the conclusion or when explicit Socratic tutoring is provided.

Weakness of the warrant in someone who accepts the requirement of total evidence is, we see, a matter of departing from a custom or habit. In such a case, weakness of the warrant shows inconsistency and is clearly irrational. But what if someone does not accept the requirement? Here a very general question about rationality would seem to arise: whose standards are to be taken as fixing the norm? Should we say that someone whose thinking does not satisfy the requirement of total evidence may be irrational by one person's standards but not (if he does not accept the requirement) by his own standards? Or should we make inner inconsistency a necessary condition of irrationality? It is not easy to see how the questions can be separated, since inner consistency is itself a fundamental norm.

In the case of fundamental norms the questions cannot be clearly separated. For in general the more striking a case of inner inconsistency seems to an outsider the less use the outsider can make, in trying to explain the apparent aberration, of a supposed distinction between his own norms and those of the person observed. Relatively small differences take shape and are explained against a background of shared norms, but serious deviations from fundamental standards of rationality are more apt to be in the eye of the interpreter than in the mind of the interpreted. The reason for this is not far to seek. The propositional attitudes of one person are understood by another only to the extent that the first person can assign his own propositions (or sentences) to the various attitudes of the other. Because a proposition cannot maintain its identity while losing its relations to other propositions, the same proposition cannot serve to interpret particular attitudes of different people and yet stand in very different relations to the other attitudes of one person than to those of another. It follows that unless an interpreter can replicate the main outlines of his own pattern of attitudes in another person he cannot intelligibly identify any of the attitudes of that person. It is only because the relations of an attitude to other attitudes ramify in so many and complex ways – logical, epistemological and etiological – that it is possible to make sense of some deviations from one's own norms in others.

The issue raised a few paragraphs back, whether irrationality in an agent requires an *inner* inconsistency, a deviation from that person's own norms, is now seen to be misleading. For where the norms are basic they are constitutive elements in the identification of attitudes and so the question whether someone 'accepts' them cannot arise. All genuine inconsistencies are deviations from the person's own norms. This goes not only for patently logical inconsistencies but also for weakness of the will (as Aristotle pointed out), for weakness of the warrant and for self-deception.

We have yet to say what self-deception is, but we are now in a position to make a number of points about it. Self-deception includes, for example, weakness of the warrant. This is clear because the proposition with respect to which a person is self-deceived is one he would not accept if he were relieved of his error; he has better reasons for accepting the negation of the proposition. And as in weakness of the warrant, the self-deceiver knows he has better reasons for accepting the negation of the proposition he accepts, in this sense at least: he realizes that conditional on certain other things he knows or accepts as evidence, the negation is more likely to be true than the proposition he accepts; yet on the basis of a part only of what he takes to be the relevant evidence he accepts the proposition.

It is just at this point that self-deception goes beyond weakness of the warrant, for the person who is self-deceived must have a *reason* for his weakness of the warrant, and he must have played a part in bringing it about. Weakness of the warrant always has a *cause*, but in the case of self-deception weakness of the warrant is self-induced. It is no part of the analysis of weakness of the warrant or weakness of the will that the falling off from the agent's standards is motivated (though no doubt it often is), but this is integral to the analysis of self-deception. For this reason it is instructive to consider another phenomenon that is in some ways like self-deception: wishful thinking.

A minimal account of wishful thinking makes it a case of believing something because one wishes it were true. This is not irrational in itself, for we are not in general responsible for the causes of our thoughts. But wishful thinking is often irrational, for example if we know why we have the belief and that we would not have it if it were not for the wish.

Wishful thinking is often thought to involve more than the minimal account. If someone wishes that a certain proposition were true, it is natural to assume that he or she would enjoy believing it true more than not believing it true. Such a person therefore has a reason for believing the proposition. If he or she were intentionally to act in such a way as to promote the belief, would that be irrational? Here we must make an obvious distinction between having a reason to be a believer in a certain proposition, and having evidence in the light of which it is reasonable to think the proposition true. (Sentences of the form 'Charles has a reason to believe that *p*' are ambiguous with respect to this distinction.) A reason of the first sort is evaluative: it provides a motive for acting in such a way as to promote having a belief. A reason of the second kind is cognitive: it consists in evidence one has for the truth of a proposition. Wishful thinking does not demand a reason of either sort, but, as just remarked, the wish that *p* can easily engender a desire to be a believer in *p*, and this desire can prompt thoughts and actions that emphasize or result in obtaining reasons of the second kind. Is there anything necessarily irrational in this sequence? An intentional action that aims to make one happy, or to relieve distress, is not in itself irrational. Nor does it become so if the means employed involve trying to arrange matters so that one comes to have a certain belief. It may in some cases be immoral to do this to someone else, especially if one has reason to think the belief to be instilled is false, but this is not necessarily wrong, and certainly not irrational. I think the same goes for self-induced beliefs; what it is not necessarily irrational to do to someone else it is not necessarily irrational to do to one's future self.

Is a belief deliberately begotten in the way described necessarily irrational? Clearly it is if one continues to think the evidence against the belief is better than the evidence in its favour, for then it is a case of weakness of the warrant. But if one has forgotten the evidence that at the start made one reject the presently entertained belief, or the new evidence now seems good enough to offset the old, the new state of mind is not irrational. When wishful thinking succeeds, one might say, there is no moment at which the thinker must be irrational.[4]

It is worth mentioning that both self-deception and wishful thinking are often benign. It is neither surprising nor on the whole bad that people think better of their friends and families than a clear-eyed survey of the evidence would justify. Learning is probably more often encouraged than not by parents and teachers who overrate the intelligence of their wards. Spouses often keep things on an even keel by ignoring or overlooking the lipstick on the collar. All these can be cases of charitable self-deception aided by wishful thinking.

Not all wishful thinking is self-deception, since the latter but not the former requires intervention by the agent. Nevertheless they are alike

---

[4] In 'Paradoxes of irrationality', in R. A. Wollheim and J. Hopkins (eds.), *Philosophical Essays on Freud* (1982), Cambridge: Cambridge University Press. I assumed that in wishful thinking the wish produced the belief without providing any evidence in favour of the belief. In such a case the belief is, of course, irrational.

in that a motivational or evaluative element must be at work, and in this they differ from weakness of the warrant, where the defining fault is cognitive whatever its cause may be. This suggests that while wishful thinking may be simpler than self-deception, it is always an ingredient in it. No doubt it very often is, but there seem to be exceptions. In wishful thinking belief takes the direction of positive affect, never of negative; the caused belief is always welcome. This is not the case with self-deception. The thought bred by self-deception may be painful. A person driven by jealousy may find 'evidence' everywhere that confirms his worst suspicions; someone who seeks privacy may think he sees a spy behind every curtain. If a pessimist is someone who takes a darker view of matters than his evidence justifies, every pessimist is to some extent self-deceived into believing what he wishes were not the case.

These observations merely hint at the nature of the distance that may separate self-deception and wishful thinking. Not only is there the fact that self-deception requires the agent to *do* something with the aim of changing his own views, while wishful thinking does not, but there is also a difference in how the content of the affective element is related to the belief it produces. In the case of the wishful thinker, what he comes to believe must be just what he wishes were the case. But while the self-deceiver may be motivated by a desire to believe what he wishes were the case there are many other possibilities. Indeed, it is hard to say what the relation must be between the motive someone has who deceives himself and the specific alteration in belief he works in himself. Of course the relation is not accidental; it is not self-deception simply to do something intentionally with the consequence that one is deceived, for then a person would be self-deceived if he read and believed a false report in a newspaper. The self-deceiver must intend the 'deception'.

To this extent, at least, self-deception is like lying; there is intentional behaviour which aims to produce a belief the agent does not, when he institutes the behaviour, share. The suggestion is that the liar aims to deceive another person, while the self-deceiver aims to deceive himself. The suggestion is not far wrong. I deceive myself as to how bald I am by choosing views and lighting that favour a hirsute appearance; a lying flatterer might try for the same effect by telling me

I am not all that bald. But there are important differences between the cases. While the liar may intend his hearer to believe what he says, this intention is not essential to the concept of lying; a liar who believes that his hearer is perverse may say the opposite of what he intends his hearer to believe. A liar may not even intend to make his victim believe that he, the liar, believes what he says. The only intentions a liar must have, I think, are these: (1) he must intend to represent himself as believing what he does not (for example, and typically, by asserting what he does not believe), and (2) he must intend to keep this intention (though not necessarily what he actually believes) hidden from his hearer. So deceit of a very special kind is involved in lying, deceit with respect to the sincerity of the representation of one's beliefs. It does not seem possible that this precise form of deceit could be practised on oneself, since it would require doing something with the intention that that very intention should not be recognized by the intender.[5]

In one respect, then, self-deception is not as hard to explain as lying to oneself would be, for lying to oneself would entail the existence of a self-defeating intention, while self-deception pits intention and desire against belief, and belief against belief. Still, this is hard enough to understand. Before trying to describe in slightly more and plausible detail the state of mind of the self-deceived agent, let me summarize the discussion up to here so far as it bears on the nature of self-deception.

An agent A is self-deceived with respect to a proposition p under the following conditions. A has evidence on the basis of which he believes that p is more apt to be true than its negation; the thought that p, or the thought that he ought rationally to believe p, motivates A to act in such a way as to cause himself to believe the negation of p. The action involved may be no more than an intentional directing of attention away from the evidence in favour of p; or it may involve the active search for evidence against p. All that self-deception demands of the action is that the motive originates in a belief that p is true (or recognition that the evidence makes it more likely to be true than not),

---

[5] One can intend to hide a present intention from one's future self. So I might try to avoid an unpleasant meeting scheduled a year ahead by deliberately writing a wrong date in my appointment book, counting on my bad memory to have forgotten my deed when the time comes. This is not a pure case of self-deception, since the intended belief is not *sustained* by the intention that produced it, and there is not necessarily anything irrational about it.

and that the action be done with the intention of producing a belief in the negation of p. Finally, and it is especially this that makes self-deception a problem, the state that motivates self-deception and the state it produces coexist; in the strongest case, the belief that p not only causes a belief in the negation of p, but also sustains it. Self-deception is thus a form of self-induced weakness of the warrant, where the motive for inducing a belief is a contradictory belief (or what is deemed to be sufficient evidence in favour of the contradictory belief). In some, but not all, cases, the motive springs from the fact that the agent wishes that the proposition, a belief in which he induces, were true, or a fear that it might not be. So self-deception often involves wishful thinking as well.

What is hard to explain is how a belief, or the perception that one has sufficient reasons for a belief, can sustain a contrary belief. Of course it cannot sustain it in the sense of giving it rational support; 'sustain' here must mean only 'cause'. What we must do is find a point in the sequence of mental states where there is a cause that is not a reason; something irrational according to the agent's own standards.[6]

Here, in outline, is how I think a typical case of self-deception may come about: in this example, weakness of the warrant is self-induced through wishful thinking. Carlos has good reason to believe he will not pass the test for a driving licence. He has failed the test twice before and his instructor has said discouraging things. On the other hand, he knows the examiner personally, and he has faith in his own charm. He is aware that the totality of the evidence points to failure. Like the rest of us he normally reasons in accordance with the requirement of total evidence. But the thought of failing the test once again is painful to Carlos (in fact the thought of failing at anything is particularly galling to Carlos). So he has a perfectly natural motive for believing he will not fail the test, that is, he has a motive for making it the case that he is a person who believes he will (probably) pass the test. His practical reasoning is straightforward. Other things being equal, it is better to avoid pain; believing he will fail the test is painful; therefore (other things being equal) it is better to avoid believing he will fail the test. Since it is a condition of his problem that he take the test, this means it would be better to believe he will pass. He does things to promote this

---

[6] The idea that irrationality always entails the existence of a mental cause of a mental state for which it is not a reason is discussed at length in 'Paradoxes of irrationality'.

belief, perhaps obtaining new evidence in favour of believing he will pass. It may simply be a matter of pushing the negative evidence into the background or accentuating the positive. But whatever the devices (and of course these are many), core cases of self-deception demand that Carlos remain aware that his evidence favours the belief that he will fail, for it is awareness of this fact that motivates his efforts to rid himself of the fear that he will fail.

Suppose Carlos succeeds in inducing in himself the belief that he will pass the test. He then is guilty of weakness of the warrant, for though he has supporting evidence for his belief, he knows, or anyway thinks, he has better reasons to think he will fail. This is an irrational state; but at what point did irrationality enter? Where was there a mental cause that was not a reason for what it caused?

There are a number of answers that I have either explicitly or implicitly rejected. One is David Pears' suggestion that the self-deceiver must 'forget' or otherwise conceal from himself how he came to believe what he does.[7] I agree that the self-deceiver would *like* to do this, and if he does, he has in a clear sense succeeded in deceiving himself. But this degree and kind of success makes self-deception a process and not a state, and it is unclear that at any moment the self-deceiver is in an irrational state. I think self-deception must be arrived at by a process, but then can be a continuing and clearly irrational state. Pears' agent ends up in a pleasantly consistent frame of mind. Luckily this often happens. But the pleasure may be unstable, as it probably is in Carlos' case, for the pleasing thought is threatened by reality, or even just memory. When reality (or memory) continues to threaten the self-induced belief of the self-deceived, continuing motivation is necessary to hold the happy thought in place. If this is right, then the self-deceiver cannot afford to forget the factor that above all prompted his self-deceiving behaviour: the preponderance of evidence against the induced belief.

I have by implication also rejected Kent Bach's solution, for he thinks the self-deceiver cannot actually believe in the weight of the contrary evidence. Like Pears, he sees self-deception as a sequence,

---

[7] See David Pears, 'Motivated irrationality', in *Philosophical Essays on Freud* (see note 4 above), and Pears' contribution to this volume. The differences between my view and Pears' are small compared to the similarities. This is no accident, since my discussion owes much to his earlier article and to his paper in this volume.

the end product of which is too strongly in conflict with the original motivation to coexist with an awareness of it.[8] Perhaps these differences between my views and those of Pears and Bach may be viewed as at least partly due to different choices as to how to describe self-deception rather than to substantive differences. To me it seems important to identify an incoherence or inconsistency in the thought of the self-deceiver; Pears and Bach are more concerned to examine the conditions of success in deceiving oneself.[9] The difficulty is to keep these considerations in balance: emphasizing the first element makes the irrationality clear but psychologically hard to explain; emphasizing the second element makes it easier to account for the phenomenon by playing down the irrationality.

I have yet to answer the question at what point in the sequence that leads to a state of self-deception there is a mental cause that is not a reason for the mental state it causes. The answer partly depends on the answer to another question. At the start I assumed that although it is possible simultaneously to believe each of a set of inconsistent propositions, it is not possible to believe the conjunction when the inconsistency is obvious. The self-deceived agent does believe inconsistent propositions if he believes that he is bald and believes he is not bald; Carlos believes inconsistent propositions if he believes he will pass the test and believes he will not pass the test. The difficulty is less striking if the conflict in belief is a standard case of weakness of the warrant, but it remains striking enough given the assumption (for which I argued) that having propositional attitudes entails embracing the requirement of total evidence. How can a person fail to put the inconsistent or incompatible beliefs together?

It would be a mistake to try to give a detailed answer to this question here. The point is that people can and do sometimes keep closely related but opposed beliefs apart. To this extent we must accept the idea that there can be boundaries between parts of the mind; I postulate such a boundary somewhere between any (obviously) conflicting beliefs. Such boundaries are not discovered by introspection;

---

[8] See Kent Bach (1981), 'An analysis of self-deception', *Philosophy and Phenomenological Review* 41, 351–70.
[9] Thus I agree with Jon Elster when he says that self-deception requires 'the simultaneous entertainment of incompatible beliefs'. *Ulysses and the Sirens* (1979), Cambridge: Cambridge University Press, p. 174.

they are conceptual aids to the coherent description of genuine irrationalities.[10]

We should not necessarily think of the boundaries as defining permanent and separate territories. Contradictory beliefs about passing a test must each belong to a vast and identical network of beliefs about tests and related matters if they are to be contradictory. Although they must belong to strongly overlapping territories, the contradictory beliefs do not belong to the same territory; to erase the line between them would destroy one of the beliefs. I see no obvious reason to suppose one of the territories must be closed to consciousness, whatever exactly that means, but it is clear that the agent cannot survey the whole without erasing the boundaries.

It is now possible to suggest an answer to the question where in the sequence of steps that end in self-deception there is an irrational *step*. The irrationality of the resulting state consists in the fact that it contains inconsistent beliefs; the irrational step is therefore the step that makes this possible, the drawing of the boundary that keeps the inconsistent beliefs apart. In the case where self-deception consists in self-induced weakness of the warrant what must be walled off from the rest of the mind is the requirement of total evidence. What causes it to be thus temporarily exiled or isolated is, of course, the desire to avoid accepting what the requirement counsels. But this cannot be a *reason* for neglecting the requirement. Nothing can be viewed as a good reason for failing to reason according to one's best standards of rationality.

In the extreme case, when the motive for self-deception springs from a belief that directly contradicts the belief that is induced, the original and motivating belief must be placed out of bounds along with the requirement of total evidence. But being out of bounds does not make the exiled thought powerless; on the contrary, since reason has no jurisdiction across the boundary.

[10] I discuss the necessity of 'partitioning' the mind in 'Paradoxes of irrationality'.

4. Deception and self-deception in Stendhal: some Sartrian themes

JON ELSTER

Sartre, in *L'Etre et le Néant*, observes that 'on peut devenir de mauvaise foi à force d'être sincère. Ce serait, dit Valéry, le cas de Stendhal' (Sartre 1943, p. 105). Against this we can set some recent attempts to see Stendhal as a Sartrian hero of authenticity (Starobinski 1961; Brombert 1968). Since I do not claim to understand Sartre's notions of bad faith, good faith and authenticity, I cannot tell which of them, if any, is embodied by Stendhal. But I shall try to offer some considerations on what, broadly speaking, are Sartrian themes.

Henri Beyle, known as Stendhal, was obsessed with the problem of the self. His obsessions can be summed up in four maxims, which I shall first state briefly and then discuss more fully. They are: 'know yourself', 'be yourself', 'shape yourself' and 'hide yourself'.

'Know yourself', 'Nosce te ipsum', is a recurring phrase in Stendhal's diary, which he kept more or less continuously from 1801 (when he was 18) onwards. In the diary, self-knowledge is at first harnessed to the goal of self-transformation. 'Faire incessamment . . . l'examen de ma conscience: comme homme qui cherche à se former le caractère.' Later on he abandoned this idea, yet continued to believe in the need for self-knowledge. 'On se connaît et on ne se change pas, mais il faut se connaître' (*OI*, pp. 508, 907).[1] In the autobiographical writings, the desire for self-knowledge is unadulterated by any desire for change. He wants to know who he has been: 'je devrais écrire ma vie, je saurai peut-être enfin, quand cela sera fini dans deux ou trois ans, ce que j'ai été, gai ou triste, homme d'esprit ou sot, homme de courage ou peureux, et enfin au total heureux ou malheureux' (*HB*, p. 533).[2]

---

[1] All references in this form are to Stendhal (1981).
[2] All references in this form are to the edition of *Vie de Henry Brulard* in Stendhal (1982).

'Be yourself', or 'be natural', is perhaps the most constant theme in Stendhal's work. For him, the natural is 'la terre promise', as Jean Starobinski has put it (1961, p. 228). Yet it is highly unclear what this term means, and we shall see that Stendhal seems to use it in several distinct and hardly compatible senses. Here I shall only mention some of his invocations of what he calls the 'divin naturel' (*OI*, p. 157). He wants to become natural: 'je pense au naturel qu'il faut avoir dans mes manières' (*OI*, p. 59). He instructs himself, 'écouter et suivre davantage le naturel dans ma conduite et mon style'. And he applauds himself, 'J'ai été très naturel hier dimanche' (*OI*, pp. 149, 267). To be natural involves, at least, not to give an impression that one is trying to make an impression. 'Rien n'était agréable comme ces folies qui semblent ne supposer aucun esprit dans celui qui les fait, qui vous font rire sans que vous soyez contraint d'admirer' (*OI*, p.124).

'Shape yourself', 'Me former le caractère, en un mot' (*OI*, p. 326). In his diary Stendhal refers constantly to various bad habits that he must rid himself of by character planning. He notes, for instance:

> Mon peu d'assurance vient de l'habitude où je suis de manquer d'argent. . . Il faut absolument m'en guérir; le meilleur moyen serait d'être assez riche pour porter pendant un an au moins, chaque jour, cent louis en or sur moi. Ce poids continuel, que je saurais être d'or, détruirait la racine du mal. (*OI*, p. 96)

The plan can be compared to a strategy for overcoming vertigo by walking on a narrow plank laid out on the ground, in order to be able to walk on the same plank when suspended in air. The idea is clearly, if distantly, related to various strategies of behavioural therapy. It is doubtful whether it would have been successful.

The supreme goal of the character planning, however, is to become natural, whatever that may mean. I discuss this plan at some length later on. Here I shall only observe that in addition to the idea of shaping the character in some desired way, specified in advance, there is also in Stendhal the idea of acquiring *a* character, whatever it might turn out to be. 'Dans ma conduite future, rechercher toutes les occasions d'aller, agir sans cesse, fût-ce pour des bêtises' (*OI*, p. 327). Thirty years later there is an echo of this phrase in *Lucien Leuwen*: 'j'ai besoin d'agir et beaucoup' (*LL*, p. 778).[3]

---

[3] All references in this form are to the edition of *Lucien Leuwen* in Stendhal (1952).

'Hide yourself', 'cache ta vie', as Stendhal notes in 1814, after the defeat of Napoleon and the probable ruin of his own career (*OI*, p. 907). His obsessive use of pseudonyms, more than one hundred, is the most obvious sign of this concern for secrecy. The need for hiding oneself follows from two central beliefs. The first was alluded to earlier: 'On peut tout acquérir dans la solitude, hormis du caractère' (*DA*, fr. 1).[4] Or again, 'Avoir de la fermeté dans le caractère, c'est avoir éprouvé l'effet des autres sur soi-même, donc il faut les autres' (*DA*, fr. 92). Secondly, Stendhal believed from his early years that the world was inhabited by charlatans and hypocrites, with very few exceptions. Moreover, the latter would tend not to reveal themselves, as we shall see. His liberal and, in many respects, advanced views on social issues went together with a deep distaste for the verbosity of liberal politicians, not to speak of the 'people' (e.g. *OI*, p. 923; *HB*, p. 686). He decided, then, to go out in the world, to live with others in order to know himself and to shape himself, yet hide himself from their view. What he had to hide was the one character feature that must constrain any Stendhalian self, constructed or discovered: his belief that the vast majority of men and women are vain, pompous, pretentious. The object he must hide is his belief that men are such that he must hide his belief from them.

The central and constant project in the first half of Stendhal's adult life was, I believe, to *become natural*. When he came to realize that this goal was contradictory, or at least unattainable, he turned to fiction as a way of realizing it by proxy. He came close to succeeding, but ultimately failed to stay at arm's length from his characters. I shall now try to substantiate these propositions.

Some plans are contradictory in the strong logical sense, that the planned state could not exist. For Sartre, the paradigm would be the desire to be at once *en-soi* and *pour-soi*; to be present at one's own funeral oration and finally to know what one is; to turn around, very swiftly, to catch one's own shadow. This can never succeed, however, since these are states that could never come about, let alone be brought about by deliberate action. Sartre no doubt would say that the very idea of wanting to be natural, or spontaneous, is contradictory in this strong sense, since it involves the impossible coexistence of *en-soi* and

---

[4] All references, by chapter or by fragment number, are to Stendhal, *De l'Amour*. A recent edition is Stendhal (1980).

pour-soi. I shall postpone the discussion of this view, and for the time being proceed on the assumption that the desire to be natural may at least be inconsistent in a weak, pragmatic sense. Some states, that is, are such that although they come about as a result of action, they cannot be brought about by action, intelligently and intentionally, at least not just on the will's saying so. We may call these 'states that are essentially by-products', and refer to the desire to bring them about as 'excess of will'.[5]

We may take sleep as a paradigmatic instance of the states that are essentially by-products. The example is appropriate, in view of Sartre's comment that one cannot *decide* to be in bad faith; rather 'on se *met* de mauvaise foi comme on s'endort' (1943, p. 109). The phenomenology of insomnia includes the following stages. First, one tries to will an empty mind, to blot out all preoccupying thoughts. The attempt, of course, is contradictory and doomed to fail, because it requires a concentration of mind incompatible with the absence of concentration one is trying to bring about. Secondly, when one understands that this is not going to work, one induces a state of pseudo-resignation to insomnia. One acts, that is, as if one were persuaded that sleep is going to elude one, by taking up a book, having a snack or a drink. But at the back of one's mind there is the idea that one can cheat insomnia by ignoring it, that the cheerful indifference to sleep will make sleep come at last. Thirdly, one understands that this is not going to work either. Real resignation sets in, founded on a real, not sham, conviction that the night will be long and bleak. And then, finally and mercifully, sleep comes. For veteran insomniacs, who know the game inside out, the last stage never arrives. They know all too well the benefits of resignation ever to be able to achieve it. Stendhal, we shall see, soon become a veteran in the fight for spontaneity.

Let us follow the corresponding stages in Stendhal's diary, in their phenomenological rather than chronological order. His desire is to be natural, 'dire tout bonnement ce qui me viendra, le dire simplement et sans aucune prétention; fuir toujours de faire un grand effet dans la conversation'. The next step is the following reflection: 'Il ne me manque, pour être sûr du succès, que d'apprendre à laisser paraître mon indifférence' (*OI*, pp. 117, 837). The phrase, to be sure, involves a contradiction in terms, since the intentional element involved in the

---

[5] See Elster (1983), Ch. II for an analysis of this notion.

desire to appear indifferent is compatible with the lack of intention-ality that characterizes indifference. A related inconsistency is embodied in the following strategy: 'Pour être aimable, je n'ai qu'à vouloir ne pas le paraître' (*OI*, p. 896). This, if anything, is excess of will, willing what cannot be willed (Farber 1968). A true statement might have been, 'Pour être aimable, je n'ai qu'à ne pas vouloir le paraître.' To confuse these two statements is to commit the modal fallacy of confusing external and internal negation, such as the absence of a desire for something and the desire for its absence.[6]

Of course, Stendhal is too intelligent not to recognize that these are fallacies; at least he does so intermittently. He knows from experience that the attempt to appear indifferent will give neither the advantages of real indifference nor those of an unfeigned interest. 'Puisque je ne puis pas être assez de sang-froid pour avoir quelque esprit, être au moins tout bonnement moi-même pour avoir les grâces du naturel. Autrement, entre deux chaises le cul par terre. Pas assez de sang-froid pour bien suivre mes projets de rouerie, et point de grâce ni de touchant' (*OI*, p. 222). But of course he will then find that the attempt to be natural fails, just as does the attempt to be indifferent. He has come full circle.

Let me pause here to point out what may not be clear from these passages: Stendhal in these years was pursuing two goals which may not always work in harness. He wants to achieve spontaneity in conversation, and to impress women. On 20 April 1804 he notes his 'dessein d'être simple, naturel et vrai dans le monde'. Only four days later, he tells himself: 'A l'avenir, lorsque je devrai être présenté a quelqu'un, écrire le compliment que je veux lui faire' (*OI*, pp. 65, 67). His profound desire, of course, is to be loved by virtue of his natural and spontaneous behaviour, not in spite of it. Yet the failure of excess of will in one direction always leads him to another excess in the opposite direction, as of course he knows well enough: 'Craignant d'exagérer le galop, j'exagère l'action de la bride, ce qui est mauvais' (*OI*, p. 197).

At this point we might want to question the assumption that there are states which are essentially by-products, in the sense that all attempts to bring them about deliberately are bound to fail. True, it might be conceded, some states have the peculiar property that they

---

[6] See Elster (1984a) for this distinction.

cannot be set up just on the will's saying so, yet it might be possible to bring them about by indirect means. Take the case of deciding to believe – a project that would not have appealed to Stendhal,[7] but which exhibits many of the paradoxical features of his own desire to be natural. It is in an obvious sense impossible to decide to believe something on the sole ground that having the belief will be useful. It may be true, for instance, that in order to achieve something at all you have to believe – erroneously – that you will achieve much, but on these grounds one can hardly decide to believe that one's achievements will in fact be great.[8] Similarly for Pascal's wager: even if one is persuaded by Pascal's argument that the expected utility of belief is larger than that of not believing, this will not by itself set up the requisite belief. Yet even though belief in this sense is essentially a by-product, one might try to set up a causal process that will ultimately produce the belief one desires. The process would have to include a self-erasing component, since the belief would hardly be stable if its non-cognitive causal origin was known. Pascal's advice – to acquire belief by acting as if one believes – takes care of this problem, since 'cela vous fera croire *et* vous abêtira'.[9]

Similarly, it might be possible to bring about spontaneity by acting deliberately, to use the will to phase out the will. This indeed is a central idea in Buddhist thought.[10] One then has to take care, of course, that one never requires more will for the next step than what is left after the preceding step. Also, one might try to overcome timidity by using what little courage one has got to build up a bit more, which can then be employed to further development. 'Les petits succès de mes hardiesses me donnant du coeur, je me suis développé', notes Stendhal (*OI*, p. 175). This is character planning by bootstrap-pulling.

Such strategies might conceivably succeed. Yet I do not think Stendhal was even remotely successful, and the reason may have been that the process of character planning did not have the necessary convergence properties. If once again we take the paradigmatic case of sleep, we may refer to this difficulty as 'the hammock problem', after the following experience. Gently rocking myself to sleep in a hammock, I found that just as sleep was coming, my body became so

---

[7] Cp. Valéry (1957), p. 578.

[8] Hirschman (1967) explains why such erroneous beliefs can be useful.

[9] Pascal, *Pensée* 233; cp. also Elster (1984b), pp. 47ff.

[10] Cp. Kolm's contribution to the present volume.

relaxed that it could no longer sustain the rhythmic motion that led me to sleep, and so I woke up and had to start all over again. Similarly, when planning for spontaneity, might there not come a point when one is too spontaneous to carry on with the plan and yet not spontaneous enough for the plan to have been fulfilled? Even if it may be possible to develop one's courage by using what little one has got, could not the successive increments add up to a smaller total than desired? And finally there is a similar problem in Pascal's wager: in the gradual process of a growing belief and a dwindling reason, might there not come a point where the first is not yet strong enough to support the religious behaviour and the second no longer strong enough to do so?

Starobinski (1961, p. 232) asks a different question, 'si l'authenticité n'est pas à tout jamais compromise par une longue accoutumance à la feinte'. Since hypocrisy is part of Stendhal's plan for becoming natural, the end might be infected by the means. In Pascal's wager this is, of course, just the point: the means *shall* turn into the end. Stendhal evidently believed that his corrosive distaste for cant would not itself be corroded by cant, and his life proved him right. Yet there surely is a problem here, for could he really know this in advance? If character planning and character discovery go together, the robustness of the initial plan can only be assessed after the fact.

Stendhal intermittently, and then definitively, came to see that he would never experience happiness in love through being natural. In the first place, he questions the possibility of being natural when in love; and in the second place that of attaining mutual love by being natural. For the first idea, there is a capital passage in *De l'Amour* (chap. 32):

Un homme sensible, dès que son coeur est ému, ne trouve plus en soi de traces, d'habitude pour guider ses actions; et comment pourrait-il suivre un chemin dont il n'a plus le sentiment? Il sent le poids immense qui s'attache à chaque parole qu'il dit à ce qu'il aime, il lui semble qu'un mot va décider de son sort. Comment pourra-t-il ne pas chercher à bien dire? ou du moins comment n'aura-t-il pas le sentiment qu'il dit bien? Dès lors il n'y a plus de candeur. Donc il ne faut pas prétendre à la candeur, cette qualité d'une âme qui ne fait aucun retour sur lui-même. On est ce qu'on peut, mais on sent ce qu'on est.

At other times Stendhal, looking back, observes himself to have been natural, yet to have failed to benefit from it. This, I believe, is a central problem in Stendhal's life and fiction: a person who is capable of inspiring love in another is so by virtue of character traits that also make it impossible for him or her to reach out to the other and consummate the love. The happy few, the great souls, do not reveal themselves to each other. Indeed they cannot, for in doing so they would reveal themselves not to be among the elect. Stendhal frequently refers to his *pudeur*, a term with overtones of modesty, delicacy and shame.[11] By implication, this is what makes him worthy of being loved; by definition, it is what prevents him from telling his love.

The first appearance of this theme, which is to reverberate throughout his life, comes in an entry in his diary from 14 March 1805:

> Voici peut-être la raison qui fait que je n'avance pas mes affaires auprès d'elle; je l'aime tant que, lorsqu'elle me dit quelque chose, elle me fait tant de plaisir, qu'outre que je n'ai plus de perception et que je suis tout sensation, quand même j'aurais la force de percevoir, *je n'aurais probablement pas la force de l'interrompre pour parler moi-même*. Ce qu'elle fait m'est trop précieux. Voilà peut-être pourquoi les véritables amants souvent n'ont pas leurs belles. (*OI*, p. 265).

In less cloying language, the same idea reappears in *De l'Amour*, when Stendhal looks back upon his unhappy love for Méthilde Dembowski: 'On ne peut avoir de courage envers ce qu'on aime qu'en l'aimant moins.' Or again, 'L'âme vulgaire . . . calcule juste les chances de succès . . . et . . . se moque de l'âme tendre, qui, avec tout l'esprit possible, n'a jamais le plus assuré' (*DA*, fr. 47, chap. 24). The superior soul, when in love, always does too much or too little.

Stendhal has painted himself into a corner. The women he loves are like himself: tender, proud, modest. They can only love others like themselves, and the smallest sign of self-assurance or rakish behaviour would be proof that the man is not worth loving. The situation of two such beings is frustrating, since their mutual love, once declared,

---

[11] For instance, in *Souvenirs d'Egotisme* (Stendahl 1982, p. 495): 'Je suis comme une femme honnête qui se ferait fille, j'ai besoin de vaincre à chaque instant cette pudeur d'honnête homme qui a horreur de parler de soi.'

would be indestructible, yet it will not be declared. This is how Stendhal to some extent tends to look at his relationship with Méthilde Dembowski, although he also recognizes the possibility that she may never have loved him at all. Conversely, for Stendhal, a woman he can persuade by outward self-assurance is *ipso facto* not a woman worth taking seriously. This is not the Groucho Marx syndrome: a woman who would stoop to love *me* is not worth loving. On the contrary, Stendhal thinks highly of himself and of the happy few worthy to be his admirers. But these are largely unknown, they hide themselves, as does he. 'Les grandes âmes ne sont pas soupçonnées, elles se cachent; ordinairement il ne paraît qu'un peu d'originalité. Il y a plus de grandes âmes qu'on le croirait' (*DA*, fr. 68). Rather, the syndrome has the following form: a woman who would accept my advances is not worth loving, since to make advances betrays a calculating spirit and the failure to recognize this betrays an inferior spirit.

After his failure to realize love, as he conceives it, in life, Stendhal turned to fiction. It is often said, and often contested, that Stendhal's novels are exercises in revenge or in wish-fulfilment. I believe it is obviously false to say that they are only this, yet there is an important element of truth in the idea that he tried to realize by proxy what he failed to do himself. This is most clearly true of *Lucien Leuwen*, which is why in the following I shall focus on this work. But it is also true of *Le Rouge et le Noir*, *La Chartreuse de Parme* and even – perhaps especially – of *Lamiel*. The protagonist of the latter is a girl, who more than any other character in Stendhal's novels has the trait which he finds in himself, 'cette gaieté qui fait peur, qui est devenue mon lot' (Stendhal 1982, p. 518).

Stendhal's presence in his novels takes several forms (cp. Jones 1976). There is the voice of the narrator, who intrudes with ironical and affectionate comments on the behaviour of his heroes and heroines, mock protestations when they behave too outrageously and so on. There are the young protagonists who enact, by proxy, Stendhal's desire for requited love. And there are older, wise, often cynical, always gay father figures, such as Count Mosca or Leuwen *père*. The relation between Lucien Leuwen and his father is especially instructive.

To explain the problem of satisfaction by proxy, it is necessary to begin with some comments on the psychology of literary creation. The closest analogy to the relation between an author and his creatures would seem to be that between God and the world he created. Sartre's claim that man always and everywhere has the freedom of the Cartesian God, unbound by any constraints, is clearly exaggerated (cp. Føllesdal 1981). Yet the act of literary creation approaches that total freedom in which to name something is to create it. Perhaps only mathematical work offers the same scope. If fiction may be seen as the author daydreaming, the world may be seen as God daydreaming. But daydreams obey laws of their own, if they are to give satisfaction to their creators. Unconstrained freedom is unsatisfactory.

The basic obstacle to unconstrained daydreaming is that there is 'a shortage of scarcity', in George Ainslie's wonderful phrase (see p. 156). If there are no obstacles, there can be no feeling of 'la difficulté vaincue' that Stendhal often stresses as crucial to the aesthetic experience (e.g. *OI*, p. 896). One can easily see this in children, who begin fantasizing about what they would do if they had a million pounds, and then are irresistibly driven toward hyper-inflation: why not ten million, or a billion? Or again, the temptation is one of premature satiation. In daydreaming, nothing prevents me from instant success. For Ainslie, this answers the question 'Why do we wait for other people to congratulate us, rather than arbitrarily congratulating ourselves, a behaviour that is certainly in our repertoire? Why is a book better than a daydream?' Yet Stendhal writes: 'Pour qui a goûté de la profonde occupation d'écrire, lire n'est plus qu'un plaisir secondaire.'[12] So if Stendhal in writing his novels is daydreaming, and if Ainslie is right, there must be constraints that prevent premature satiation.

Why did God create the world? Traditional answers have involved the notion of 'enriching alienation', of God externalizing himself in the world he creates so as to increase his fullness of being. Leszek Kolakowski cites the following passage from Eriugena, which can also be applied to the act of literary creation:

> God, in a marvellous and inexpressible way, is created in creation in so far as he manifests himself and becomes visible instead of invisible, comprehensible instead of incomprehensible, known instead of unknown; when instead of being without form or shape he

[12] Stendhal (1980), p. 512. *Souvenirs d'Egotisme.*

becomes beautiful and attractive; from super-essential he becomes essential, from supernatural natural, from uncompounded compound, from non-contingent contingent and accidental, from timeless temporal, from spaceless located in space, from the creator of all things to that which is created in all things.[13]

God in the world is no longer short of scarcity. Yet this cannot be the whole story and not the most relevant part of the story, for God created a world with men in it, as does the novelist. Kolakowski has the following explanation:

God created the world for His own glory. This is an indisputable fact and one, moreover, that is quite understandable. A greatness that nobody can see is bound to feel ill at ease. Actually, under such circumstances one has no desire whatsoever to be great. Greatness would be pointless, it would serve no purpose . . . Holiness and greatness are possible only in a concrete setting . . . And only then [after the creation of the world] did He really become great, for now He had someone who could admire Him and to whom He could compare Himself – and how favorably![14]

Yet the story is still incomplete, for the question remains whether men are to be given free will or not, whether they are to be programmed into admiring God or are to have a say of their own in the matter. People often do engage in self-congratulatory behaviour; experiments in social psychology show people to be avid readers of advertisements for goods in their own possession (Festinger 1957). Yet we would certainly expect God to be more rational, and to see that there is no satisfaction derived from being admired by puppets set up for this purpose. Men, therefore, must be free.[15]

Similarly, the creatures of literary fiction must be free if they are to fulfil the wishes of their author. It has often been observed that there is a stark contrast between the mechanistic psychology that Stendhal professed and which governs the behaviour of many of his characters, and what has been called the 'fairylike' psychology of his heroes and heroines (Starobinski 1961, p. 240). Stendhal tried to temper his

[13] Quoted after Kolakowski (1978), vol. 1, p. 25.
[14] Kolakowski (1972), p. 3, quoted after Brams (1980), p. 12.
[15] Brams (1980, 1983) pursues the argument in great, if not always convincing, detail.

hedonism with ethics and even generosity, and yet remain within his utilitarian framework, but his main characters cannot be understood in this way.

Why must the creatures be free if their author is to derive satisfaction from what he makes them do? Indeed, what does freedom mean here? I think the relevant sense of freedom is that of an undeveloped character. One is unpredictable for oneself and for others as long as one has not been hammered into shape by experience. One is free when acquiring a character, but the freedom disappears as it becomes increasingly difficult to surprise oneself. I am not saying this is what freedom means in all contexts, nor that one cannot be free when 'acting in character'. I am only saying that this is the freedom which an author must give his creatures if they are to be vehicles of his wish-fulfilment. It is only in early youth that one has the open-ended character that can plausibly be extended counterfactually towards some desired target state.

Wish-fulfilment, indeed, typically takes the form of counterfactual thought experiments, 'if only . . .' The cruder form of wish-fulfilment in which one benefits from some improbable accident is, as I said, subject to premature satiation. It is more gratifying to construct an alternative past in which one could plausibly have said or done the right thing at the right moment. Stendhal's fiction and autobiographical writings are replete with such thought experiments. One critic has distinguished between the 'système des oufs' and the 'système des hélas', that is, between the occasions when something almost went wrong and those when one just missed the train. He asserts, moreover, that in *Vie de Henry Brulard* the dangers avoided outnumber the occasions missed by five to one. In his fiction, and especially in *Lucien Leuwen*, Stendhal explores the missed occasion, the 'système des hélas'. The same critic makes the acute observation that the basic principle of this mode of writing is that 'le narrateur continue à juger ces possibles, qui n'ont pas été, en fonction de ce qu'il est devenu, et non de ce qu'il serait devenu, si cela avait été' (Lejeune 1976, p. 31). When I undo my life to construct a new one, the purpose is to create something that will be appreciated by my actual self and not only by that counterfactual self. Perhaps we tend to construct something that will be appreciated by both, but surely not something that will only satisfy the self I did not become.

I now turn to some passages in *Lucien Leuwen* where Stendhal gives free rein to his desire for vicarious satisfaction. These are the love scenes between Lucien and Madame de Chasteller, among the most moving in all fiction. Valéry – that arch-cerebral writer – reports that reading these scenes 'opérait en moi le miracle d'une confusion que j'abhorre' (Valéry 1957, p. 555) that between the emotional life of the protagonists and the emotions of the reader. And we may add that they certainly also rest on a fusion – I would not say confusion – of the author and the protagonists. In studying this fusion we have the benefit of Stendhal's marginal comments on the progression of the manuscript, his difficulties in making his characters go the way he wanted them to, and his plans for their further development. The work is unfinished; I shall suggest that Stendhal once again may have painted himself into a corner.

Le Rouge et le Noir was built on a *fait divers*, which spared Stendhal the necessity of inventing. With *Lucien Leuwen* he had to invent. His marginal comments on this difference are strikingly contradictory. Early in *Lucien Leuwen* he writes: 'Je ne puis mettre de *haute portée* ou d'esprit dans le dialogue tant que je songe au fond. De là l'avantage de travailler sur un conte tout fait, comme Julien Sorel.' A few hundred pages later he writes: 'On ne va jamais si loin que quand on ne sait où l'on va. Ceci ne ressemble pas *à Julien*, tant mieux' (*LL*, pp. 1492, 1539). In between there is the extraordinary interplay between Lucien and Madame de Chasteller. Clearly, Stendhal must have appreciated the freedom he had in writing about them, which cannot be dissociated from the freedom he lent them.

I shall single out two scenes. The background is the following. Lucien and Madame de Chasteller have come to love each other deeply, yet are uncertain about each other. Madame de Chasteller fears that Lucien may be no more than a rake, Lucien that she does not really love him. Whenever he makes a clumsy and tentative advance, she tends to see it as a reason for doubt about his character; she grows haughty, he is made desperate. Yet they gradually grow closer to each other. Lucien writes her a letter; she, after some soul-searching, replies, in what she believes to be a severe and uncompromising tone. Stendhal comments as follows:

A quoi bon noter que la réponse fut écrite avec la recherche des tournures les plus altières? On recommandait trois ou quatre fois à Leuwen de perdre tout espoir, le mot même d'espoir était évité avec une adresse infinie, dont madame de Chasteller se sut bon gré. Hélas! Elle était sans le savoir victime de son éducation jésuitique: elle se trompait elle-même, s'appliquant mal à propos, et à son insu, l'art de tromper les autres qu'on lui avait enseigné au *Sacré-Coeur*. Elle *répondait*: tout était dans ce mot-là, qu'elle ne voulait pas regarder. (*LL*, p. 959)

As an analysis of self-deception, this is strikingly similar to Sartre's example of the woman who lets a man take her hand, yet refuses to admit to herself the meaning of this act (Sartre 1943, pp. 94ff). Sartre's woman lets her companion take her hand, and finds refuge in lofty and exalted conversation; Madame de Chasteller replies to Lucien's letter, and finds refuge in the severity of her tone.

If Madame de Chasteller will not admit the significance of replying, Lucien does not understand it. Here is Stendhal's affectionate aside:

'Ah! Madame de Chasteller répond!' aurait dit le jeune homme de Paris un peu plus vulgairement élevé que Leuwen. 'Sa grandeur d'âme s'y est enfin décidée. Voilà le premier pas. Le reste est une affaire de forme; ce sera un mois ou deux, suivant que j'aurai plus ou moins de savoir-faire, et elle des idées plus ou moins éxagérées sur ce que doit être la défense d'une femme de la première vertu.'

Leuwen, abandonné sur la terre en lisant ces lignes terribles, ne distinguait point encore l'idée principale, qui eût dû être: 'Madame de Chasteller répond!' Il était effrayé de la séverité du language et du ton de persuasion profonde avec lequel elle l'exhortait à ne plus parler de sentiments de cette nature. (*LL*, p. 960)

In this tender and comic ballet, Madame de Chasteller deceives both herself and Lucien: herself, because she is in the habit of deceiving others about the nature of her real feelings, and Lucien because he is too blind to perceive that the message is not in the letter, but is the letter itself. But her deception of Lucien is of another kind than the deception she learned to practise in Sacré-Coeur. He accepts her self-deceptive beliefs about herself, because to do otherwise would be incompatible with his love for her. And, of course, her love for him depends on his being the kind of person who would not see through her deception. But observe that the original cause of this shared deception is located outside the lovers, in her Jesuitic education. Stendhal had a horror of Jesuits, going back to his own Jesuitic tutor whom he hated even more intensely than his father. What he had against Jesuits was not their hypocrisy, since in a sense he also practised this himself. Rather, he abhorred their open and self-complacent hypocrisy. His tutor taught Stendhal the Ptolemaic system of astronomy. His grandfather asked why he taught a system that he knew to be false, whereupon the tutor answered: 'Monsieur, il explique tout et d'ailleurs est approuvé par l'Eglise' (*HB*, p. 611).[16]

The two lovers go on like this for a while, almost succeeding in telling each other about their love, yet never quite. At one point Madame de Chasteller scolds him for his frequent visits, which could damage her reputation:

> Eh bien? dit Leuwen, respirant à peine.
> Jusque-là, le ton de Madame de Chasteller avait été convenable, sage, froid, aux yeux de Leuwen au moins. Le son du voix avec lequel il prononça ce mot, *eh bien*, eût manqué peut-être au Don Juan le plus accompli; chez Leuwen il n'y avait aucun talent, c'était l'impulsion de la nature, le naturel. Ce simple mot de Leuwen changea tout. (*LL*, p. 1035)

Madame de Chasteller, moved, almost fails to go on, but Lucien of course fails to see that she fails. So we seem to have got no further. Lucien leaves her, he is almost incapable of walking straight. 'Madame de Chasteller eut pitié de lui, elle eut l'idée de lui prendre la main à l'anglaise, en signe de bonne amitié' (*LL*, p. 1037).

At this point Stendhal seems on the point of giving up. Lucien really is too clumsy, and Stendhal after all cannot push him towards Madame de Chasteller. He writes in the margin of the manuscript: 'Sur quoi

---

[16] There is another key episode that shows Stendhal's horror of conventionalism in science, and his way of linking this mode of reasoning to Jesuitism. Referring to his teacher of mathematics, he recalls that 'le monstre, s'approchant de son tableau en toile cirée et traçant deux lignes parallèles et très voisines, me dit: "Vous voyez bien qu'à l'infini on peut dire qu'elles se rencontrent." Je faillis tout quitter. Un confesseur, adroit et bon jésuite, aurait pu me convertir à ce moment en commentant cette maxime: "Vous voyez que tout est erreur, ou plutôt qu'il n'y a rien de faux, rien de vrai, tout est convention. Adoptez la convention qui vous fera le mieux recevoir dans le monde . . ."' (*HB*, pp. 858–9).

l'historien dit: on ne peut pas espérer d'une femme honnête qu'elle se donne absolument; encore faut-il la prendre. *For me.* Le meilleur chien de chasse ne peut que passer le gibier à portée du fusil du chasseur. Si celui-ci ne tire pas, le chien n'y peut mais. Le romancier est comme le chien de son héros' (*LL*, p. 1537). Even though Lucien is superior to 'le don Juan le plus accompli', he is also inferior to 'le jeune homme de Paris un peu plus vulgairement élevé'. The net effect is that he gets nowhere. Stendhal *has* to push him into the arms of Madame de Chasteller – or should we say that Lucien finally decides to take the step? 'Leuwen, voyant la main de madame de Chasteller s'approcher de la sienne, la prit et la porta lentement à ses lèvres' (*LL*, p. 1037). There follows a period of extreme happiness, two or three weeks during which Lucien and Madame de Chasteller are constantly together, innocently but intensely in love.

Yet Stendhal clearly felt that this was a case of premature satiation. The Lucien who achieves this bliss is not yet quite him, Henri Beyle. Lucien has no character yet, he knows nothing about the world, he has not exposed himself to action, he is pure sensibility. Stendhal then introduces a ridiculous and implausible event to separate the two lovers, by making Lucien believe that Madame de Chasteller, whom he has seen daily at close quarters, has suddenly given birth to a child. He escapes from Nancy, where this part of the novel has taken place, returns to Paris and enters the bureaucracy of the July Monarchy. He does indeed see action, quite a lot of it in fact, some of which would have been dishonourable had it not been for his fundamental integrity. Eventually the two lovers were to be reconciled and marry – an outcome that would have made the novel unique among Stendhal's major works. But the final part was never written, and the manuscript ends before the reconciliation has taken place.

There is an additional point about *Lucien Leuwen* to be made. Stendhal seems to be almost as enamoured of Lucien's witty and worldly father as of Lucien himself. While Lucien has all the awkward grace of a naive youth, his father has the uncontrived charm of the born *raconteur*. He has the same tender impatience towards Lucien as has Stendhal himself. Like Stendhal, he tries to steer Lucien into the right channels by arranging for him to have a post in the bureaucracy, a left-hand mistress and then a right-hand mistress, etc. Yet, like Stendhal, he tells his son: 'Soyez libre' (*LL*, p. 1069). I do not claim to fully understanding this intricate relationship, but I do think that the following statements can be supported. Stendhal identifies closely both with father and son. His ironic asides on Lucien parallel the attitude of Leuwen *père* towards his son. Moreover, they closely parallel Stendhal's own entries in his diary, when he comments on what he wrote some years before. In 1815, for instance, rereading his amorous notes from 1810, he remarks: 'Si je n'avais pas été amoureux, je lui aurais dit ce soir-là, au milieu de tout le monde, à voix basse: "Je vous aime éperdument." Je l'aurais eue deux mois plus tôt' (*OI*, p. 645). Also, there is evidence for Stendhal's desire to be several persons at the same time. In *Les Privilèges* – an extraordinary exercise in wish-fulfilment – we find the following statute: 'Ainsi, le privilègié pourra quatre fois par an et pour un temps illimité chaque fois occuper deux corps à la fois' (Stendhal 1982, p. 984).

Let me try to draw the argument together by offering some conclusions. I shall do so by confronting Stendhal and Sartre – a confrontation not undertaken by Sartre himself, for reasons we can only speculate about. The confrontation cannot be conclusive or systematic, since Sartre notoriously was better at raising important problems than at constructing an analytical framework for discussing them.

As an apparently trivial fact, we may note that Stendhal in his youth entertained that typical adolescent belief which for Sartre is epitomized in the title of a play by Sarment, 'Je suis trop grand pour moi' (Sartre 1943, p. 96). This holds in relation to women: 'Si Victorine me repousse, elle en refuse une autre que moi, mes lettres ne me montrent pas tel que je suis' (*OI*, p. 178). It also holds for his artistic career: 'Si je ne me corrige pas, j'aurai été *the greatest bard* au fond de mon coeur, de moi-même, et n'ayant jamais pu me montrer aux hommes, je passerai *without fame*' (*OI*, p. 208). We might dismiss this as bad faith of the kind classically embodied in Garcin, in *Huis Clos*: the belief that one can have an inner essence totally at odds with one's overt behaviour. The existentialist reader of Stendhal appreciates him precisely because he overcame the cult of the mute and beautiful soul: 'A hundred years before Malraux, Stendhal might have said that man is what he does, not what he hides' (Brombert 1968, p. 174). Now this seems to me to be clearly false, given Stendhal's constant and I believe veridical emphasis on the joys of the inner life. In society he prefers listening to talking; he talks only as a way of paying his entry ticket

(*HB*, p. 804). But this is not the main point I want to make. Rather, I would query the easy assumption that Stendhal in these diary entries was in bad faith, for would we not in retrospect say that he was right? Moreover, did he not have reasons for believing what he did? We could not say, of course, whether he believed what he did for these reasons. His confidence in his own superiority may have stemmed from desires of a kind shared with many adolescents who do not have Stendhal's reasons for it. Yet I believe the case drives a wedge in Sartre's argument at the very place where it might seem most unassailable.

According to Valéry and Sartre, Stendhal was guilty of bad faith by his desire to be sincere. There may be an element of truth in this assertion, but if so a very small one. First, it should be clear that one can be sincere with respect to one's own past. One can say, sincerely, 'I did such and such', 'I felt such and such' and even 'I was such and such', if by that phrase one only means to point to a certain pattern in one's behaviour. Incidentally, of these phrases the most suspicious in Stendhal's eyes would be the second, 'I felt such and such'. For him it is almost a criterion of a genuine sentiment that one should be unable to remember it. 'Il est très difficile de peindre ce qui a été *naturel* en vous, de mémoire, on peint mieux le *factice*, le *joué*, parce que l'effort qu'il fallu pour *jouer* l'a gravé dans la mémoire.' This corresponds to his remark that there is no greater absurdity than when Voltaire has a person saying, 'Je sens telle et telle chose' (*OI*, pp. 267, 124).

Next, I believe that Valéry at least was guilty of a logical mistake when he attributed to Stendhal the desire to impress by his sincerity. 'J'y crois distinguer un certain calcul, une spéculation sur le lecteur futur, une intention sensible de séduire par le négligé et l'impromptu apparent' (Valéry 1957, p. 569). Now it is true that Stendhal in his autobiography has a reader in mind; also that he may well have anticipated and rejoiced in the possibility that the reader might be seduced by his frankness. But this does not imply that he wrote in order to seduce the reader by his frankness. We must distinguish between the consequences of an action for the sake of which it is undertaken, and the consequences that may arise as predictable and possibly welcome by-products. If we ask an artist what he is doing, he would say 'trying to get it right', not 'trying to impress the public', although he may well know that the public will be impressed if he gets it right.

Moreover, it is not clear that Stendhal's sincerity consists in attributing to himself any permanent qualities or features. For Sartre, of course, bad faith does not consist in getting hold of the *wrong* attribute, but in attributing to oneself *any* determinate characteristic (Caws 1979). Now Stendhal, throughout his life, refused to attribute any permanent qualities to himself. In a diary entry from 1804, he notes that 'l'âme n'a que des *états* et jamais des *qualités* en magasin' (*OI*, p. 114). Thirty years later he writes, 'je ne sais pas ce que je suis: bon, méchant, spirituel, sot' (*HB*, p. 804). But – and this is where the Valéry–Sartre objection might apply – he also adds that 'Ce que je sais parfaitement, ce sont les choses qui me font peine ou plaisir, que je désire ou que je hais.' If such likes and dislikes are taken as character features, then Stendhal does impute to himself a permanent core which, as I said, any Stendhalian self must respect. If, however, character is understood as a disposition to act, then he does not see himself as having a character, nor as being a character. On Sartrian premises Stendhal's belief in his fixed preferences might count as bad faith, but perhaps this should rather make us question those premises themselves.

If there is a Sartrian criticism to be made of Stendhal, its thrust must be elsewhere. I promised that I would have more to say about Stendhal's notion of natural behaviour, and indeed this may be the weak point in his enterprise. From Stendhal's diary, it is clear that, for him, to be natural means two different things, embodied in Lucien Leuwen and Leuwen *père* respectively. There is, first, the unreflected spontaneity that we may refer to as naiveté. Of women with this quality, Stendhal says that 'Leur pudeur délicate communique à leurs actions quelque chose de contraint; à force de naturel, elles se donnent l'apparence de manquer de naturel; mais cette gaucherie tient à la grâce céleste' (*DA*, chap. 26). Secondly, however, there is the natural wit which Stendhal found in good company – that which delights not by clumsy grace, but by throwaway perfection; evoking admiration, yet not striving for it; knowing well that one may evoke admiration, yet not acting for the sake of it. Stendhal, clearly, wants to have both of these graces. Now I believe that each of these virtues, taken separately, is essentially a by-product: the attempt to achieve one of them is contradictory in the weak sense, assuming that any attempt at character planning will be frustrated by the hammock problem. In addition Sartre would argue, and I think correctly, that the idea of having both of these virtues simultaneously is contradictory in the strong sense, being essentially a variety of the notion of being at one and the same time and in one and the same respect *en-soi* and *pour-soi*.

However, there are reasons for believing that Stendhal abandoned the attempt to achieve these virtues for himself, and tried to satisfy his desires by proxy. In *Lucien Leuwen* this attempt takes two forms – one that failed, one that could succeed. First, he tried to endow Lucien with both innocence and character. The innocence is the key to his love for Madame de Chasteller, and hers for him; the character is what he sets out to acquire when returning to Paris. In the third act, presumably, he would marry Madame de Chasteller and enable Stendhal, by proxy, to have his cake and eat it too. But there is no reason to believe that Madame de Chasteller would recognize in the lucid cynic, who Lucien by that time would have become, the awkward young man whom she had loved. In fact, it is hard to escape the conclusion that Lucien would turn out to be like his father.

On the other hand, Stendhal could have achieved the impossible feat of being *en-soi* and *pour-soi*, naive and witty, by firmly distinguishing between son and father. This would enable him to be two persons simultaneously, to laugh at himself without the object of amusement being infected and corroded by the irony. Stendhal almost succeeded in this ingenious exercise in wish-fulfilment, but failed because he tried to fuse his two personae into one. *Lucien Leuwen* remained unfinished because its separate parts converge to a non-existent point.

REFERENCES

Brams, S. (1980) *Biblical Games*, Cambridge, Mass.: MIT Press.
Brams, S. (1983) *Superior Beings*, Cambridge, Mass.: MIT Press.
Brombert, V. (1968) *Stendhal: Fiction and the Themes of Freedom*, Chicago: Chicago University Press.
Caws, P. (1979) *Sartre*, London: Routledge and Kegan Paul.
Elster, J. (1983) *Sour Grapes*, Cambridge: Cambridge University Press.
Elster, J. (1984a) 'Active and passive negation', in P. Watzlawick (ed.), *The Invented Reality*, pp. 175–205, New York: Norton.

Elster, J. (1984b) *Ulysses and the Sirens*, rev. edn, Cambridge: Cambridge University Press.

Farber, L. (1968) *Lying, Despair, Jealousy, Envy, Sex, Suicide, Drugs and the Good Life*, New York: Basic Books.

Festinger, L. (1957) *A Theory of Cognitive Dissonance*, Stanford University Press.

Føllesdal, D. (1981) 'Sartre on freedom', in P. A. Schilpp (ed.), *Sartre* (The Library of Living Philosophers), pp. 392–407, La Salle, Ill.: Open Court.

Hirschman, A. (1967) *Development Projects Observed*, Washington, D.C.: The Brookings Institution.

Jones, G. C. (1976) 'Le Moi qui se regarde: les problèmes de l'autobiographie dans le roman stendhalien', in V. del Litto (ed.), *Stendhal et les Problèmes de l'Autobiographie*, pp. 11–20. Grenoble: Presses Universitaires de Grenoble.

Kolakowski, L. (1972) *The Key to Heaven*, New York: Grove Press.

Kolakowski, L. (1978) *Main Currents of Marxism*, Oxford: Oxford University Press.

Lejeune, P. (1976) 'Stendhal et les problèmes de l'autobiographie', in V. del Litto (ed.), *Stendhal et les Problèmes de l'Autobiographie*, pp. 21–36, Grenoble: Presses Universitaires de Grenoble.

Sartre, J.-P. (1943) *L'Etre et le Néant*, Paris: Gallimard.

Starobinski, J. (1961) 'Stendhal pseudonyme', in *L'Oeil Vivant*, pp. 189–240. Paris: Gallimard.

Stendhal (1952) *Romans et Nouvelles* vol. 1 (edn. Pléiade), Paris: Gallimard.

Stendhal (1980) *De l'Amour*, Paris: Flammarion.

Stendhal (1981) *Oeuvres Intimes*, vol. 1 (edn Pléiade), Paris: Gallimard.

Stendhal (1982) *Oeuvres Intimes*, vol. 1 (edn Pléiade), Paris: Gallimard.

Valéry, P. (1957) 'Stendhal', in *Oeuvres* (edn Pléiade), vol. 1, pp. 553–82, Paris: Gallimard.

5. Self-deception, *akrasia* and irrationality*

AMÉLIE OKSENBERG RORTY

Self-deception and *akrasia* present severe problems for certain theories of rational agency, problems that have provoked an astonishing exercise of philosophic self-deception in denying the phenomena, redescribing them in ways that attempt to preserve the theories they jeopardize. Such philosophical self-deception is often also accompanied by philosophic *akrasia*: standard practices violate the preferred philosophic theories.

There have of course also been attempts to save the phenomena – to explain, rather than explain away, self-deception and *akrasia* so that they do not present embarrassments for the theory of rational agency. But these attempts rarely question the centrality of rationality and rationally oriented motivation that self-deception and *akrasia* seem to challenge. Rather than trying to save the phenomena by still keeping them at the fringe suburbs of the theory, I want to bring *akrasia* and self-deception in from the beggarly outskirts, the slums of the self and theories of the self. I want to examine them to see how they force revisions on our theories of agency.

Behind standard theories of rational agency there is a picture of the self: it can be represented as a map, a plan of a city, a city of broad avenues radiating from a grand central square with the federal government buildings, with magesterial façades and elegant capitols. At the centre of the city, in the square from which all avenues radiate, are the judicial, legislative and executive branches of the self: although the governmental functions are distinguished, they are presumed to act

*An earlier version of this chapter was read at a colloquium on 'Irrationality: Explanation and Understanding' held in Paris at the Maison des Sciences de l'Homme. That paper was published in *Social Science Information* (1980) 19, 6. I am grateful to the members of that colloquium, and especially to Sissela Bok, for suggestions and comments.

from a single set of rules, with clearly defined priorities fixed by a classical conception of rationality. Decisions emanate directly from the centre, along the broad boulevards to the outskirts, to the commercial and industrial centres, to the suburbs. Even foreign relations are presumed to be regulated by the same systematic rational plan.

The phenomena of self-deception and *akrasia* lead us to a different image of the structures of the self. It is the older medieval city of relatively autonomous neighbourhoods, linked by small lanes that change their names half way across their paths, a city that is a very loose confederation of neighbourhoods of quite different kinds, each with its distinctive internal organization, and distinctive procedures for foreign relations, even different conditions for entry into the federation: a city of guilds, the courts of grand families, religious orders, and old small towns. Imposed over the medieval city there is the grand plan of radial avenues emanating from the centre to the outskirts: the rational plan of the city that one can see from an aerial view. But the new main arteries do not necessarily provide the best routes from one part of the city to another, and they do not give the most perspicuous idea of the working relations among the various parts of the city. The radiant city does indeed exist and function over the medieval configuration: our task is to understand how the two cities both serve and block each other's operations. An examination of the strategies exercised in *akrasia* and self-deception reveal the various strata and layers of the self, its complex archaeology.

I

What is the theory of rational agency that self-deception and *akrasia* challenge? Against what background assumptions do akrasia and self-deception seem puzzling? We have good working distinctions among the varieties of rationality – the rationality of formal consistency and entailment; prudential or *Zweckrationalität*; and what we might call the substantial rationality that not only orders actions to ends but also examines those ends critically for hidden disorientations that might not be revealed by the self-fulfilling practices of prudential rationality.[1] Against the background of this work, we can begin with the recog-

[1] Cp. Jon Elster (1979) *Ulysses and the Sirens*, Cambridge: Cambridge University Press.

nition that the dimensions of rationality are not only complexly interrelated, but that there are conflicting views about their respective priorities.

According to all these theories of rational agency, an agent capable of voluntary action, and certainly of responsible agency, must be rational, at least by prudential and formal criteria. But even an agent who fulfils all those requirements, in a strong substantive way – an agent who knows what he is doing, who is aware of the natural primary standard consequences of his actions, and of his priorities, and is capable of standard valid references, accepting the consequences of those inferences – even such an agent who also can weigh and assess his ends as well as his course of action, might have judicious judicial capacities whose powers and capacities do not necessarily automatically dominate the entire variety of his motives. Even if his rational evaluations carry his desire, they need not carry his intellectual habits, the patterns salient in his perception, his ways of interpreting his particular situation.[2] Even a strongly rational person also daydreams and acts from habit. Furthermore, even when a person's rationality has strong legislative power, it does not automatically have strong executive power. Even if the large variety of his motivational determinations conform to his rationality he can, in the event, be voluntarily swayed against his better judgment, to follow a charismatic leader, allow himself to be cast into a role that does not coincide with his preferences, to be moved by empathy or by the excitement of crowd behaviour.[3]

But questioning the model of the legislative and executive centrality of the various forms of rationality, and seeing that even these forms can conflict with one another, should not – does not – force us to obscurantist Whitmanesque poses on the propriety and necessity of irrational inconsistency, with a different self for every occasion. If philosophers who deny *akrasia* are self-deceptive and akratic, so are those who deny the integrative functions of the varieties of rational strategies, the ways in which they genuinely do operate in decision and action. Our practices of assigning responsibility, distinguishing friends from enemies, the practices of planning for the future on an assump-

---

[2] Cp. A. O. Rorty (1983) 'Akratic believers', *American Philosophical Quarterly* 20, 175–83.
[3] Cp. A. O. Rorty (1980) '*Akrasia* and conflict', *Inquiry* 23, 193–212.

tion that one's present self bears a strong continuity to one's future self, the plans of weighing and assaying alternatives towards ends which are themselves also evaluated would become incomprehensible illusions if we abandon the view of the self as engaged in rational attempts at integration.

There is a question of whether these practices of planning, assigning responsibility, shame, etc. are the stale leftovers of a bad education based on a mistaken or a dated and ideologically slanted conception of individuality. Or perhaps they are a canny move on the part of an ideological view that builds certain sorts of benign and functional misconceptions into the educational system, the modern version of the Platonic lie. Perhaps our practices as rational planners and evaluators are self-mesmerizing exercises, designed to assure the élan, style and conviction necessary for successful action. Perhaps their success is simply a function of their working as a self-fulfilling prophecy. No doubt there is something to the view that what we boldly call rational evaluation is a way of steeling ourselves to endow our actions with the shimmering look of conviction. After all, our best rational actions are called so, by an extension of courtesy. What commonly passes for responsible deliberation is rarely sound, rarely even reconstructible as sound. It is our magic for acquiring a brave face and a sureness of manner. It is no accident that philosophical scepticism has such power as a philosophical position: we are all too keenly aware of the differences between the psychological and the logical accounts of our beliefs and actions, their causal descriptions and their rational reconstruction.

But deliberation does after all generally provide better assurance than six Hail Marys and a somersault. Deliberation is after all truly directed to getting things right. Sane scepticism stops short of cynicism: rational deliberation succeeds in helping us whistle in the dark because there is some conceptual connection between success and truth, and between truth and careful investigation. Even if they are merely self-fulfilling ideologically oriented prophecies, the assumptions of the theory of rational agency require to be reformulated rather than abandoned. After all, even sceptical detractors of theories of rational agency are presenting argumerts designed to convince rational agents.

Self-deception and *akrasia* are so pervasive, prevalent and powerful because the psychological processes that are operative in them are by no means distinctive to them, and by no means pathological in their normal use. Self-deception and *akrasia* are by-products of psychological processes that make ordinary rational action possible. Of course not each and every case of *akrasia* and self-deception is benign; but the capacities which are exercised in self-deception and *akrasia* are common, and perhaps even necessary for sane rational action. In some cases, self-deception and *akrasia* may even be a miserable agent's best options, though of course not one that he – or we – could coherently choose under that description. There is a strong hidden rationale behind the persistent strategies that are commonly called irrational.

II

What are the respective attractions of self-deception and *akrasia*? In what does their respective irrationality consist? Because *akrasia* is the less dangerous and the far more ingrained and pervasive complaint, let us start there.

First, a rough and crude characterization of *akrasia*: X has performed an action *a* (where *a* can be a psychological action, like perceiving or deciding) akratically when X has acted voluntarily and intentionally under a description of *a* that on some level he takes to be contrary to his judgment about the preferred course for him to take in that situation.

Now why is *akrasia* so pervasive and attractive?

An agent capable of responding appropriately to the potentially conflicting demands of a rich and rapidly changing environment is an agent with potentially conflicting traits. On the one hand, he requires strong relatively conservative habits of behaviour and thought, of interpretation and understanding, habits that provide action outcomes even when the person's motivational scheme is indeterminate or fluid. On the other hand, he requires the critical capacities of unbounded inquiry, of rational thought that is not formed, determined or directed by his habits. A voluntary agent requires Tory habits, and Whig critical capacities. Furthermore, an agent living in a complex heterogeneous social world requires strong empathic capacities for acquiring the interests and motives of the members of his community. Rousseau and Freud have shown us that the mechanisms that make social cooperation easy and natural are mechanisms that also internally divide a person. Precisely to the extent that a person can empathize with, and acquire the interests of the various members of society, to that extent he will be divided. On the other hand, the capacities that help overcome the internal divisions of a genuinely social and empathetic person, the capacities of strong critical and often unswerving autonomy are also clearly necessary. Reconciling the narcissistic, the empathic and the autonomous capacities involves a long-range integrative project for a conflicted agent. Integration is not his automatic starting-point and inheritance. (In drawing the contrasts between habit and rationality, between autonomy and strong empathy, I do not want to suggest that habits are a-rational or that reason is not thoroughly imbued with its own routines and habits. Habits could not operate in their reliable conservative ways if they did not have a cognitive component.) Similarly, the capacities for autonomy and empathy are by no means mutually exclusive. Indeed, Rousseau and Freud argued that their development is interdependent; nevertheless, we can profitably contrast the conservatism of rational habits with the critical self-corrective rational capacities that can in principle detach us from those habits. Similarly, even though empathy and autonomy do not in principle conflict, they often do so in normal, and not merely in pathological, practice.

If, then, a complex agent capable of voluntary responsible agency is not merely capable of conflict but often also drawn to it, he will frequently find himself in situations where his preferred course – even when it is rationally formed, and linked to some rational habits – will fail to draw the rest of his motivational structure with it. The usual story about the attractions of the akratic alternative are far too simple. Often what explains *akrasia* is not the strength of the akratic alternative, but the relative psychological weakness of the preferred course. The agent need not want to perform the akratic action: it frequently does not stand very high in his preference rankings. It need not even be a close contender to the preferred course. Sometimes the attraction of the akratic alternative is simply the attraction of a strongly entrenched habit: the akratic course is then the easy course. Moreover, the sorts of conflict that produce, and are expressed in *akrasia*, need not be the conflict of desires, needs or wishes; they can be conflicts between other sorts of motivationally functioning psychological processes: habits of perception and interpretation, behavioural habits of all sorts, habits of social sensitivities. When an agent is conflicted, without a taste for conflicts and without approved strategies for resolving them, then akrasia sometimes provides a way out. It at least settles *what to do*. And it does so, because the strategies represented in the akratic alternative are strongly entrenched: they work to produce an action or thought outcome, no matter what the agent's motivational condition may be. That is precisely the strength and function of habit: it is capable of being exercised relatively independently of the agent's occurrent motives.

One of the ways that the phenomena of *akrasia* and self-deception illuminate the shortcomings of the standard model of action as an outcome of beliefs and desires, an outcome that can be overridden by rational will, is that they show how complex and varied the class of motives is. The class of motives is highly heterogeneous; various members of that class function in quite distinctive ways in forming actions, and the conditions for their satisfactions are quite distinctive. Wishes, religious and moral commitments, wants, needs, fantasies and habits are often standardly classified as desires or wants or preferences. But their respective relations to beliefs are quite distinctive in form; they determine the details of the action outcome in distinctive ways; the formal conditions of their satisfaction are distinguishable. The complete description of the actions which issue from each of these – the description that identifies the significance of the action by tracing its aetiology – has a different form. In principle, such attitudes can be formulated as reasons and beliefs, as propositionally defined desires by procrustean moves: either they are capable of being propositionalized, or off-with-their-heads: they are irrational. While this procrustean procedure may reveal the structure of the logical justification of our actions and attitudes, it does not reveal the ways in which such intentional proto-rational motives really function. Even when such reconstructions reveal the *structures* of the rational reconstruction of our attitudes, they do not by themselves provide the basic premises that are the substance of that reconstruction.

So though the akratic action formally satisfies some motive simply because it is, after all, voluntarily performed, the motive can be extremely general in character: it need not specify a particular desire. But explaining actions – particularly actions that appear deviant –

requires specifying the level of generality of the intentional component that identifies the action. Is there a feature about the particular action that sets the satisfaction conditions, or will *any* action of a quite general similar structural type satisfy? Sometimes an action satisfies a motive simply because the motive is strongly entrenched; but a motive can become entrenched accidentally rather than because it consistently leads to satisfactions. Not all motives are desires *sub specie boni*; nor is whatever is seen as *sub specie boni* so seen because it has been taken *sub specie rationis*.

Standard theories of rational agency trade on important ambiguities in the notions of preference and satisfaction. Because they take satisfactions and preferences at face value, they do not give explanations of an agent's desires; their accounts of motivation are simplistic. An agent's felt preferences$_1$ are what he believes and senses himself to want: standardly, these are desires for felt satisfactions$_1$. Such felt satisfactions$_1$ are defined by their corresponding desires. But since there are also preferences that are not phenomenologically experienced, and since a person can be mistaken about his preferences$_1$, *preference* becomes a theoretical term that encompasses a wide range of motives, only some of which are phenomenologically experienced as such, and only some of whose satisfactions are phenomenologically experienced. Habits, moods, emotions, religious or moral commitments, aesthetic reactions like disgust or admiration and other sorts of character traits are, in the larger sense, motivational. They form a person's preference$_2$ system, and often explain the structure of a person's preference$_1$ rankings.

The psychological explanation of the agent taking the akratic course need not appear, even in disguised form, in the intentional description of the akratic course. What draws the agent to the akratic course is not necessarily the surface description of his preferences$_1$ for the akratic alternative, but the psychological mechanisms – his preferences$_2$ – that operate in standard rational habits. These preferences$_2$ can operate without the agent having to act from an occurrent desire, in ways that preserve the voluntary character of the action. When the agent is conflicted or debilitated, he lacks a reigning occurrent desire. So he turns himself into what we might call the lower gear of standard operating procedures, of a large variety of psychological processes, which can all roughly be characterized as habitual because they operate without the intervention of a current desire. Acting on such procedures satisfies preferences$_2$. A satisfaction$_2$ of a preference$_2$ is the state of affairs that represents the realization of a preference$_2$ where that preference$_2$ may conflict with the agent's felt desires, his preference$_1$ rankings.

There are, roughly, three attractive strategies of *akrasia*. These are of course not mutually exclusive, nor are they exhaustive. Indeed, they often augment and supplement each other.

1.   The akratic alternative sometimes acquires its attractions by its power to dominate the agent's attention: it has more salience for him than the preferred course. It draws and focuses the agent's attention on some feature of the akratic alternative; by filling the experiential field, it drowns out the preferred alternative. The akratic alternative can be dominant by default: a person's preferred judgments may fail to magnetize or hold his attention. There are of course a number of ways in which an alternative can dominate attention: it can be immediately present, filling the visual field; it can have imagined intensity or excitement; it can promise absorbing pleasure. It can be represented in vivid detail, with a high degree of specificity and determinateness. It can be physiologically or psychologically salient. It can represent the satisfaction of a frustrated need. There is of course a continuum between constitutionally fixed, although relatively plastic patterns of salience and dominance, their strong cultural formation and reinforcement, and patterns of dominance fixed by the vicissitudes of an individual's biological and psychological history. It is not always easy to identify the attention-dominating features of an akratic alternative: their dominance can be symbolically coded in ways that could only be deciphered by tracing the aetiology of the formation of an individual's habits of intentional focusing.

2.   The attractions of the akratic alternative are sometimes those of the familiar, the habitual, the easy course. The more the akratic alternative seems composed of action routines that are strongly habitual, and the more distant the preferred alternative is from such habitual action routines, the more attraction it acquires above its surface attractions. The habitual course presents ready-made action solutions; the ease of following it is a function of its not requiring any extra motivation. Perceptual habits of attending and focusing, cognitive habits of structuring or interpreting situations, habits of inference

and narrative expectations are as voluntary as many behavioural habits. They often support the akratic alternative against the preferred course.

3. Social streaming can pull in the direction of the akratic alternative: the akrates can follow the charismatic leader, or be influenced by the mechanisms of sympathy or antipathy to take a position or adopt an attitude that conflicts with his judgment, being impelled into action routines that conflict with the preferred alternative. It is just these strategies of social streaming – our capacities to take in, to acquire the beliefs and desires of others – that enable us to be social agents, capable of quick cooperative action; these capacities also simultaneously set the conditions for *akrasia*.

Once we have demystified *akrasia*, we can see that the attractions of the akratic alternative are those of the most ordinary and common sorts of psychological activities. Far from being pathological, these activities are automatically and constantly functional, not only in pre-intentional behaviour, but also in the most considered, most rational considered action. In the larger sense, these psychological habits provide the very stuff of rational thought. They can provide the rational explanation of the agent's beliefs and desires, a rational explanation that the agent accepts as accounting for what he did. In this way he can think of them as *general principles* that he would underwrite, without thinking that they justify what he did in the instance; they justify the most general *type* of his action, without justifying the particular action. It is this that allows us to see how *akrasia* can be voluntary – since it falls within the agent's character structure, following general principles that he accepts – and yet to be against his better judgment.

In any case, even when a person takes rationality to be more than a crucial criterion for the legitimization of his various ends, even when he takes the exercise of rationality to be the end with which he primarily identifies himself, it cannot provide the sole or sufficient principle of choice. It cannot by itself provide the range of aims and directions required for a recognizably human life. The Platonic dream of integration is that the direction of rationality will coincide with the direction of other goods. And perhaps, for a happy few, it does. But it is not part of that dream that rationality can provide the substance of our goods.

III

Let us now turn to the irrationalities of self-deception. Briefly and crudely, X is self-deceived when by some criterion for attributing belief and action (a criterion that allows a person to be self-deceived about his actions as well as about his beliefs), he believes *p* and he believes not-*p* or denies that he believes *p*. While on some level he sees that his beliefs conflict, he engages in a strategy of denying that conflict, a strategy of the sort that he would normally recognize as merely masking their incompatibility. This strategy is exercised in the interests of maintaining, advancing, developing some conception of himself as the sort of person he takes himself to be. Self-deception involves deception of the self, by the self, for or about the self.[4]

We shall set aside the familiar epistemological problems of identifying bona fide cases of self-deception that do not reduce to conflict or to being mistaken about one's beliefs and actions, and instead consider the attractions that self-deception has for us, attractions that explain its pervasiveness and power.

The attractions of self-deception come from its involving the exercise of several psychological processes which it is difficult to distinguish. Although these strategies are not in themselves necessarily self-deceptive, their exercise is frequently highly benign. Because the success of these strategies depends on their unselfconscious and relatively automatic use, it is natural that they should often lead to self-deception. Given a choice between being unable to exercise these psychological strategies, and being prey to self-deception, one might well choose and even perhaps rationally choose to retain the capacities.

The first strategy involves self-manipulation in situations of indeterminacy. We often deliberately trade on the ambiguities of asserting a potentiality and its fulfilment. 'That is very good!', we say to children, 'How responsible you are!' We mean they are doing very well for what they are; but the energy and enhancement for the child comes from his taking what we say in the stronger sense. We practise the same sorts of deflection on the child within, carefully using ambiguities that we interpret in the strong sense when doing so is often

---

[4] Cp. A. O. Rorty (1972) 'Belief and self-deception', *Inquiry* 15, 387–410 and A. O. Rorty (1975) 'Adaptivity and self-knowledge', *Inquiry* 18, 1–22.

a crucial condition for generating a self-fulfilling prophecy. Such bootstrap operations in situations of indeterminacy allow us to act energetically and loyally beyond our standard emotional means, in ways we might not be able to do if we were careful to avoid manipulative shadow-falsification in the service of making it all come true. Marriages, work, devotion to children, friendships and causes do not of course absolutely require such self-manipulation. Nevertheless, they involve risks we would find difficult to accept with absolutely clear and open eyes: carefully directed ignorance and blindness are wonderfully enheartening. Frequently, in any case, such manipulative enterprises are initially non-deceptively naive. Yet successful naive habits quickly become strongly entrenched. Even when we know better, we connive in our projections, being careful to hide the traces of the enlarged slightly misleading description, the carefully preserved myopia, the averted gaze.

Of course these strategies are not in themselves self-deceptive. They only become so when the person actively resists acknowledging them, refusing correction that he would normally recognize. But since the successes of these enterprises often require that we do not focus on ourselves as being engaged in carrying them out, there is some resistance to their acknowledgment, a resistance that can become self-deceptive.

The second strategy involves the strong conservation of beliefs and motives that we have come to regard as suspect. Latitudinarian soft believers, who adopt a policy of holding to a well-entrenched dispositional belief until there is good reason to doubt it, sometimes still actively resist revising beliefs when they do indeed take themselves to have reason to doubt. The holism of the mental and the psychological requires sanity-preserving compartmentalization and regionalization that blocks the correction and revision of the ramified consequences of changed beliefs. We also resist revisions in our priorities even when we think (on some level) that such changes would appropriately follow significant changes in preferences. We resist the decisions and perhaps even the renunciations that we would like to avoid.

Descartes and Hume joined in refusing to follow the practical implications of their philosophical investigations. They set limits on the disquieting if not actually sceptical force of their respective versions of the method of doubt. In its benign forms, this is the conservativism built into the habits of our Tory minds. When, like Descartes and Hume, we advance Burkean justifications of such conservatism in practical though not in philosophical matters, we need not be self-deceived. Resisting the ramification of corrections – even when they seem, on strictly logical grounds, to be required – can be a sound and rational policy.[5] Without self-deception, it increases adaptability and flexibility by keeping options open. Yet the transition from justified conservativism to dangerous self-deception is quick and subtle: it is difficult to notice, even more difficult to prevent. Such compartmentalization and regionalization works best precisely when it is relatively unself-conscious; the transition from a compartmentalization that is still sensitive to the needs of appropriate correction and a compartmentalization that actively resists correction might not only go unnoticed, but be judged to be worth the cost.

IV

What can we learn from the differences between the strategies of self-deception and those of *akrasia*? How do their respective forms of irrationality differ?

One theory is that self-deception concerns beliefs while *akrasia* concerns actions. But self-deception can be behavioural and non-propositional. A person can present false appearances, not only to others but to himself, without actually ever saying anything, without taking an explicit propositional attitude to the description of what he does. For instance, someone might behave as if he were devoted to his family or to his teaching: he may take himself to be the sort of person who gives these commitments first priority. But a closer observation can belie that story. While overtly he gives priority to his family and to his teaching, he does so in a way that actually undermines those projects. The manner of his actions undermines their apparent direction and intent. He takes his children to the zoo, but in such a way as to make it all go wrong. He devotes himself to his students, but in such a way as to damage their real development. Of course he might well be conflicted or mistaken about his priorities. But there can be overwhelming behavioural evidence that he recognizes what he denies. Of

[5] Cp. Gilbert Harman, 'Coherence and foundations: positive versus negative undermining'. Unpublished paper.

course that evidence will not have the force of certainty; but ascriptions of behavioural self-deception are no more unsound than are attributions of psychological states in opaque contexts generally are.

On the other hand, *akrasia* need not be behavioural. A person can voluntarily perceive, categorize, intend and decide in ways that violate his primary preferences, and do so without necessarily being self-deceived about what he is doing.

Another theory is that self-deception is always motivated while *akrasia* is not. But, as we have seen, sometimes *akrasia* is motivated by the agent's strategies in avoiding or temporarily resolving conflict. Still, the motivational intervention works differently for the two. The psychological explanation of the akratic action need not appear, even in an encoded form, in the intentional description of the akratic course. The intentional description of the akratic action need not obliquely refer to the agent's motive. The details of the akratic action need not reveal the agent's debility or conflict: the action indicates his situation without representing it. What explains the details of the akratic action is not the person's preference$_1$ ranking, but his preference$_2$ character structure. Like *akrasia*, self-deception need not always be motivated: it can occur as the result of a person's psychological habits and patterns of attention.[6] But when it is motivated, the content of the deception is usually significant. Though that content may be symbolically encoded, it is linked to a person's conception of himself, of what is centrally important to him. Even when a person's conception of himself is not flattering or idealized, the content of the deception serves an image the person has of himself.

Akrasia and self-deception are often subtly interlocked. For a person committed to a strong integration, self-deception is akratic. In deceiving himself, the person has failed to follow what he takes to be the best course, all things considered. But a person who does not adopt strong principles of integration might deceive himself without doing so akratically. Similarly, the akratic can, but need not, cover themselves with self-deception. Of the two, self-deception is the more dangerous. It can block the movement to correction, block the logical rational processes oriented towards truth. Akrasia blocks *Zweckrationalität* without necessarily blocking its own correction.

---

[6]   Cp. Brian MacLaughlin and A. O. Rorty (eds.) (1986) 'The deceptive self: liars and layers', in *The Forms of Self-Deception*, California: University of California Press.

V

A brief and highly programmatic summary is in order. First, these accounts of the strategies and attractions of *akrasia* and self-deception suggest that the picture of a rational agent as someone whose actions are outcomes of beliefs and desires, with a capacity to override these by some act of rational will, requires to be supplemented. The class of beliefs, the class of motives and the class of acts of will are heterogeneous. They form and rationalize actions in quite distinctive ways.

Secondly, we cannot distinguish the good guys so clearly and simply from the bad guys, separating psychological functions that are as such irrational, from those that are rational. Psychological functions that are in some contexts irrational, or at best a-rational are necessary to the rational functions. Self-deception and *akrasia* are pervasive because they are closely connected to strongly entrenched functional psychological processes. Attempts to eradicate *akrasia* and self-deception would jeopardize these processes.

It does not follow of course that we can forthwith justify or accept *akrasia* and self-deception. As they are standardly defined, such an enterprise would be incoherent. Even when we can recognize that *akrasia* or self-deception can sometimes be the agent's best option, he cannot himself choose that course under a description that justifies it. Although *akrasia* and self-deception are not by any means the worst among the psychological and intellectual vices, there is no way of underwriting them in general. Yet is it important to remember that the correction of self-deception and *akrasia* can sometimes lead to consistent unconflicted vice or equally dangerous (though moral) floundering vacillation. Self-deception and *akrasia* are among the phenomena of conflict: as such they are potentially dangerous, because conflicted agents are often unpredictable, and at worst quite destructive. But there are worse dangers, and the strongly righteous determination to wipe out self-deception and *akrasia* can sometimes lead to strong vice.

There is a general lesson in this: for many reasons, we concentrate on establishing that certain practices (like lying for instance) are prima facie, other things being equal, absolutely wrong for a rational agent; and that other practices (like being just for instance), are prima facie, other things being equal, absolutely required of rational agents. It is important to establish such proprieties. But standardly such accounts fail to analyse the relative priorities of those practices which, while absolutely just, nevertheless sometimes conflict with one another, or those which, while being absolutely unjust or wrong, are nevertheless sometimes the best option. Naturally one would not expect a decision on these matters: but as agents we generally need to know how to weigh conflicting goods and wrongs, more than we need to assure our certainties about absolutely binding rights and wrongs. The account of rational agency that is simply concerned to determine the rationality or irrationality of various types of psychological processes or activities sometimes blocks investigations into their respective priorities and proprieties. Not every lie is equally pernicious: we need to investigate the relative advantages of these courses.

VI

Now what about the self and city? These explorations suggest, although of course they by no means establish, that we can regard the agent self as a loose configuration of habits, habits of thought and perception and motivation and action, acquired at different stages, in the service of different ends; some are acquired accidentally and incidentally; others are constitutionally based. Among these habits are a wide ranging variety of what we consider habits of rationality: patterns of inference, of calculation, of interpretation. Closely allied are habits of the imagination, of association, narrative construction, expectation. Agents vary in the ways their habits are structured; some form quite strictly unified systems with strong centralization, others are quite loosely connected, with different habits coming to the fore in response to situational variations. For some, the various strategies of rationality are dominant and integrative; for others, rationality is not the dominant integrative function and some of the integrative processes are served by such other psychological activities as aesthetic disgust or delight, or certain intentional habits of style, ways of interpreting situations as (say) occasions for combat or for adventure. Not all subsystems of habits cooperate in the integrative processes, or cooperate in the same way, on every occasion.

Following this line, it might seem as if the agent disappears into a loose community. It might seem as if the notion of agency disappears;

and with it, too, the very phenomena we set out to explain. It is not the *same* agent who accepts one judgment but acts on another, or the *same* person who both knows and does not know what he is doing.

This brings out an interesting irony in the centrality of self-deception and *akrasia*. It is only when an agent takes the unification of his traits, his thoughts and his actions, as a central project that he is capable of self-deception and *akrasia*. A person who just is a loose confederation of habits is an agent only in the loosest sense. For someone to be capable of agency in the strong sense, to hold himself responsible for avoiding self-deception and *akrasia*, requires that he – or at any rate some relatively central set of his habits – reflexively underwrite his integrative processes. He must declare his various friendly neighbour-hood habits to be one city, the *I*.

The *persona* who says *I* is not necessarily central, not an absolute ruler or even surveyor of the complex actions of the subsystems of habits. In one sense, the *I* is the entire configuration, the loosely connected system seen as a whole. In another, it is the claimant of centrality, the centrality of legitimized governing functions. That articulate voice does indeed represent the varieties of rational strate-gies. But the claimant of centrality has not always or necessarily achieved its aim. And it certainly can fail to acknowledge the necessary contributions of other psychological processes, sometimes charac-terized as irrational.

6. Beyond microeconomics. Conflict among interests in a multiple self as a determinant of value*

GEORGE AINSLIE

Since ancient times people have tried to understand the nature of value, that is, how events motivate us. Two kinds of good have been described: what might be called visceral satisfactions, closely associated with the consumption of a concrete object and usually in the service of an obvious biological need; and more subtle satisfactions, such as knowledge of 'the ideal' (Plato), pursuit of wisdom (Aquinas), 'the good will' (Kant) or self-actualization (Maslow). Human behaviour towards concrete goods has been by far the easier subject to study systematically. Subtle goods defy precise characterization, and so have often seemed to be irrational or at least to be members of a different motivational system than the one people use to evaluate concrete goods.

Value in economics

Quantitative description of the value of concrete objects became the science of economics. By restricting its attention to goods that trade in a cash market, this discipline has been able to describe striking regularities in how we value these goods. It has created a nucleus of well-articulated rules for understanding value. However, this restriction of attention has had a distorting effect. The territory of monetary transactions has sometimes become disconnected from the broad realm of human choice. Money has often been spoken about as 'behaving' in various ways, almost as if it had a life outside the minds of its owners. For all the usefulness that this analytic fiction may have had, it has tended to create a self-contained body of procedures

*Delivered at a conference on the multiple self, Maison des Sciences de l'Homme, Paris, 4–7 January, 1982.

133

without reference to the human motivational processes that actually determine value.

There has always been dissatisfaction with this insular approach to economics. Early economists looked for broader sources from which the power of money might be derived: gold, land, labour. Recently economists have taken increasing notice of the people who spend the money, and have developed means of studying individual households – 'microeconomics'. Bargaining theory has arisen to study the precise ways prices are agreed on, and the spending decisions of individual subjects are studied using real and hypothetical games. It has even been noted that people's behaviour towards unpriced objects, still concrete but removed from the market for one reason or another, resembles their behaviour towards market goods and can sometimes be studied in a similar way. For instance, Gary Becker (1976) has shown that such diverse activities as marriage, prostitution and burglary follow the rationality described by economic laws.

However, as economics examines individual human behaviours more closely, it discovers examples of apparent irrationality that are not accounted for by existing theory. This is true even of purely monetary transactions. For instance, people value sunk costs more than the equivalent opportunity costs, and in experimental gambling situations frequently do not maximize expected value (Thaler 1980; Tversky and Kahneman 1981). In the real world, of course, any gambling reduces one's expected income, and yet gambling is a popular activity.

Gambling may even become an addiction, a circumstance that raises even harder conceptual questions. The victim of an addiction reports himself to be trapped in a consumption pattern which he wants to abandon but cannot. Although some of his behaviour can be described in conventional economic terms, for instance as the combination of an inelastic demand curve for the addictive good with an increasing price for that good (Stigler and Becker 1977), the simultaneous existence of a demand curve for *avoiding* the good requires special treatment.[1]

Most troublesome of all are the examples where contingencies of

---

[1] Winston (1980) has offered a formal solution to this particular problem – two competing, independent consumption patterns. However, once economics has recognized more than one consumer within the individual, it must specify some rules for how these consumers interact.

concrete reward simply fail to control choice. Sometimes this is only because such contingencies have blind spots, where the attitudes and practices Leibenstein (1976) described as 'X-inefficiency' can flourish without penalty. Often, however, there is evidence that the subtle kind of rewards earlier described only by philosophers have become a factor in the marketplace. Looking not only at people's life strategies broadly (Scitovsky 1976) but also at workers' motives to perform on the job (Levinson 1973) economists are becoming aware of the importance of non-concrete, often non-purchasable rewards. There is more and more reason to re-connect economics with other approaches to human choice-making, in the hope of finding ways to rationalize what now seems irrational.

Value in psychology

Unfortunately, the psychological study of motivation has paralleled rather than complemented the economic one. Concrete rewards have been studied thoroughly, but this nucleus of knowledge has not been successfully expanded to include the subtle rewards.

The study of concrete rewards has produced a wealth of quantitative detail about how reinforcement (the internal mechanism of reward) depends on previous deprivation, rate of delivery, the presence or absence of other sources of reinforcement, etc. However, in a prosperous society, most behaviour is not motivated by literal biological needs. Most of our activity is rewarded by emotional processes that are occasioned by other people's social responses, or by tasks or games which are rewarding in their own right. It would clearly be desirable if these subtle reward factors could be understood in the same framework as visceral ones, but psychology has had difficulty bridging the gap.

One approach has been to make classical conditioning ('learning by association') the bridging mechanism. For instance, the rewarding value of an intangible reward like fame might be attributed to an infantile association between getting attention and getting food, thus in effect backing the soft currency of an activity reward with the hard currency of a visceral reward (Miller and Dollard 1941). However, observation has not traced and perhaps cannot trace such tortuous paths of association. Such derivations strain credulity, and in any case there is no reason to expect that the conditioned rewards should remain powerful once the person has discovered direct ways of getting the original visceral reward. The person who is not hungry should stop valuing the conditioned food stimulus, attention.

More recently, psychologists have argued that there are elementary drives for the game-like rewards (Fowler 1967; Hunt 1963). The problem with their exploration, curiosity and mastery drives, and with the related concept of maintaining an optimal level of arousal, is that the properties of the situation needed to satisfy the drive are hard to specify. In general, objects with moderate degrees of complexity, as opposed to very high or very low degrees, have been found to be the most desirable as objects of attention (Berlyne 1971; Chevrier and Delorme 1980); but the correlation with desirability has been only approximate, and important questions about what limits satisfaction from this kind of activity have not been answered. The attempt to predict higher motives from this kind of elementary drive was pronounced a failure by Coombs and Avrunin (1977).

Discouraged in the attempt to account for subtle motives with simple principles, psychologists have recently turned to the same kind of 'shopping list' concept of reward that economists use: 'That which a person will pay money for is a good.' For instance, David Premack (1959) has pointed out that activities the person will indulge in frequently when free to do so can be used as rewards for activities he ordinarily performs less frequently. There is still argument as to the proper form of this principle (Timberlake 1980), but its effect has clearly been to pull motivational psychology out from inside the individual subject, making it something like a branch of micro-economics.

The blind, functional definition of reward runs into the same problem in psychology that the simple marketplace model has encountered in economics: people often fail to maximize any shopping list of goods, but rather behave in ways that look internally contradictory. At least seven such problems can be defined:

Problem 1.   Many rewards seem to function simultaneously or in close succession as both rewards and punishments. For instance, a person may in the same day or at the same instant both pay for cigarettes and pay for a smoking cure. Such conflictual rewards utterly defeat the Premack strategy of functional definition.

Problem 2. Even harder to understand is human abstemiousness in areas where we are freely able to reward ourselves. The emotions which we hope to have in our human relationships, and which we pay to experience in a play or movie, are nothing we cannot generate on our own, just by thinking about the appropriate subject. Some researchers have taken the trouble to demonstrate this ability under controlled conditions (Koriat *et al.* 1972; Lazarus 1975a and b), but it is familiar enough. Why do we wait for other people to congratulate us rather than arbitrarily congratulating ourselves, a behaviour that is certainly in our repertoires? Why is a book better than a daydream, sexual intercourse better than masturbation, or a back rub better than a back-scratcher? Under hypnosis, which is the directed concentration of attention, people can enjoy virtually any familiar reward. Many people can learn to hypnotize themselves, but they subsequently have little or no tendency to spend their time coining such rewards. What process can it be that keeps most of us from becoming autistically self-absorbed, and why should it be an unhappy fate when this protective process fails?

Problem 3. The events that can serve as rewards are changeable: an object which is highly desirable to a person or to a whole society in one time period may be worthless in the next (see Stigler and Becker 1977 for an economic exploration of the problem of fashion). Thus the scientist cannot simply observe what has been rewarding and assume that it will continue to be so. Even goods which are widely regarded as rock-hard reinforcers – food, sex, aggression, life itself – not infrequently lose their motivating power. In anorexia nervosa a physically healthy person may voluntarily starve to death; in sexual frigidity, the chance for sexual activity may become actually disgusting; many people develop a similar disgust for anger; and more than 1 per cent of deaths are suicides.

Problem 4. Many apparent rewards cannot be produced by direct effort. These are the states which usually occur as by-products, like sleep, laughter, happiness, and dignity, and which are lost in any systematic attempt to attain them (well defined and discussed at length in Elster 1981). Such states may be highly valued, but how can they be called operant reinforcers if they lack a behaviour to reinforce?

Problem 5. As has been mentioned already, people often fail to maximize their expected incomes or minimize their costs; this behaviour is characteristic of some individuals, and a temporary pattern for others. The difference in importance that various people give to money is notorious. Some people think about it constantly and analyse most of their decisions in terms of it. Some people seem fundamentally unable or unwilling to think economically and are forever buying irrationally, giving capriciously, etc. Not only are there individual differences, but seemingly irrational considerations regularly alter the value of money from time to time in the same person. The value of an amount of money, as measured by its tendency to be chosen, seems to be significantly affected by such circumstances as the terms in which it is presented to the person (Wasson 1975), whether it represents a gain or an avoided loss (Tversky and Kahneman 1981), whether the person already has money at stake (Thaler 1980) and whether or not the current choice is an obvious example of a larger set of choices (see below). Why should these seemingly value-less factors have such an impact on choice?

Problem 6. The converse of the problem of how people abstain from self-reward is that of why people consent to undergo pain. Attention is now understood to be a motivated response (Moray 1969) so that attention to painful stimuli requires motivation (Ainslie, forthcoming). Under many circumstances pain cannot in fact compete for the person's attention: soldiers preoccupied by battle frequently do not feel their wounds, hypnotic subjects may undergo major surgery while merely directing their attention voluntarily from the pain, expectant mothers may learn attention-directing exercises to greatly reduce the pain of labour and dentists find that trivial distracting stimuli reduce the pain of dental procedures (Beecher 1959, pp. 157–90; Melzack et al. 1963; Sternbach 1968, pp. 140–1). How does nature induce people to take an interest in their pains and other aversive stimuli in such a free market as this?

Problem 7. Finally, quantitative study of the function by which rewards lose their power with delay have shown it to be very steep (Renner 1964), even in man. For instance, both normal and impulsive human subjects, reporting how long they would wait to get double a hypothetical prize, usually generate answers reflecting annual discount rates in the billions, trillions, or quadrillions of per cent; and a large proportion of adult human subjects who could wait 3 days to receive 25 per cent higher subject pay chose not to do so, a choice which represents rejection of an annual 5 billion per cent interest rate (Ainslie and Haendel 1982). How may we reconcile this finding with the widespread savings ethic? What would even give primitive farmers a sufficient savings tendency to get through the winter?

Intra-personal bargaining

It may be that economics and psychology must stop at the boundaries of the individual subject – that he must be regarded as a black box, and that his idiosyncrasies can only be catalogued as well as possible and added as epicycles to the rational model of economic man. However, some recent findings in behavioural psychology suggest a way to go beyond microeconomics by defining durable interests within the individual person. These interests, in their dealings with each other, follow some of the rules of interpersonal bargaining, and may provide a systematic explanation for the phenomena just listed.

It is not a new idea that the self is multiple. Philosophers and psychologists since Plato have described competing principles of decision-making, usually a lower, impulsive principle and a higher, rational principle (Kenny 1963, Ch. 8; Kant 1960, pp. 15–49; Ricoeur 1971, p. 11; Freud 1923); but the relationship between these principles has been elusive. If the parts of the self can be clearly articulated, they may be suitable material for a model more microscopic than microeconomics, 'picoeconomics' perhaps, in which the elements that combine to determine the individual person's values can be described. Freud proposed such an economic model and kept it in mind as he modelled motivational conflicts, but he never achieved a coherent system (1916–17, pp. 356–7). This chapter will present some preliminary suggestions about how a multiple self may be simply described.

I will argue that problem 7 contains not only its own solution but a practical approach to the first six. This solution is apt to be counter-intuitive, since it relies on the fact that the curve describing how people discount delayed rewards is warped: not only steep, but markedly bowed downwards. Carrying this observation to its logical conclusions may seem unnatural. We do not like to think of our world as being curved: people resisted the Greeks' deduction that the world was round until Magellan made the conclusion inescapable, and we have been equally queasy in modern times about the curves that relativistic physics has introduced into our space and time. Nevertheless, the concept of a highly concave discount curve is not only supported unanimously by the available evidence, but is most useful in understanding 'irrationality'.[2]

Temporary changes of preference

Two decades ago, Richard Herrnstein (1961) proposed his matching law, a formula which summarized the choices animals made on concurrent variable interval schedules. This formula was parsimonious in the extreme, containing no empirical constants:

$$\frac{B_1}{B_2} = \frac{R_1}{R_2} \times \frac{A_1}{A_2} \times \frac{D_2}{D_1}$$

where B_1 and B_2 are the amount of time spent in each of two alternative behaviours, and the Rs, As and Ds are the rates, amounts and delays of the consequences of these behaviours. A variety of subsequent experiments have found this formula to give the best least-squares fit of preference data in animal and human subjects (deVilliers and Herrnstein 1976). For our purposes, its major prediction is that preference for a reward will be inversely proportional to the delay of that reward from the moment of choice, a function that can be graphed as a hyperbola. Delay has its effect independently of rate and amount. Its inverse is multiplied by them to obtain actual value. This value declines steeply in the range of delays close to zero, a behaviour that fits the experimental findings just described; but it levels out into a long tail at long delays, a property which, as we shall see, produces a contrary tendency towards 'objective' valuation of rewards.

Subsequent experiments have suggested that the original matching law is not the last word on discounting reward. Some predictions it makes have not held up; for instance, alternative rewards delayed by the same amount from the moment of choice should be preferred in the same proportion whatever that delay is, but in fact preference for the larger reward increases as the delay increases (Navarick and Fantino 1976). It also does not account for individual variations observed in the

[2] This argument has been developed more fully in Ainslie (1982).

tendency to discount delayed rewards, an observation which has led Herrnstein (1981) to add an empirical constant. Furthermore, the matching law may be only a corollary to more fundamental laws only partially discovered; its predictions with respect to rate of reward, which have been the ones best validated, can be predicted by a more fundamental kinetic equation (Myerson and Miezin 1980).

However, the aspect of the matching law which is important to our discussion of value does not depend on its precise shape. It requires only that the discount curve of delayed rewards be more bowed than the standard per-cent-per-unit-time (exponential) curve by which ordinary interest and discount rates are calculated. Exponential curves drawn from rewards of different sizes at different delays will never cross one another if they have the same time constant (as in Fig. 1). Their relative heights, describing the adjusted values of the rewards from which they are drawn at any particular time, will be the same at every moment. With more concave curves, however, there will be some pairs of alternative rewards such that a larger, later reward is

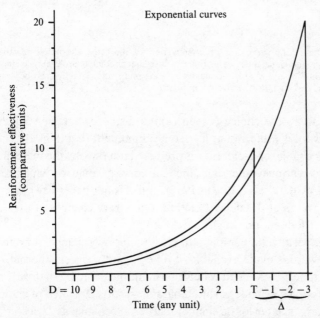

Fig. 1. Exponential curves of the effectiveness of a reward available at time T and an alternative which is objectively twice as great, available three units of time later, as a function of decreasing delay before they become available.

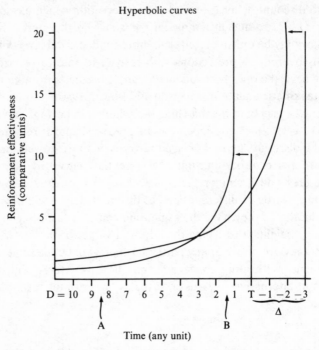

Fig. 2. Hyperbolic curves of the effectiveness of the same alternative rewards, available at the same times as in Fig. 1. Note that predicted preference changes between time A and time B. As delays become minuscule, effectiveness becomes enormous, making objective size unimportant.

preferred when the choice is seen from a distance, but the smaller, earlier reward is preferred as it becomes imminent (e.g. Fig. 2). This temporary change of preference is predicted not only by the matching law but by various other hypothetical curves, some of which are supported by data (e.g., Logan 1965). But it is not necessary even to know the shape of the delay function; temporary changes of preference can be looked for directly.

In the experimental paradigm to elicit temporary change of preference, a reward is made available at time T, and a larger, alternative reward at time $T + \Delta$. With Δ held constant, the delay (D) before T at which the choice is made is varied parametrically. A switch of choice from the larger, later to the smaller, earlier alternative as D becomes smaller represents the temporary change of preference that is important for the study of value. Such temporary change of preference has been obtained in animals (Rachlin and Green 1972; Navarick and Fantino 1976; Ainslie and Herrnstein 1981); in undergraduates choosing between longer or shorter periods of relief from noxious noise (Solnick *et al.* 1980); in substance abuse patients choosing between different amounts of real money (Ainslie and Haendel 1982); and even in the conscious self-reports of various human subjects choosing between hypothetical amounts of money (Ainslie and Haendel 1982). For instance, most people say they would rather have a prize of a $100 certified cheque available immediately rather than a $200 certified cheque that could not be cashed for 2 years, but do not prefer a $100 certified cheque that could be cashed in 6 years to a $200 certified cheque that could be cashed in 8 years, even though this is the same choice seen at 6 years' greater delay (D).[3]

Intra-personal interests

Temporary preference for inferior alternatives during the time they are imminently available seems to be a universal feature of the way we perceive delay. Its obvious consequence is the creation of two distinct interests in many choice situations: a short-term interest based on the proximity of a poorer reward, and a long-term interest based on the 'objective' sizes of the alternative rewards. The long-term interest is based on heavily discounted incentives but has the advantage of foresight – it can take steps in advance to forestall the temporary change of preference towards the poorer alternative, like Ulysses tying himself to the mast.[4] The short-term interest is powerfully motivated and can be expected to prevail if it has not been forestalled in advance. These two interests will tend not to come into equilibrium with each other, that is, not be weighed against each other to produce a simple preference, because they are dominant at separate times.

It is these interests, based on alternative rewards and motivated by their temporal relationships to act upon one another, that would be the choice-making agents in a picoeconomic approach. I will argue that the moves they are motivated to make can be expected to generate the

[3] These normal subjects generally do not notice that these choices differ only in the time they are made, and cannot give a rational explanation of their reported intention to change their choice when this is pointed out to them.
[4] This comparison was first suggested by Strotz (1956), and is explored in detail by Elster (1979).

otherwise paradoxical phenomena listed above. For instance, the spontaneous preference not to save at an enormous interest rate, by subjects without apparent problems in the area of compulsive spending (problem 7, above), may be seen as an example where subjects' short-term interests are not forestalled by their long-term interest. Why this might be true some but not all of the time depends on the properties of the precommitting devices open to the long-term interest.

Precommitting devices

Psychologists have long had an intuitive awareness of the need for long-term interests to forestall the temporary dominance of competing short-term interests, and have discussed the means by which they do so under the name of defence mechanisms or coping mechanisms. As described by the literature of ego psychology, behaviour therapy and self-help, these mechanisms follow one or more of four distinct strategies (Ainslie 1982).

1. Extrapsychic devices. People may set up physical or social constraints to limit their future range of choice. Such devices include taking pills to change appetitite, locking up temptations or moving away from them, asking friends or parents for supervision, making public promises to avoid temptation or getting themselves locked up. Psychoanalytic writers refer to some of these devices as 'asking for controls'.

2. Control of attention. People may keep the opportunity to behave impulsively out of sight or out of mind, so that they cannot receive or process the information that the inferior reward is at hand. For instance, an overeater may keep food out of sight or keep busy so as not to think about food. Behaviour therapists have referred to similar activities as 'stimulus control' (Kanfer and Phillips 1970; Goldiamond 1965), and psychoanalysts have called them suppression, repression or denial.

3. Control of emotion. People may use the self-perpetuating quality of affects to influence their motivational state in the near future. One can cultivate an emotional process that is incompatible with an impulse one fears; the person who is afraid of getting too angry may cultivate loving feelings, and the person who is afraid of being seduced may start a quarrel. Behaviour therapists have described 'coverants' that function this way (Homme 1966), and psychoanalysts have called this process reversal of affect or reaction formation. Conversely, a person may nip in the bud emotions that increase the likelihood of impulses, maintaining an attitude of neutrality that is sometimes called isolation of affect. Anger and love will not overwhelm the person who is not emotionally involved to begin with.

4. Private rules.   People may make private rules that group their temptations into sets, so that each choice involving a temptation becomes a precedent predicting all their future choices within the set. By this perceptual change, they are able to stake their expectation of reaching some major goal against each small step in the wrong direction (Ainslie 1975). For instance, an overeater can adopt a diet which each act of eating must either violate or not; thereafter any act of overeating will lead not only to a small gain in weight but to a major fall in the person's expectation that he would stick to his diet in the future. This tactic of staking the credibility of a long-term goal on each choice that threatens it has been described as will-power, acting on principle, making promises to the self, and beta control (Kanfer and Karoly 1972). It does not correspond to any single psychodynamic defence mechanism, but seems to be at the heart of what are called 'compulsive controls' (Ainslie 1984).

Making private rules is a side-betting tactic familiar to bargaining theorists. Schelling (1960, p. 30) describes the position of a bargainer who must face an opponent in repeated transactions: 'If I conceded to you here, you would revise your estimate of me in our other negotiations. To protect my reputation with you, I must stand firm.' In effect, the value of the series of future transactions forms a 'kitty' which both sides can see to be at stake in each current transaction. Similarly, the person making a private rule tests the rule against each successive temptation. If he goes off his diet, or takes his first drink or breaks his budget this time he will lose his expectation of following his rule in the long run, since it was this expectation that formed the 'kitty' of the bet: the next time he faces the same temptation he will have that much less weighed against it and so will be even more apt to give in. This effect is most palpable in the case of the alcoholic trying to avoid drinking, where the force of temptation after the first drink is so strong that it is called a 'loss of control', and for a long time was falsely thought to have a reflexive basis (Marlatt 1978).

This fourth strategy, making private rules, seems to be the most effective means of precommitment, and it will be the most useful in understanding the seeming irrationalities mentioned above.

Bright lines

The implementation of private rules depends a great deal on the availability of external criteria for their application. Facts that are outside of the person's control can act as truce lines between his long- and short-term interests. Again, Schelling provides a succinct analogy:

> Two opposing forces are at the points marked X and Y in a map similar to the one [in Fig. 3]. The commander of each force wishes to occupy as much of the area as he can and knows the other does too. But each commander wishes to avoid an armed clash and knows the other does too. Each must send forth his troops with orders to take up a designated line and to fight if opposed. Once the troops are dispatched, the outcome depends only on the lines that the two commanders have ordered their troops to occupy. If the lines overlap, the troops will be assumed to meet and fight, to the disadvantage of both sides. If the troops take up positions that leave any appreciable space unoccupied between them, the situation will be assumed 'unstable' and a clash inevitable. Only if the troops are ordered to occupy identical lines or lines that leave virtually no unoccupied space between them will a clash be avoided. In that case, each side obtains successfully the area it occupies, the advantage going to the side that has the most valuable area in terms of land and facilities. (1960, p. 62)

Schelling goes on to argue that the only good solution for each commander is to order his troops up to the river. The river has no military value *per se*, but it is the only boundary that stands out from other possible boundaries, and each commander should assume that that is what the other is looking for.

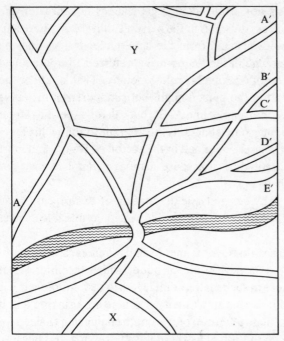

Fig. 3. Map of hypothetical terrain, explained in text (from Schelling 1960).

In the case of private rule-making, the problem is not one of blocked communication but of leaderless troops, say on the X side, who share a common interest in holding ground for their side but who have an individual urge to flee. These troops represent successive motivational states in an individual person, which are individually lured in the X direction by temptation but are less likely to succumb if doing so will end the general resistance to the temptation. Temptation is greatest the furthest one goes in the Y direction. At each choice the person picks a position he thinks he will be motivated to maintain in the future, say along line A–B′. He gives up on positions on the Y side of this line as posing irresistible temptations, a self-confirming prediction. At his chosen line he is somewhat protected from succumbing by the fact that his holding or failing to hold the line represents a precedent, which he will recall at all subsequent choices. A lapse would have much the same effect as a soldier running away: the other soldiers would follow him and the line would crumble.

When a choice is not a precedent, a lapse does not threaten the larger series of choices; thus, it is in the person's short-term interest to distinguish the choice at hand from the larger category, so that the person can both indulge in the temporarily preferred alternative and keep an expectation of obeying his rule generally. That is, under the pressure of temptation the person might not simply retreat from his chosen boundary, for example, line A–B', but call for a specific retreat to line A–C'; in doing so he abandons the attempt to follow his long-term interest in any cases contained in the sector A–B'–C', and must hope that this retreat does not cause a more general retreat, for example, to the river.

William James provides a classic description of this process in an alcoholic defining the line between forbidden and permissible drinks:

How many excuses does the drunkard find when each new temptation comes! It is a new brand of liquor which the interests of intellectual culture in such matters oblige him to test; moreover, it is poured out and it is a sin to waste it; or others are drinking and it would be churlishness to refuse; or it is but to enable him to sleep, or just to get through this job of work; or it isn't drinking, it is because he feels so cold; or it is Christmas day: or it is a means of stimulating him to make a more powerful resolution in favor of abstinence than any he has hitherto made; or it is just this once, and once doesn't count, etc., etc., *ad libitum* – it is, in fact, anything you like except *being a drunkard. That* is the conception that will not stay before the poor soul's attention. But if he once gets able to pick out that way of conceiving, from all the other possible ways of conceiving the various opportunities which occur, if through thick and thin he holds to it that this is being a drunkard and is nothing else, he is not likely to remain one long. The effort by which he succeeds in keeping the right *name* unwaveringly present to his mind proves to be his saving moral act. (James 1890, p. 565)

James is pointing out that if the person believes he can get away with loopholes, he may find so many that his rule becomes worthless. If he does *not* believe this, he can probably hold the line.

In any given choice, the person's long-term interest is to say, 'It's a matter of principle', while the short-term interest proposes, 'Just this once.' If the person expects the proposed exception to produce a greater rise in imminent reward than a fall in (discounted, delayed) aggregate reward, it will succeed and in all probability be institutionalized as a loophole: 'I always get drunk on New Year's Eve', or 'We mustn't stint expenses on Johnny's birthday.' A rare windfall like a game-show prize or one's earnings as an experimental subject, the rewards so steeply discounted in problem 7, are in a prime position to become exceptions to the person's usual rules of thrift.

The availability of boundaries which cannot be moved just a little bit is very important to the long-term interest. Activities like smoking and drinking have such a line in an obvious place, that is, between any indulgence and no indulgence; but people who eat too much or spend too much money cannot completely give up these activities, and so must find some way to make a single diet, or budget, stand out from all the others to which they are apt to retreat under pressure. Lawyers call such a unique boundary a 'bright line'. The concept is familiar to people whose profession it is to negotiate between interests in the larger world. It expresses why countries blessed with unique boundaries like a mountain range or a river without large tributaries have fewer wars than countries just set out on a plain.

How the conflict of interests creates seeming irrationality

The basis for a durable ambivalence between larger, later and smaller, earlier rewards should now be apparent. A person's short-term interest in smoking a cigarette may take turns indefinitely with his interest to obtain a smoking cure (see above, problem 1). In a bargaining situation brought about by his use of private rules, he might even want the two alternatives simultaneously: a cigarette just this once to be followed by abstention ever afterwards, a deal which, if credible, would be acceptable to both his long- and short-term interests.

Constraints on self-reward

This intra-personal bargaining model is important to the problem of self-reward because it applies not only to the choice of competing rewards like drink vs. sobriety, but also to alternative rates of consuming the same reward. As was noted in problem 2, it does not seem to be difficult to short-circuit the 'normal' dependency of rewards on external events. Insofar as emotions, the main rewards in humans, are within each person's power to evoke in himself, the question must be asked: why don't people become totally involved in rewarding themselves? What would happen if someone decided to become self-sufficient, and to reward himself without regard to environmental input?

Freud believed that infants had just such omnipotence (1900, p. 598; 1915, p. 135). He said that the 'demands of reality' ended their self-sufficiency; but if he meant the threat of starvation he was certainly not referring literally to modern society. In fact, young children reduce their fantasy lives gradually, not because their parents and teachers beat them into line but because their fantasy becomes relatively less satisfying and fails to compete with other forms of play.

Further observations come from two kinds of psychiatric patients who try to bring their sources of reward into their own hands by withdrawing their investment in chancy activities: schizoid characters feel threatened by social give-and-take and often contrive to live entirely in their rooms, or in a cabin in the woods. Insofar as they succeed in doing this, their solitary activities mysteriously become stale, and they often fall prey to worries, fears or rituals. At a higher level of functioning, narcissistic characters choose their activities and companions so that continual success is a foregone conclusion. They, too, report a mysterious reduction in satisfaction that cannot be accounted for by any confrontation with reality; on the contrary, their problem is that they have managed to get reality to obey them almost as well as their fantasies do. Thus, the harshness of reality does not seem to be the factor that limits arbitrary self-reward. It looks more as though self-reward, indulged in *ad libitum*, becomes unsatisfactory for that reason itself.

The staleness of reward reported by self-absorbed people makes one think of habituation or fatigue. Any neuronal process, if repeated frequently during a short period of time, will lose vigour. For instance, if one stares at a solid colour for any period of time, the visual pigment that subtends that colour will be depleted, so that if one then stares at a neutral screen one will see the complementary colour. Data about the generality of this phenomenon in psychophysiology have been summarized by Solomon (1980), who proposed an increasing recruitment of antagonistic processes as an explanation; but the simple fatigue of the process in question should account for its decreasing ability to compete with its fellows. If the physiology of reinforcement is not an exception, then repeated attempts to invoke a given kind of reward should produce diminishing returns. Even self-reinforcement should be expected to satiate.

It is also important that satiation is not simply proportional to the amount of rewarding activity that has occurred. A person will get more or less satisfaction from a given opportunity for reward (i.e. drive) depending on how he consumes the reward. For instance, a person is less rewarded by a given amount of food if he pays attention to something else while eating, a practice thus forbidden by behaviour therapists of obesity. Likewise, a person would not want to bolt a gourmet meal, but rather space out consumption to take maximum advantage of his available appetite. In fact, the problem of premature satiation is widely noted in other activities as well, from sexual intercourse to the writing and reading of fiction. The writer must not resolve the story's problems too soon, nor the reader peek ahead to the end (other examples in Ainslie 1975). It seems that intense or rapid consumption of a reward often leads to disproportionally rapid satiation, perhaps because some kind of threshold is reached too soon – a phenomenon certainly present in premature orgasm. Thus, within a given reward modality the person faces choices involving the pace at which he will consume the reward. If he maximizes the rapidity with which reward reaches peak intensity, he may reduce rather than increase his aggregate reward.

This situation is shown graphically in Fig. 4. The solid lines depict two possible curves of reinforcement over time, where rate of satiation is proportional to the initial intensity of reinforcement. The choice between intense, brief periods of reward and less intense, more prolonged periods of equal frequency clearly poses the smaller–earlier vs. larger–later reward problem we have just discussed. If the discounted value of every moment of consumption is calculated according to the matching law and added together, and the resulting values plotted for each moment before consumption occurs, the curves (broken lines) favour the slower consumption of reward when the two consumption patterns are viewed at a distance, but temporarily favour the rapid, less productive consumption pattern when it is imminently available.

Highly bowed curves other than the matching law generate the same result: rapid consumption can be an impulse that threatens the most efficient consumption pattern for the reward in question.

Inefficient consumption would not matter if the amount of drive that could enable comparable reward were limitless and could be tapped without delay. Neither of those conditions is apt to be true, however. We do not know how many processes there are that can satiate separately – that is, sources of reward that can remain productive when other sources have fatigued, as when one is hungry but not thirsty. If we had this information, we would be able to count the number of

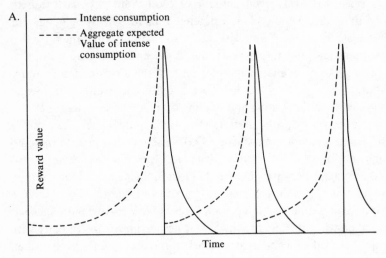

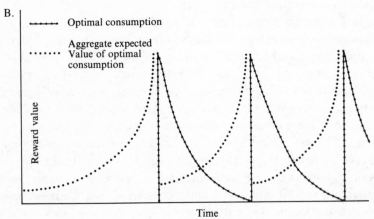

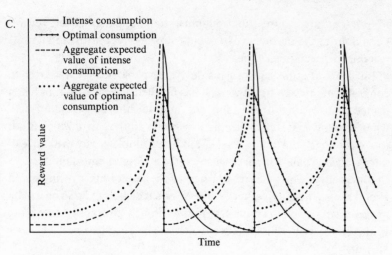

Fig. 4. Two consumption patterns of reward over time (solid lines), and the aggregate value of all remaining moments in each, discounted in hyperbolic curves (broken lines): (A) Rapid, intense consumption; (B) more gradual consumption; (C) the two patterns compared.

separate drives it defined. However, we can deduce that the number must be small for practical purposes from the fact that appetite is so widely regarded as a precious commodity: people not uncommonly work up an appetite for dinner, boast of an appetite for sex, complain of a jaded appetite for entertainment and so on. Furthermore, it seems that to indulge an appetite requires a period of relatively unrewarding setting up: one must change one's interests, 'settle down' to the new task, 'get in the mood', and if one's attention is distracted in the midst of this process, the task must be partially repeated. Distractions have an aversive impact.

For these reasons, inefficient use of available drive will reduce a person's aggregate reward. It will be in his long-term interest to adopt any available precommitting devices that prevent premature satiation. It is not hard to think of concrete devices that seem to serve this purpose: banquets with many courses which pace their consumption, eating lobsters or crabs out of the shell, retarding orgasm with anaesthetic creams, etc. However, these mechanical devices are apt to be of limited availability and usefulness. Against the ultimate temptation – the availability of purely intrapsychic self-reinforcement – such devices would be of no use whatsoever. A really practical device to prevent premature satiation must tie the person's self-reward behaviour to the occurrence of events outside his control, and it must use purely psychological ties.

But a private rule is just such a device. A person can make a rule to congratulate himself only when he has finished a certain task, or when someone else congratulates him; he may let himself be elated only when a friend is, or only when he wins some kind of prize which is not too easy to get. He can make binding gambles. He can 'invest' importance in a person, or a cause or just a piece of entertainment, so that his self-reward is thereafter tied to the fate of his investment. In Freud's term, he may 'cathect' objects, and if he fails to do so he will be at the mercy of his own natural greed; he will be trapped like King Midas in a sterile omnipotence which might be called narcissism or autism.

The activity of investing objects with importance can be detected under perfectly ordinary circumstances, despite the fact that the investor has usually let the rule grow spontaneously rather than creating it deliberately.[5] For instance, if I have a friend who sometimes drops by and suggests we take a coffee break during the work day, and if he does not come too rarely or too often, I am spared the need to regulate my breaks. If I have to decide arbitrarily when to take a break, I cannot take it whenever I feel ready, for fear the sensation of readiness will come with increasing frequency and make me unable to complete any difficult task. Rather than take the chance of an arbitrary decision, I may go without breaks altogether. But if my rule merely says I can have a break when my friend invites me, and if my friend is a 'good' friend in this respect, my problem is solved.

The same considerations apply to purely mental self-reward. If I reward myself in fantasy arbitrarily, that is, without regard to events outside of my control, my fantasies will slide into premature satiation. At the very least I will have to fantasize enemies to my imaginary goals, who operate according to inexorable rules to restrict my self-rewarding behaviour. In fact, people who dwell extensively in fantasy are usually driven to paranoid scripts to maintain the vigour of their fantasies. For instance, the unreal world of the schizophrenic often evolves from a

[5] See Ainslie (1984) for a discussion of how private rules can grow without the person's being able to report them.

heaven to a hell, a process well depicted in Hannah Green's *I Never Promised You a Rose Garden* (1964).

When I make a rule that my self-reward will hinge on hard facts, my task becomes easier. Such facts may merely be fictions created by someone else: a book or movie is apt to be preferable to my own unrelieved company. A person is not usually conscious of investing importance in a movie, but the existence of this importance is shown in the infrequent case when a movie becomes too punishing and the person withdraws the importance. He says to himself, 'It's only a movie', and yet he is not giving himself new information – he has never ducked when guns pointed towards the audience. Rather he is announcing his disinvestment: 'This movie shall no longer be important to me. I shall no longer reward myself according to its vicissitudes.'

A person can always abandon a rationing device, and is sometimes forced to do so by the unusual strength of a short-term interest or the unwise choice of a device by the long-term interest. However, when this happens the long-term interest is somewhat undermined. The person who withdraws his investment during the scary part of the movie loses his chance to be rewarded by the movie afterwards; to some extent he will lose his ability to keep his investment in subsequent movies when they tempt him to disinvest. The person whose long-term interests combine through the use of private rules thereby stakes more on each choice. Thereafter each competing short-term interest is less apt to prevail, but if it does the disaster to the long-term interest is so much the greater.

If a situation is 'real' rather than fictional it will be more dangerous to disinvest in, even if the person's physical safety is not at risk. There are many fictions that can be chosen, but there is only one reality. If a person abandons that bright line as a criterion for self-reward, he is in danger of autism. Of course, many realities are a matter of interpretation ('Can I expect to be rich?', 'Am I a good guitar player?', 'Is my missing spouse alive?'). The set of beliefs which the person qualifies as real must be protected from inflation by another set of private rules, governing what psychiatrists call 'reality testing'. Like all private rules, they can be hedged by finding loopholes.

In this model of value, the availability of environmental reward is not the limiting factor in the operation of the person's internal reinforcing mechanism. The limiting factor instead is the availability of discipline, that is, of means of restricting self-reward according to a pattern that makes the best use of the underlying drive. External objects are valued not because they can peremptorily bestow or withhold reward, but rather insofar as they serve as useful boundaries between the person's long-term interest in maximal aggregate reward and his short-term interest in immediate reward. If a private rule can turn upon a particular situation in a way that permits a large amount of self-reward aggregated over time and is not very vulnerable to the competition of brief, intense self-reward patterns, this situation will be valued, for the same reason that Schelling's battle commander valued the river. The person will pay money to obtain it and learn behaviours which increase its availability.

This is the solution to our second problem: how an organism that has an extensive capacity to reinforce itself can take an interest in the outside world. An omnipotent organism has a shortage of scarcity; it needs objects that can maintain appetite if it is to get the greatest possible reward.

Fashion

It is not clear why nature should have selected rationing devices for self-reward as the goods which people will value, rather than a turn-key kind of reward which must always come from outside the person.[6] It can only be said that inventors have often found the most direct solution to a problem to be too rigid; the device that works in practice is often engineered to allow slippage among the parts. Perhaps the constitution of rewards as rationing devices rather than as absolute determinants of reinforcement permits the most flexible adaptation to the environment.

For instance, such a mechanism may motivate maximal environmental exploration over a wide range of success rates, both by the naive youngster and by the experienced problem-solver. If internal

[6] Other animals, too, have been found not to be entirely dominated by concrete rewards. Hungry monkeys have been observed to prefer exploration tasks to tasks which obtained food; and even in lower animals like rats the power of visceral rewards such as food and sexual activity are modified by factors like variety, which are wholly unnecessary to the physical consumption of those rewards (Fisher 1962; Wilson, Kuehn and Beach 1963; Walker and King 1962).

reinforcement were strictly proportional to the amount of some external stimulus, a proportion sufficient to shape behaviour in a beginner might lead more advanced problem-solvers to rest on their laurels. But instead, as a person becomes increasingly skilled in an activity, this activity is apt to become more rewarding only at first, and then to become less rewarding again because of the person's increasing speed at achieving the criteria for self-reward. As long as games of tic-tac-toe dole out wins and losses in a pattern that repays the cost of paying attention to the game, a child will value them. When the range of possible outcomes is so familiar that he anticipates them all at the outset of the game, it ceases to be a useful rationing device for self-reward and is no longer valued. To go on with this method of disciplining reward, the child must take up draughts or checkers, and perhaps chess in turn. Similarly, when a daydream or a joke becomes familiar the mind leaps ahead to the ending, dissipating the suspense and poorly repaying the cost of paying attention to it in the first place. The person must search for new daydreams or new jokes, or undertake an activity even less under his control, such as a challenging relationship with another person. To remain useful as a rationing device, the activity must either: (1) change so that it remains novel (golf on new courses, new foods, new sexual partners, new tunes and, as the style in which the tunes are produced becomes increasingly familiar, new styles of tune) or (2) be intricate enough to defy total comprehension – this is the quality a work of art must have to save it from the obsolescence of fashion (Empson 1930).

Thus problem 3, with susceptibility of some but not all rewards to changes of fashion, can be brought within a consistent behavioural framework.

Rewards that are essentially by-products

The fourth problem, why many significant rewards cannot be sought directly, can be discussed within the same framework. The direct production of a reward implies control, and increasingly masterful exercise of the person's control is apt to attenuate the reward through premature satiation. If a person could make himself laugh, or make himself content, he would probably keep himself satiated in these modalities. In doing so he would make them trivial as sources of reward, unless he found it practical to bind their consumption to rationing devices: flexing one's leg is a powerful reward to someone who has been tied up or splinted, but it is insignificant to people who can move freely, because direct action harvests the potential pleasure as soon as the least bit has built up. However, building up appetite in this modality is not worth the effort, or we would see examples of physical confinement used as a rationing device, in the same way that saunas seem to build up potential reward by depriving people of comfortable temperatures.

It may be that a 'by-product' reward is noticed as a reward precisely because there is some natural impediment to obtaining it by direct action. It may still motivate behaviour to obtain it, of course; but insofar as ostensible 'tries' to obtain it are counter-productive, they may pose the same problem as other temporary preferences pose to other long-term interests. To obtain the by-product reward, the person may have to precommit himself not to try to seize it directly. He may even have to be unaware that the behaviour he finally adopts is a means to get that reward (the precommitting device of attention control, discussed above). Thus, while a person will probably not undermine his wish to laugh if he buys a joke book, he may find no conscious strategy that brings contentment. The only way to defeat his tendency to make selfish grabs at it may be to tell himself that virtue is its own reward, keeping in the distant back of his mind the idea that virtue may also be rewarded by contentment. This situation is not an exception to the usual laws of operant reward – only a ticklish impulse control problem.

The irrational valuation of money

The literal function of money is to induce other people to give us goods or services. Insofar as it functions reliably, it poses the same opportunities and dangers as the available goods and services do. In people's spontaneous perceptions, it should be highly valued when something that can be bought is both intensely rewarding and imminently available, and less valued at other times. Unless a person takes steps to stabilize this value, he will earn and spend impulsively, behaviours that will not only fail to serve his own long-term interest, but make him a poor competitor with respect to other earners and shoppers. He should thus be motivated to adopt precommitting devices to control his future behaviour towards money, the most powerful of which will be private rules.

Financial behaviour is especially suited to control by private rules, since it is by its nature concrete and quantifiable. For most people in Western society, money ceases to be a simple means to immediate ends, valued when we need it for a specific purchase but not otherwise. Instead it is assigned value according to an extensive set of private rules designed to maximize objective income despite fluctuations in one's spontaneous preference. Various private rules require a person not to live on capital, not to go into debt or to go into debt only under specific conditions, to live within a budget, to discount future income only at the bank rate, to buy large items only when they are on sale, etc. Where the discipline of financial planning would undermine other valued activities, the person defines exceptions: money is not to be weighed against affairs of the heart, or counted as a reason to obey or disobey the law or considered when seeking medical care.

Private rules will dampen swings in the person's valuation of money but, as with other behaviours, they will also introduce a characteristic artificiality into the choice-making process (see Ainslie 1982). Their failure to make financial behaviour simply objective can be seen in occasional examples where a chance for a tiny gain is valued beyond what would be expected, apparently because it serves a precedent. Some people will not allow themselves to pass a penny in the street without picking it up, or to put more postage than necessary on a letter to avoid searching for the right stamps, to be short-changed in any amount by a shopkeeper or vending machine, or to get petrol at a convenient station when an out-of-the-way station is one or two pence cheaper. These are not spontaneous behaviours, but are performed because money 'shouldn't be wasted'. A violation of this rule undermines the person's long-term interests with respect to money in general, and thus has much greater importance than would the loss of the single economic opportunity which was literally at stake. If the person perceives himself to have wasted money, this perception in itself might actually increase his future tendency to waste money in more significant ways. Of course, the person who is afraid of his impulses or unwise in his choice of rules may carry this concern to an inefficient extreme and become a miser, in the same way that anorectics starve themselves to death for fear of seeing themselves give in to their hunger.

Where a long-term interest has created rules, we should see short-term interests negotiating loopholes on the basis of 'just this once', and the rules establishing the value of money are no exception. Entrepreneurs of lotteries seem to find that they can further appeal to people's short-term interests by offering specific, extravagant prizes like sports cars and vacations rather than money, which the person might feel he had to spend sensibly; designating the prize in this way seems to be enough to create the desired exception, even though the person could sell the item or take cash instead under the rules of the contest. It is also well known that tourists on their vacations will buy things they would not ordinarily buy.

Vendors may find they can profit by allying themselves with a customer's short-term interests and providing these interests with the bargaining points they need. If a person rewards himself especially for finding bargains, he may become the willing prey of a vendor who sells inferior goods 'marked down'; this person evades his rule for thrift by claiming that he has found a bargain, and thus his short-term interest is perfectly willing to pay the price of getting inferior goods. Similarly, a person may attach different rules of scrutiny to different price categories, which he divides by the natural bright lines, round figures; the vendor who marks his goods with a price ending in $9.95 invites the person's short-term interest to plead a lower price category against the long-term interest's rules for thrift, without really having created the illusion that the merchandise is substantially cheaper.

When a person gets more money than is necessary to satisfy his visceral needs, he must confront another of its properties: it is a natural counter in game-like activities. He may perceive himself to be earning money simply as a means to various ends, but these ends often have to compete for his attention with the activity of earning (or saving) money *per se*. Insofar as the latter activity predominates, money itself becomes valuable as a rationer of self-reward, and the person starts to behave so as to maximize the aggregate reward realized from this rationing effect rather than to maximize his actual income. Naturally, the rules of this activity will still call for him to maximize income (or minimize expense); otherwise the game will not be 'real', but will be only one of any number of arbitrary activities, thus losing much of its value as a rationing device. However, maximizing income is a very general criterion, and is susceptible to hedging. For instance, a person may congratulate himself on how much money he saves by recycling glass or using food store coupons, even though if he audited the activity strictly it would not pay for his time.

This example of cheating on rules for realistic money-making is trivial, but some are not. Even professional investors are prone to it, and must be cautioned against it in business schools: For instance, a person who has made a bad investment might be obliged by his rules for valuing money to reduce his rate of self-reward; but if he can regard this investment as part of a larger investment which still stands a chance, he can defer this duty or, if he is lucky, evade it altogether. Thus, protecting his sunk cost, although objectively less adaptive, will be in his best short-term interest. There are many times everyone is motivated to 'fool himself', as it is often called; more properly, what he is doing is finding loopholes in his own private rules on the basis of one short-term interest or another.

Another example, mentioned in problem 5: most people's rules for reality testing will not allow them to entertain the belief that they are rich, but if they buy a lottery ticket they may allow themselves to say, 'I have a finite chance to get rich.' They can permit themselves the self-reward attached to this perception even though they squeaked into it with a one-in-a-million chance. Thus a person's short-term interest may find it worthwhile to buy a situation that reduces his objective expectancy of reward.

Finally, neither money-getting itself nor the activities money makes possible are the only efficient ways to ration self-reward. Indeed, there is much hoary wisdom which says that they are relatively poor at this in the long run. Thus some people may value money extensively, and among these some will be better than others at playing a disciplined game that maximizes the aggregate reward realizable from this activity. Some people will not value money much, and will tend to seek only as much as they need for other ends. And some may change from one to the other in the course of their lives.

These examples of a continuing struggle between spending and saving suggest that the value of money is not established simply by a mental substitution of an amount in pounds for the goods to which a person is attracted, but rather by the personal legislation of a discipline which requires the person to act 'as if' the money had a certain value, legislation which is modified by a variable amount of evasion. This value ceases to be anything like a scalar quantity, and becomes rather the arbiter of an intricate set of internal conflicts. No wonder the person looks irrational to an observer who thinks he is just trying to maximize income.

Pain as temporary preference for inferior reward

There remains the question of how nature can inflict pain on an organism that can control its own reinforcement. Modern operant theory has corrected many of the awkward features of older, two-factor theories of punishment (Herrnstein 1969); it portrays pain as simple non-reward, to which an organism attends because it contains adaptive information. However, pain cannot be just the absence of reward or, in terms of the model just presented, the absence of effective rationing devices for self-reward. The person in pain is not just bored, as he would be in a stimulus deprivation situation, but feels attacked by a process that prevents him from enjoying food, entertainment or whatever other sources of reward may be available. And yet the person must perform a motivated act, the direction of his attention to the pain, in order for it to have its effect. As we have seen, pain can be and sometimes is deliberately shut out of consciousness. How does nature get people to open their gates to pain?

To function as a deterrent, the reward level of the pain would have to be well below the ambient reward level of the person's usual activities. What, then, could induce the person to give up his usual reward level and pay attention to the much less rewarding, painful stimulus? Hypothesizing that attention to pain is an operant which is necessary to maximize reward in the long run does not solve the problem. For one thing, delayed rewards are heavily discounted; it will be hard to convince anyone who has seen emphysema patients smoking in their hospital beds that people can be relied on to accept pain or deprivation in the present to better their situation in the future. Furthermore, if attention to pain is a goal-directed behaviour, people should be able to stop performing it if they know it is useless in the case at hand; yet the patient who has already arranged for his aching tooth to be pulled is not thereby able to ignore the pain, nor is he able to ignore the sore socket when the tooth is gone. Even if these problems could be solved, the effect of simple non-reward following a behaviour should be to select against not only the behaviour but the rehearsal of memories of the behaviour, so that the punished person should find himself doing alternative activities without recalling why. This prediction is not supported by the subjective experience of pain as a vivid, hard-to-forget event. Thus the conventional operant theory of pain is inadequate.

Rescue from this quandary, too, comes from the highly bowed discount curves of delayed reward. We have already seen that an immediate but brief reward can temporarily dominate a much more substantial reward that is delayed. This has been found in experiments using a wide variety of time intervals, anywhere from seconds to years. In real-life activities, the conflicts between poorer–earlier and better–later rewards also seem to occur with a wide variety of time bases. The length of time that the smaller reward is dominant will obviously have a great effect on the way the choice is experienced, as will the length of the refractory period between when a reward is consumed and when the choice is again available. Choices that recur in seconds will demand very different responses from choices that do not recur for years. It is apt to take several cycles of preference reversal before the person identifies a short-term interest as a threat to his long-term interest and begins being moved by the latter interest to counteract it. An inferior behaviour pattern that was well rewarded for years before exerting its inhibiting effect on a greater source of reward might never be discovered, or might be discovered only late in the person's life, having been seen up until then as an unmixed blessing. An inferior behaviour for which the reward was dominant for only a split second might never be perceived as rewarded at all; and yet if the split second of dominance was enough to control a behaviour it might seriously lower the person's average level of reward. This last possibility will prove a way to understand pain as part of the temporary preference problem we have been discussing.

Some familiar motivational patterns are classified in the table, according to the probable periodicity of the preference involved. Actual cycle durations probably form a continuum, more or less smooth as particular evolutionary factors have dictated; but it will be illustrative to describe five ranges of this duration, defined by how the

Table 1. *Zones of temporary preference duration*

Descriptor	Distinguishing feature	Duration of cycle	Time until recognized as a problem	Examples
1. Optimal	Never aversive	Life or no cycle	Never	'To love and to work', non-conflictual pleasure
2. Sell-outs	Ambiguous feeling of aversion	Months to years	Decades	7 deadly sins
3. Addictions	Clear periods of pleasure and aversion	Hours to days	Years	Substance abuse, gambling, perversions, kleptomania
4. Itches	Ambiguous pleasurable phase, but person is conscious of participating	Seconds	Minutes	Physical itches, mannerisms, satiated self-reward, compulsions
5. Pains	Never pleasurable, no participation	Fractions of second	Fractions of second	Physical pain, phobias

person tends to report the positive and aversive phases. In the highest range are activities which never undermine more productive ones, even when viewed over the perspective of a lifetime. These activities vary from the ordinary, like eating and sleeping, to the most profoundly meaningful experiences.

In a lower range are activities which people usually find limiting to their life enjoyment, but only after many years. These tend to be the concrete, highly involving, single-goal activities that religious and philosophical books warn us about; they are usually not considered psychopathological unless they lead to life crises, and many people never identify them as a cause of lost reward.

Beneath them are the addictions, in which a phase of clear, conscious preference for the addictive activity alternates with the phase of conscious avoidance of it. Note that this is a psychological definition of addiction, not a physiological one; for instance, not all people who become physiologically dependent on alcohol are ambivalent about drinking. Rewarding substances like alcohol, tobacco or drugs are often the bases of addictive cycles, but so are substance-unrelated activities such as gambling, compulsive sexual activities (exhibitionism, paedophilia, fetishism), and other compulsive behaviours like kleptomania and spree-buying.

In a still lower range, rewarding and unrewarding phases alternate rapidly, leading to rapidly repeated behaviours that generate what is experienced as insubstantial pleasure. The addiction to cigarettes verges on being in this range. Clear members of the range are annoying activities that are hard to give up: itches, behavioural tics, nail-biting and other mannerisms, playing with a sore, etc. A major category are activities that have fallen prey to premature satiation: the desultory rehearsal of worn-out fantasies, listening to stale jokes, or being at an over-familiar movie and feeling intermittent temptation to pay attention. Often the person is not conscious of a pleasurable phase, but he has some sense of participation in paying attention to the relevant cues. Pathological self-consciousness, obsessional doubts or worries and compulsive rituals belong here.

In the lowest range, a rewarding phase is never evident; it can only be inferred from the fact that people repeatedly direct their attention towards the painful stimuli. Presumably the act of attention is sufficient to produce both the reward that motivates it and the interference with other rewards which soon follows. Repeated rapidly, perhaps too rapidly for the person to distinguish the separate components, this cycle of brief reward and longer inhibition of reward forms a continuing activity that is both unrewarding and hard to resist. This is an adequate operant mechanism for pain. Such a mechanism would explain pain's property of rewarding attention but punishing behaviour (Ainslie 1975, pp. 489–92; and forthcoming).

Phobias may also be in this range, although it might be argued that phobic patients' participation in attending to the relevant cues is no less than that of the obsessive-compulsives I have put in the 'itch' category. Too much should not be made of exact categorization. Insofar as the major mental illnesses have a voluntary component, it is also apt to be in the itch or pain range; for instance, schizophrenics often report that they can 'set up' hallucinations or other forms of regression, and do so repeatedly even though they perceive themselves as suffering from them in the long run.

These examples illustrate how pain can be included in a consistent picoeconomic approach – not the simple negative it has been since before Bentham, but not an exception to the rules of the marketplace.

The results of intra-psychic bargaining

Given the many possible turns of the intra-psychic bargaining process, what will an individual value? In general, he will try to obtain situations which permit a stable compromise between his long- and short-term interests. He will especially seek rationing devices that restrict his self-rewarding activity, but which are not so stringent or rigid that they either reduce his long-term reinforcement rate or make possible a successful rebellion by his short-term interests. For instance, a good game does not let a player win too often, but is not too frustrating, either. To take a more important example: in a robust personal relationship people give each other adequate occasions for self-reward without becoming predictable. The amount of actual supportiveness does not matter, since each person can adjust his own rules for self-reward to accommodate another's scanty approval or even sheer enmity. The unpredictability is what is needed; evasion of this requirement in the interest of short-term comfort leads to stereotyped, mechanical social roles like nurse and dependant, nag and Rip Van Winkle, etc., which reduces the amount of surprise produced by the relationship and hence its value to the participants.

Surprise is at the heart of the matter. If one word can express the antidote for premature satiation, 'that which cannot be generated by the self but must be obtained from outside', it is surprise. Surprise, not gold, or land or labour, should be the epigrammatic font of value.

If there is no rationing process so challenging that it can overcome the temporary dominance of an available short-term reward, then the person will value anything that directly removes or restricts the opportunity for this short-term reward. For instance, it is usually not practical to engage in activities that motivate ignoring physical pain for long periods of time, and so people buy analgesic drugs to reduce the lure of the painful stimulus itself. Similarly, an alcoholic may obtain disulfiram (Antabuse), and the person who cannot save money may accept the poor interest rates of a Christmas club to make himself do it.

Finally, if the person has not found some way to forestall the attractiveness of a short-term reward, he will ultimately seek this reward. However, as the table indicates, the short-term nature of an interest is apt to be relative. What looks to an observer like a person's capitulation to his short-term interest may in fact be a realistic attempt to forestall a still shorter-term one. For instance, it is not uncommon for people to cultivate a rigid, narrowly self-righteous personal style (Level 2) in order to avoid becoming alcoholic or to overcome alcoholism (Level 3). Similarly, it is said in the psychiatric lore that marginally psychotic people often become alcoholic (Level 3) to avoid regressing into psychosis (? Level 4 or 5). A person may sometimes not aspire higher for fear of sinking lower.

Furthermore, the shape of a hyperbola will permit the interaction of more than two levels (Fig. 5). A high-level interest may ally with a low-level interest to undermine one in the mid-range. For instance, if a person values altruism (Level 1) but is usually too avaricious (Level 2) to give money to charity, he may arrange to gamble (Level 3) in such a way that his expected outcome is to lose money to a 'good cause'. Hence, perhaps, the enduring success of church bingo games and lotteries for charity. Similarly, if a person has good reason to tell someone off (Level 1) but has rigid rules against aggression (Level 2), he may allow himself to get drunk (Level 3) in order to create a situation where he does not feel responsible for his aggressive

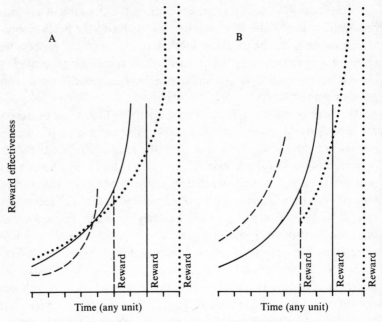

Fig. 5. Hyperbolic curves of the effectiveness of three rewards: A, if each reward is an exclusive alternative to each other reward; and B, if the earliest reward precludes the middle one and the middle one precludes the last one, but the earliest one does not preclude the last one. The summed effect of the earliest and last rewards is depicted by the dashed curve. Note that the curve from the middle reward dominates that from each other reward at some time before the first reward is available in contingency A, but in contingency B never rises above the summed curve from the first and last rewards during the time before the first reward is available.

behaviour. Longer-term interests may 'use' short-term ones in the same way that kings of olden time are said to have allied with commoners to restrict the power of the noble class. The interaction of motivational interests within the individual, although simple in principle, may become as complex as any power struggle between individuals.

Can individual cases be studied empirically?

This chapter has described some of the logical consequences of the highly bowed discount curve described by experimental psychology. The predicted patterns are identifiable in many familiar life situations. In some additional areas where they are not directly observable, they can be inferred as mechanisms for seemingly irrational choices, since they reconcile these choices with a strictly economic view of human behaviour. Given these highly bowed curves, all behaviour can be interpreted as dependent on operant reward. A corollary of this interpretation is that the laws of bargaining which determine the value of goods in commerce can be extended to deal with the conflict of interests within individuals.

It remains to be seen whether these principles, however internally consistent they may be, will be of practical value in understanding individual people with motivational conflicts.

Certainly the collection of data will be harder than it is with commercial activities. Unlike cash transactions, bargains struck in the mind are not a matter of record. Sometimes an interest will require a transaction to be unavailable to memory. For instance, a short-term interest may be able to prevail by disguising the fact that a particular transaction violates a private rule. Whether or not this occurs in the way Freud described (see Ainslie 1982), it renders the subject unable to report the transaction to the observer.

However, much information may appear unavailable not because people are motivated to be unaware of it, but because they are not in the habit of noticing it. We learn internal bargaining intuitively, by trial and error, in much the way we learn language. The study of this process may parallel linguistics, which has not collected new kinds of data so much as examined ordinary speech in a systematic way. For centuries people spoke well without knowing what nouns, verbs and adjectives were, much less tacts and mands; but these concepts are not hard to teach, even to children, who can subsequently describe their speech quite accurately in such terms. In many cases, the task of understanding an individual's internal interests may be a matter of asking the right questions.

Simple tests can determine whether a behaviour pattern is part of a motivational conflict. For instance:

(1) When temporary preferences persist, that is, when they are incompletely controlled or are controlled only by extrapsychic devices, they are easily identified by the fact that the person foresees them with apprehension and looks back on them with regret.

(2) Private rules can be distinguished from 'rules of thumb' or simple habits by the presence of motivational pressure which is not

accounted for by the outcomes of the choice literally being made, or by the fear of loss of control if a choice is not made in the prescribed direction. Trying an unaccustomed behaviour has little consequence for a simple habit; but if it is a habit of will, the kind of habit with 'force', then, as one Victorian psychologist said, 'It is necessary above all things never to lose a battle. Every gain on the wrong side undoes the effect of many conquests on the right' (Bain 1886).

(3) A criterion for conduct may be understood as a bright line if the subject expresses the idea that change would make the relevant rule meaningless or harder to obey, or if the possibility of changing it raises a feeling of guilt or a fear of loss of control.

Structured interviews to elicit this information about patients' most important behaviours are now being developed.

It may be possible to go beyond subjects' self-reports in getting information about their internal bargaining processes. Subjects' actual behaviour in tests resembling story-telling video games may reveal their tendency to respond in similar situations in real life. The ability of computers to simulate part of a conflictual situation, and to record a subject's response to the computer-generated situation, is just beginning to be explored (e.g. Ainslie and Haendel 1982, pp. 136–8). Motivational patterns elicited in human subjects by such means can then become the basis for fully articulated computer models like those that have been useful in other branches of economics.

However, it is not yet clear whether data gathered in these ways can become the basis of a practical scientific discipline. This approach may be defeated by uncooperative or deceptive subjects. There may also be a psychological analogue of Heisenberg's uncertainty principle which leads a subject to treat all testing situations as special cases, thus rendering important private rules inapplicable. The outcome of these possibilities will determine whether the analysis of bargaining among parts of a multiple self will be a method of gathering useful information about individuals, or just a conceptual boundary for microeconomics.

REFERENCES

Ainslie, G. (1975) 'Specious reward: a behavioral theory of impulsiveness and impulsive control', *Psychological Bulletin* 82, 463–96.

Ainslie, G. (1982) 'A behavioral economic approach to the defense mechanisms: Freud's energy theory revisited', *Social Science Information* 21, 735–79.

Ainslie, G. (1984) 'Behavioral economics II: motivated involuntary behavior', *Social Science Information* 23, 247–74.

Ainslie, G. (forthcoming) 'Aversion with only one factor', in M. Commons, A. Nevin and H. Rachlin (eds.), *The Effect of Delay and of Intervening Events on Reinforcement Value: Proceedings of the Fifth Harvard Symposium on Quantitative Analyses of Behavior*, Cambridge, Mass.: Ballinger.

Ainslie, G. and Haendel, V. (1982) 'The motives of the will', in E. Gottheil, A. T. McLellan, and K. Druley (eds.), *The Etiology of Addiction*, Springfield: Charles Thomas.

Ainslie, G. and Herrnstein, R. J. (1981) 'Preference reversal and delayed reinforcement', *Animal Learning & Behavior* 9, 476–82.

Aquinas, St T. *Summa Theologica* I–II, 94, 2, in A. Pegis (ed.), (1948) *Introduction to St. Thomas Aquinas*, New York: New York Modern Library, p. 635.

Bain, A. (1886) *The Emotions and the Will*, New York: Appleton.

Becker, G. (1976) *The Economic Approach to Human Behavior*, Chicago: Chicago University Press.

Becker, H. S. (1960) 'Notes on the concept of commitment', *American Journal of Sociology* 66, 32–40.

Beecher, H. K. (1959) *Measurement of Subjective Responses*, New York: Oxford.

Berlyne, D. E. (1971) *Aesthetics and Psychobiology*, New York: Appleton-Century Crofts.

Chevrier, J. O. and Delorme, A. (1980) 'Aesthetic preferences: influence of perceptual ability, age and complexity of stimulus', *Perceptual and Motor Skills* 50, 839–49.

Coombs, C. H. and Avrunin, G. S. (1977) 'Single peaked functions and the theory of preference', *Psychological Review* 84, 216–30.

DeVilliers, P. and Herrnstein, R. (1976) 'Toward a law of response strength', *Psychological Bulletin* 83, 1131–53.

Elster, J. (1979) *Ulysses and the Sirens: Studies in Rationality and Irrationality*, Cambridge: Cambridge University Press.

Elster, J. (1981) 'States that are essentially by-products', *Social Science Information* 20, 431–73. Reprinted in Elster, J. (1983) *Sour*

Grapes: Studies in the Subversion of Rationality, Cambridge, Cambridge University Press, pp. 43–108.

Empson, W. (1930) *Seven Types of Ambiguity*, London: New Directions.

Fisher, A. (1962) 'Effects of stimulus variation on sexual satiation in the male rat', *Journal of Comparative and Physiological Psychology* 55, 614–20.

Fowler, H. (1967) 'Satiation and curiosity: constructs for a drive and incentive-motivational theory of motive', in K. Spence and J. Spence (eds.), *Psychology of Learning and Motivation*, vol. 1, New York: Academic Press.

Freud, S. (1956) *The Complete Psychological Works of Sigmund Freud* (J. Strachey and A. Freud, eds.), London: Hogarth: 1900, vol. 5.

Freud, S. (1915) *ibid.*, vol. 14.

Freud, S. (1916–17) *ibid.*, vol. 16.

Freud, S. (1923) *ibid.*, vol. 19.

Goldiamond, I. (1965) 'Self-control procedures in personal behavior problems', *Psychological Reports* 17, 851–68.

Green, H. (1964) *I Never Promised You a Rose Garden*, New York: Holt, Rhinehart and Winston.

Herrnstein, R. (1961) 'Relative and absolute strengths of response as a function of frequency of reinforcement', *Journal of the Experimental Analysis of Animal Behaviour* 4, 267–72.

Herrnstein, R. J. (1969) 'Method and theory in the study of avoidance', *Psychological Review* 76, 46–69.

Herrnstein, R. J. (1981) 'Self-control as response strength', in E. Szabadi and C. Lowe (eds.), *Quantification of Steady-State Operant Behavior*, Amsterdam: Elsevier/North Holland.

Homme, L. E. (1966) 'Contiguity theory and contingency management', *Psychological Record* 16, 233–41.

Hunt, J. M. (1963) 'Motivation inherent in information processing and action', in O. J. Harvey (ed.), *Motivation and Social Interactions: Cognitive Determinants*, New York: Ronald.

James, W. (1890) *Principles of Psychology* (2 vols.) New York: Holt, p. 565.

Kanfer, F. H. and Karoly, P. (1972) 'Self-control: a behavioristic excursion into the lion's den', *Behavior Therapy* 3, 398–416.

Kanfer, F. H. and Phillips, J. (1970) *Learning Foundations of Behavior Therapy*, New York: Wiley.

Kant, I. (1959) *Foundations of the Metaphysics of Morals* (trans. L. Beck), New York: Bobbs, Merrill.

Kant, I. (1960) *Religion Within the Limits of Reason Alone* (trans. T. Green and H. Hucken), New York: Harper and Row, pp. 15–49.

Kenny, A. (1963) *Action, Emotion, and Will*, London: Humanities Press.

Koriat, A., Milkman, R., Averill, J. R., and Lazarus, R. S. (1972) 'The self-control of emotional reactions to a stressful film', *Journal of Personality*. 40, 601–19.

Lazarus, R. 1975a 'A cognitively oriented psychologist looks at biofeedback', *American Psychologist* 30, 553–61.

Lazarus, R. 1975b 'The self-regulation of emotion', in Levi, L. (ed.), *Emotions, Their Parameters and Measurement*, New York: Raven.

Leibenstein, H. (1976) *Beyond Economic Man: A New Foundation for Microeconomics*, Cambridge, Mass.: Harvard University Press.

Levinson, H. (1973) *The Great Jackass Fallacy*, Cambridge, Mass.: Harvard University Press.

Logan, F. A. (1965) 'Decision-making by rats: delay versus amount of reward', *Journal of Comparative and Physiological Psychology* 59, 1–12.

Marlatt, G. (1978) 'Craving for alcohol, loss of control and relapse: a cognitive–behavioral analysis', in Nathen, P. *et al.* (eds.), *Alcoholism: New Directions in Behavioral Research and Treatment*, New York: Plenum.

Maslow, A. (1968) *Toward a Psychology of Being*, New York: Van Nostrand.

Melzack, R. *et al.* (1963) 'Stratagems for controlling pain: contributions of auditory stimulation and suggestion', *Experimental Neurology* 8, 239–47.

Miller, N. and Dollard, J. (1941) *Social Learning and Imitation*, New Haven: Yale University Press.

Moray, N. (1969) *Attention: Selective Processes in Visions and Hearing*, London: Hutchinson.

Myerson, J. and Miezin, F. (1980) 'The kinetics of choice: an operant systems analysis', *Psychological Review* 87, 160–74.

Navarick, S. and Fantino, E. (1976) 'Self-control and general models of choice', *Journal of Experimental Psychology: Animal Behavior Processes* 2, 75–87.

Plato, *Phaedo* (trans. H. Tredennick), in E. Hamilton and H. Cairns (eds.) (1961), *Plato, the Collected Dialogues*, Princeton: Princeton University Press.

Premack, D. (1959) 'Toward empirical behavior laws', I. 'Positive reinforcement', *Psychological Review* 66, 219–34.

Rachlin, H. and Green, L. (1972) 'Commitment, choice and self-control', *Journal of the Experimental Analysis of Animal Behavior* 17, 15–22.

Renner, K. E. (1964) 'Delay of reinforcement: a historical review', *Psychological Bulletin* 61, 341–61.

Ricoeur, P. (1971) 'Guilt, ethics, and religion', in J. Meta (ed.), *Moral Evil under Challenge*, New York: Herder and Herder, p. 11.

Schelling, T. C. (1960) *The Strategy of Conflict*, Cambridge, Mass.: Harvard University Press.

Scitovsky, T. (1976) *The Joyless Economy: an Inquiry into Human Satisfaction and Consumer Dissatisfaction*, New York: Oxford.

Solnick, J., Kannenberg, C., Eckerman, D., and Waller, M. (1980) 'An experimental analysis of impulsivity and impulse control in humans', *Learning and Motivation* 11, 61–77.

Solomon, R. (1980) 'The opponent-process theory of acquired motivation', *American Journal of Psychology* 35, 691–712.

Sternbach, R. A. (1968) *Pain: A Psychophysiological Analysis*, New York: Academic Press.

Stigler, G. and Becker, G. (1977) 'De gustibus non est disputandum', *American Economic Review* 67, 76–90.

Strotz, R. H. (1956) 'Myopia and inconsistency in dynamic utility maximization', *Review of Economic Studies* 23, 166–80.

Timberlake, W. (1980) 'A molar equilibrium theory of learned performance', in *The Psychology of Learning and Motivation*, vol. 14, New York: Academic Press, pp. 1–58.

Thaler, R. (1980) 'Towards a positive theory of consumer behavior', *Journal of Economic Behavior and Organization* 1, 39–60.

Tversky, A. and Kahneman, D. (1981) 'The framing of decisions and the rationality of choice', *Science* 211, 453–8.

Walker, W. and King, W. (1962) 'Effects of stimulus novelty on gnawing and eating by rats', *Journal of Comparative and Physiological Psychology* 55, 838–42.

Wasson, C. (1975) *Consumer Behavior: A Managerial Viewpoint*, Austin, Texas: University of Austin Press.

Wilson, J., Kuehn, R. and Beach, F. (1963) 'Modification in the sexual behavior of male rats by changing the stimulus female', *Journal of Comparative and Physiological Psychology* 56, 636–44.

Winston, G. (1980) 'Addiction and backsliding', *Journal of Economic Behavior and Organization* 1, 295–324.

7. The mind as a consuming organ

THOMAS C. SCHELLING

Lassie died one night. Millions of viewers, not all of them children, grieved. At least, they shed tears. Except for the youngest, the mourners knew that Lassie didn't really exist. Whatever that means. Perhaps with their left hemispheres they could articulate that they had been watching a trained dog and that *that* dog was still alive, healthy and rich; meanwhile in their right hemispheres, or some such place (if these phenomena have a place), the real Lassie had died.

Did they enjoy the episode?

We know they would not have enjoyed the death of the dog that played Lassie. Did the adults and older children wish that Lassie hadn't died? Do the dry-eyed parents of a moist-eyed teenager wish their children hadn't watched? If he hadn't watched, what would have been his grief at breakfast, reading the news that Lassie was dead? And would he regret missing the final episode?

What about declaring that Lassie did not die and showing an alternative episode, one that was filmed after Lassie's death was screened, and explaining that, Lassie being only fictional, the screen-writers thought it best, in view of the widespread grief (evidenced by some people wanting to know where to send flowers), to rewrite the story.

I don't think it works. But maybe a substitute screen-writer could be blamed for an inauthentic episode, Lassie's true creator having been hospitalized but, now having recovered, swearing that the real Lassie hadn't been going to die and that the dying episode was a counterfeit.

But there are rules that mustn't be violated. An important one is no feedback from the audience. You cannot show two episodes and let each viewer choose, nor poll the audience to determine whether Lassie dies.

Nor can the viewers simply imagine themselves a different episode in which Lassie is spared. The problem is not the lack of imagination, but discipline and authenticity. Fantasy is too self-indulgent. George Ainslie's work illuminated the issue.[1] Daydreams escalate. Before I can spend the $10,000 that my poker partner bet because he thought that I was bluffing, I revise the figure to $100,000; then I put it in gold at $40 dollars an ounce, spend a couple of years hiking home from a plane crash in Northern Canada, phone my broker to sell and hit the $800 dollar market, and start plotting to invest my two million in something equally good . . . By then I realize that it is all counterfeit if I can make it up so easily.

There is no suspense, no surprise, no danger. Likewise there is no emergency in which Lassie can risk her life with which I can quicken my pulse as long as I know that I write the ending.

Engrossing fiction, whatever else it is, is disciplined fantasy. If you know your authors you can even choose, as people choose their opponent's skill in a chess machine, the risk of tragedy. Killing a character in whom the reader has made an investment puts the lives of the remaining characters in credible jeopardy, and some authors acquire a reputation for poignant endings.

There is something here akin to self-deception. Jon Elster's work on self-deception is persuasive.[2] His interest is rational cognitive self-deception, reasoning one's way into a belief one knew to be false, inducing the belief through practice, or permanently removing something from memory together with the memory of the decision to remove it. There are other phenomena that could be called self-deception that are less permanent and less cognitive. Riding a safe roller-coaster can give some people the same exhilaration as a genuinely risky trip. Their eyes and semi-circular canals capture the communication channels. I don't know who I thought was being stabbed in the shower in *Psycho*, but after the movie my wife and I, having arrived at the theatre in separate cars, left one car behind and drove home together. I have not been able to determine whether it is the scare that I enjoy or the relief that follows. Richard Solomon has

---

[1] 'Beyond microeconomics: conflict among interests in a multiple self as a determinant of value', xerox, January 1982, pp. 18–23.

[2] Jon Elster (1979) *Ulysses and the Sirens*, Cambridge: Cambridge University Press, Ch. 2, especially pp. 47–65, or, alternatively (1977), 'Ulysses and the Sirens: a theory of imperfect rationality', *Social Science Information*, 16, 469–526.

discussed an 'opponent process' that might generate net utility from the infliction of pain or fright; his parachutists enjoyed a high that lasted twenty-four hours after the jump.[3] I wonder whether someone thrown from an aeroplane, saved by a parachute that he didn't know he had, would be exhilarated by the experience. In sky-diving and in horror movies the sensation of risk is controlled; self-deception is partial; the glands that secrete euphoriant stimuli are encouraged to be deceived, but not the control centres that would make us sick.

A puzzle occurs to me. I have never been instructed in how to produce good daydreams. It could be that I haven't the talent to create fiction, for myself or for anybody else, and I rely on novelists to provide fully articulated fantasies with which I can identify in a participatory way. But possibly I simply don't know the rules of construction. Like a sculptor who finds challenge in the stone itself, artistic fantasy may require the challenge of self-imposed restraint. Perhaps I could be taught strategies of self-discipline to prevent that runaway inflation to which my favourite daydreams are so susceptible. There may be ways to introduce genuine surprise, perhaps by some random drawing from a library in my mind. The problem suggested by Elster's comments on self-induced beliefs, and on sneaking up on one's own insomnia, is that in the act of reigning in one's daydreams to give them greater authenticity one may not be able to hold the reins and forget one is holding them.

It does not detract, as far as I can tell, from the suspense and credibility of the fiction I read that I chose the book, that is, chose an author I knew, or knew something about the book by hearsay. (Douglas Hofstadter, in *Gödel, Escher, Bach*, pointed out that by unconsciously estimating the pages remaining we spoil some of the terminal surprise of a novel, just as by checking our watch during an adventure film we can tell whether we are on another false summit or have reached the climax.)

I doubt whether these puzzles can be resolved by just thinking about them. The rules of argument for certain philosophical problems require idealizing a person as a reasoning machine, one that not only can think logically but cannot think not logically, who has no hallucinations and no chemical or electrical means of putting things into

[3] R. L. Solomon and J. D. Corbit (1974) 'An opponent-process theory of motivation', *Psychological Review* 81 (2), 119–45.

memory or taking them out. Whether that kind of person can do something that would be called 'foolish himself', and what the limits are on what he may fool himself about, is an intriguing question.[4] But it is not the only question, because that is not the only kind of person worth studying. What makes dreams, daydreams, books and films captivating, credible and irresistible, with or without music or stimulants, requires more than reflection. Though we can often simulate by reasoning what can be done by reasoning, spellbinding requires other modes of study.

Maybe real dreams are more promising. Some work of Kilton Stewart indicated that people in the Malay peninsula have developed techniques for taming their dreams, reshaping dreams in progress.[5] Apparently they do not make up their dreams in advance, but assume enough command to keep the dreams from getting out of hand. I cannot claim even to understand what that means, but I also don't understand the particular control that I had when that nice girl was being stabbed in the shower.

Lassie represents only one of the ways that, as consumers, we live in our minds. She was fiction and her medium was television; Rin Tin Tin was radio and movies. But novels, plays, puppets and stories, impromptu or composed, new or familiar, are of the species. They are primarily for enjoyment. And they usually, but not always, capture the mind.

By capture I mean to engage it, to hold it, to occupy or to preoccupy it so that one's thoughts are not elsewhere; to give the reader or viewer or listener a stake in the outcome; to make him identify in some fashion with characters in the story, if only by caring what happens. The engagement has dynamics; it progresses. Interruption is disagreeable, though a person can sometimes go on 'hold' while the man in the projection room changes the reel.

[4] There is a probability, P, that I have a disease that will kill me suddenly during the next few years, and a reliable test for whether or not I have the disease. Do I want the test? (If I am compulsive about the test do I regret my physician told me of it?) Scoring the anticipation of death at zero and of confident good health at 1, in utility notation the issue seems to be whether $(1-P) U (1)$ is greater or less than $U (1-P)$. I doubt whether the two values are equal even for people who consider them logically obliged to be equal.
[5] Cited in Robert E. Ornstein (1977) *The Psychology of Consciousness*, 2nd edn, Harcourt Brace Jovanovich, Inc., pp. 142–3.

The characteristic that interests me is the engrossment – not merely the surrender of attention but the participation, the sense of being in the story or part of it, caring, and wanting to know. (There is some fiction that does not have that quality; irony and humour require a more conscious attention, and some plots are constructed to be admired rather than absorbed into. Some surprise turns of plot are intended to jolt the reader out of the story and into a relation with the author; and some science fiction is more like turning the leaves of a mail-order catalogue than participating in a story.)

There is also non-fiction that works like fiction. For many of us it is impossible to watch sports on television just to admire the performance. Not only do we end up caring how the game comes out, we are incapable of watching the game symmetrically. It is more fun to be engaged. And that Lassie phenomenon occurs: I cannot change the side I am on, especially not to be on the winning side, because changing sides discredits the notion that I have a side, just as I cannot mentally bring Lassie back to life without denying that Lassie is mortal and I care what happens to her.

It is this suspense and concern that qualifies certain live events to be considered as impromptu fiction. Snippets of football, like an eighty-yard punt return, can be good entertainment for a few minutes, but I have never known a TV channel to replay old games regularly; and people who look forward to a delayed broadcast do all they can to avoid overhearing the outcome in advance.

What puzzles me is how to relate these observations to a theory of what people are up to. Take the rational consumer in economic theory: what is he consuming?

What do I consume when I purchase *The Wizard of Oz*? Physically I buy a book, or a reel of videotape. But that is a raw material; I 'consume' two hours of entertainment. But should I say that, like Dorothy, I consumed a trip to Oz? Or, to phrase it awkwardly, that I procured Dorothy's trip to Oz, in which I participated? I do not mean a sight-seeing trip – television can always show me places that I cannot afford to visit – but the adventure, with the risk and poignancy and excitement and surprise.

A way to try to make sense of the question is to ask what the substitutes are. If you lower the price of air travel I may travel less by bus, but if I see *Around the World In Eighty Days* am I less likely to travel? Can I do without a dog if I have Lassie? Do I need as much romance, repartee, or fresh air and sunshine if I get plenty of it from nine until midnight on a screen in my living-room? I am not sure what I should be expected to consume less of once I have seen two killings in *Psycho*. And since some consumer goods whet appetites, the notion of substitutes may not be the correct one.

There is no question but that part of what I get from a two-hour movie or two hours in a book is 'two hours worth' of something. I get two hours of time out, of escape, of absent-mindedness. Escape from what? Certainly from boredom. Escaping boredom is escaping the tedium of consciousness, of one's own company, of being here and now and one's self, not someplace else or somebody else.

And there is escaping things the knowledge of which makes one unhappy. If 'truth' is what we know and are aware of, in the most engrossing fiction we escape truth. Whatever else it is, drama is forgetfulness. We can forget and forget that we are forgetting. It is temporary mind control. If memories are pain, fiction is anaesthesia.

But is it more than that? Is it more than time out? Do we consume the contents of the story, or just the time? And what implication does this kind of consuming have for what we are doing with our minds the rest of the time?

There is a funny correspondence between the mind and the home computer. For years, of course, the mind has been likened to a calculating machine, and much 'artificial intelligence' is an indirect way of studying the human mind. Texts in cognitive science treat perception, recall and recognition, and reasoning with the same schemata as are used in analysing electronic machines and their software, with the same flow charts and terminology. But I have in mind what families bought last Christmas.

These are the machines you use to calculate the payback period of a new furnace or the answer to a child's geometry problem and, when you have done that, to shoot down enemy missiles or go spelunking in a cave full of reptiles. The computer is a tool *and* a plaything, and *that* is what makes it like the mind.

An important difference is that to switch a computer from tool to toy or toy to tool you usually have to insert a cartridge or disc, but the mind is able to go from work mode to fantasy like a computer that, halfway through an income-tax programme, finds oil on your property.

But fantasy and fiction are not all that I have in mind. Aside from those two related forms of make-believe, most of the things that affect my welfare happen in my mind. I can say this, I suppose, because I am part of that minority of the human race that is comfortable most of the time, trained from childhood to be reflective and socially sensitive, and most of the day not required to be busily alert at tasks that entirely absorb one's attention. The things that make me happy or unhappy, at any level of consciousness that I can observe, are the things I believe and am aware of.

I like to be liked, I like to be admired. I like not to be guilty of cowardice, I like to believe that I shall live long and healthily and that my children will too, that I have done work I can be proud of and that others appreciate, that my life will be rich with challenge but I shall meet the challenges and have many accomplishments. That the talk I gave yesterday was a good one, and what I am writing today will be read and appreciated.

If I were hungry or cold or itched all over my body or had to work physically to exhaustion, those would be the conditions that determined my welfare. But I think I have stated the situation correctly for myself and for most of the people that I know.

An unavoidable question is whether I could be happier if only I could believe things more favourable, more complimentary, more in line with my hopes and wishes, than what I believe to be true. That might be done by coming to believe things that are contrary to what I know, such as that my health or my reputation is better than it is, my financial prospects or my children's prospects better than they are and that I have performed ably and bravely on those occasions when I did not. Or it might be accomplished by improving the mix of my beliefs by dropping out – forgetting – some of the things that cause me guilt, grief, remorse and anxiety.

Whether I would be happier, whether my welfare should be deemed greater, with those improved beliefs is one of the questions; another is whether, if I had the choice, I would elect a change in my beliefs. Set aside for the moment the question whether there is any way I could do that. The question whether I would choose to revise the contents of my mental library, so that even in my most rational thinking I would come to more positive conclusions, is independent of whether or not we know the technology by which it might be done. (I admit that whether I would choose it might depend on the technology.)[6]

A third question is whether you would encourage me to manipulate my own beliefs in the interests of my own happiness, or permit me to if you had anything to say about it. Maybe for that question we have to be more explicit about technologies. There are animals that reportedly self-administer pure pleasure through electrodes in their brains, to the point of endangering their survival by not stopping to eat or drink. The nature of that euphoria we may never know until we try it; and whether it sounds like music, feels like a rocking-chair, tastes like chocolate, reads like a novel, or is merely a pleasant absence of sensation may determine our attitudes. Currently it is considered all right to do it with stereo headphones but not electrodes.

Of course, if we ever can select our favourite beliefs off some menu we shall have to be practical about it. I might want to forget I had cancer but not to forget showing up for treatment. I must avoid beliefs that collide with each other or with reality in such a way that I have to confront my own confusion and recognize my beliefs as unreliable, coming to doubt the beliefs I selected off the menu. Just as lawyers advise us to stick close to the truth because the truth is consistent and easier to remember, self-deceivers will be wise to pick sparingly from that menu.

A little later I shall invite you to think about that menu, about what you would like to find on a menu of beliefs and disbeliefs, of ways to insert things into memory and to remove things, to manipulate awareness and the ease or difficulty of recall, and in other ways to affect what is resident in your mind. But first let me recall some of the methods already available, that work well or ill according to who uses them and what for. Most of them we do not think of as mind control, although several fit that description. They would not be described as *belief* control, but that may be because we speak about beliefs as if they were little entities in the mind. That notion misses some relevant dimensions. We forget things all the time, in the sense that we do not *currently* have them in mind; are unaware of them. We can be using

[6] In *Cognitive Therapy and Its Disorders* (1976) New American Library, Aaron T. Beck, describes a system of psychotherapy that can improve the quality of a patient's beliefs by substituting more favourable correct beliefs for depressing wrong beliefs. Substituting still more favourable incorrect beliefs would require a different procedure.

knowledge that is not in mind, aware of conclusions that derive from things we are momentarily unaware of. We don't usually call this forgetting; but when it is important to get things out of mind, and we make an effort at forgetting, doing things and thinking things that are incompatible with the awareness of what it is we are trying to forget, what we are doing deserves to be called 'forgetting' even though it is temporary. People do say they went to a movie to forget tomorrow's examination.

The language of belief is confusing here. I have observed in myself, so often that it no longer surprises me, that if I give a performance before some audience I am jollier at dinner, and eat more, if I am pleased with my performance. Disagreeable feedback spoils the evening. At my age the statistical record of my performance ought to reflect so many observations of good, poor and mediocre performance that one more experience at either end of the distribution could hardly affect a rational self-assessment. I try to remind myself of that on those occasions when feedback depresses me; but my welfare function apparently isn't constructed that way. It feels to me as if I am taking the audience reaction as evidence, and what makes me feel good or bad is the belief that my *average* career performance is high or low and will continue so in the future. I think it is plain bad reasoning. I am making a rudimentary statistical error, attaching weights that are distorted by vividness or recency and 'forgetting' the bulk of my experience. I mention this as evidence that there are kinds and degrees of forgetting even despite our knowing better.

Before we compose that menu of mental self-controls and self-stimuli that we might wish we could choose from, an inventory of techniques already available is useful. I offer a suggestive list. I exclude things that require a large investment in time, effort or therapeutic care, like education, psychoanalysis and hermitage, and those that entail irreversible surgery, like castration and lobotomy, and also those that cope with diagnosed pathologies and are based on prescription drugs or dietary supplements that require the attention of a physician. I am rather thinking of tranquillizers, caffeine and sleeping pills.

First is sleep itself. Sleep is somewhat addictive: giving it up each morning is for many people one of the hardest things they do. Sleep can be escape from awareness of what is fearful or hideous. Sleep with dreams can be enjoyable, but not reliably for most of us. Meditation and other modes of relaxation apparently offer escape from anxiety and mental torment for some people. Maybe the more generic term 'unconsciousness' will include the state of apparent sleep that goes with blood alcohol and other anaesthesia.

Different from sleep itself are things that bring on sleep. These can be sleeping pills, white noise, rocking, alcohol or breathing exercises. Sleep is an equilibrium state after we get there; getting there requires controlling stimuli. The distinction between sleep as a state and getting to sleep as a transition is sharp, even though some techniques for arriving at sleep, like relaxation, are also substitutes for sleep, and some of the things that induce sleep, like alcohol, help to sustain sleep.

Then we have tranquillizers – pills or alcohol – that are intended not only to relieve distress but to remove inhibitions, shyness, anxiety, specific phobias and fear in general, so that one can perform and remain calm despite stimuli that might otherwise be disabling.

We have things that help us to remain alert. Caffeine in coffee and in tablet form prevents dozing and sleep, as do some prescription drugs. Unexpected stimuli, including noise and even pain, can help, and sometimes aerobic exercise. A useful distinction here is between staying awake and enhancing awareness.

There are techniques to enhance mental concentration. These may take the form of suppressing stimuli and intrusive signals. Insulation against noise is an example. Even fatigue sometimes helps concentration.

Sensory deprivation is a technique, the purposes and results of which I am not sure. Generally it includes earplugs, masks over the eyes, avoidance of tactile sensation or stimulation of skin, and deliberate relaxation, as well as tanks of warm water. Classical and operant conditioning can affect what one likes, dislikes, fears, enjoys, remembers or forgets.

Sensory enhancement is a possibility. Marijuana is sometimes reported to make colours more brilliant, music more profound, dance more sublime.

Drive-enhancement of various kinds is apparently available to increase gustatory or sexual appetite. Aside from deliberate starvation there are visual and olfactory stimuli, conditioning, imaginative self-stimulation and the ubiquitous alcohol.

Hypnosis has been successful in affecting permanent change in desires, in the effectiveness of stimuli, in the treatment of addictions and phobias and in what one forgets or is reminded of.

Subliminal stimulation can apparently have some effect, whether in stimulating, reminding or providing information. Subliminal visual stimulation in connection with television never became the menace that some feared, but the technology remains a possibility. Cassettes are advertised that offer subliminal help.

Finally I would mention electrical and chemical control of memory and other mental processes. We should consider the possibility, which I believe not absolutely ruled out by current theories of information storage in the brain, that memories could be extinguished permanently by electrical stimulation or surgery. In science fiction this would be done by having the patient recall vividly the memory to be extinguished, in order that the memory itself or its location could be targeted, the exciting of the memory being the process that offers the target. If the act of recall produces merely a xerox and not the original, there is nothing accomplished; but there are enough ways to erase something erroneously in the memory of even good computers to suggest that deliberate memory extinction may not be forever beyond reach.

I leave to a footnote an extreme therapy that differentiates the reasoning mind from the reactive one.[7]

Now to consider that menu of believings, forgettings, awarenesses,

---

[7] I love somebody whose face is hideously disfigured in an accident. I know that it will be difficult to love her forever if I continuously see her as ugly as she is going to be. I was in the same accident; I am in the same hospital; I haven't seen her yet, I have only heard about her facial disfigurement. My doctor visits and asks if there is anything I would like.

I ask to be blinded.

This is not self-deception in the Elster sense. Not only do I know that she is ugly; every day my blindness will remind me that she must be too ugly to love if I see her. It keeps me, however, from reacting to visual stimuli that I would not be able to accommodate.

There is something here like reaction to a mask. Might the doctor propose that, though there is nothing plastic surgery can do to restore the looks of the person I love, she can wear a mask?

How does this relate to cosmetics? If I know that somebody looks prettier than she would if her face were clean of cosmetics, and if I prefer her looks with cosmetics, is it that the cosmetics make me think she is more beautiful, or do I just react to a sight that includes the cosmetics as well as the face?

Maybe the term 'self-delusion' can be used for these processes, saving 'self-deception' for the more purely intellectual.

remindings and other modes of mind control that we might be tempted to administer to ourselves if they were reliably available at moderate cost without side-effects. We need to put a boundary on what we should let ourselves wish for. Wouldn't it be delightful if we could change our taste in foods, and enjoy turnips as much as we enjoy smoked oysters? Think of the money we would save, to say nothing of calories and cholesterol. Instant wit, efficient memorization, bravery, poise, optimism and immunity to disagreeable noises would look good in a Christmas stocking. The capacity to like, even love, one's work, colleagues, neighbours, spouse and neighbourhood would make rose-coloured glasses a bargain. In contemplating the self-paternal self-deception that might interest us if only it were available, we shall get nowhere (or rather we shall get infinitely far too fast) if we let our wishes escalate the way our daydreams sometimes do.

A modest place to begin is phobias. We could wish for either of two things about phobias – that we didn't have them, or that we did. The usual definition of a phobia is a disabling or severely discomforting fear, persistent, illogical and serving no prudential purpose. The more famous of them have Greek names. Most people who react with repugnance to enclosure, open space, rodents, reptiles, insects, viscera, blood, audiences, precipices, needles and the dark suffer directly from the sensation when it cannot be avoided and suffer the costs of avoidance when it can be. Phobias appear to be based upon memories of real or imagined scenes and events or associations of real or imagined scenes or events. There are therapies like conditioning, hypnosis, relaxation and stimulus control that can weaken or extinguish the phobia, and there must be corresponding ways to enhance or aggravate them. Whether, for some phobias or most of them, there is something that could be 'forgotten' that would extinguish the phobia I do not know. But for at least some phobias some of the time it can help to forget the phobia itself. Just as closing one's eyes can sometimes eliminate a stimulus that produces vertigo or a reaction to blood or even darkness, forgetting a phobia can sometimes reduce one's awareness of the presence of the conditions that trigger the phobia. There are people who are suddenly stricken when reminded that they are in circumstances – enclosures, high places – to which their normal reaction is phobic. Thus a modest minimum that might be achieved through specific forgetfulness would be occasional neutralization of a phobia by merely forgetting it. (An analogy: forgetting one's insomnia makes it easier to get to sleep.)

Acquiring a phobia can be useful. Some of the therapies offered to people who smoke attempt to produce a mental association of cigarettes with dirty lungs, lip cancer and foul breath. If these are presented as realistic consequences of smoking and the smoker is expected to reflect on them and to decide never to smoke again, and then never to smoke again, there is no need to characterize the aversion as a phobia; but if the patient is unable to respond reasonably to the danger itself, through lack of self-control or absent-mindedness, raising the fear an order of magnitude and putting the enhanced fear itself beyond reason permits the resulting fear to be both unreasonable and useful. (The dangers of such techniques are demonstrated by extreme cases of anorexia. Cigarettes have the advantage that one needn't smoke in moderation but can quit, and the contrived horror is avoided by not smoking at all.)

The idea of deliberately cultivating latent disagreeable thoughts suggest an important distinction. Some of the things we would like to believe and forget are beliefs and memories that directly affect our internal welfare, our state of hope and happiness, regret, anxiety, guilt, fear, compassion or pride. If I am going to smoke anyway, believing that cigarettes cannot hurt me improves my welfare. That cigarettes are dangerous is a belief that, if available for adoption, I should adopt only if I thought I would act on it and quit the habit that worries me.

But the instrumental beliefs and the 'consumable' beliefs cannot always be distinguished. There is evidence that people who believe themselves to be exceptionally at risk – people who after a severe cardiac episode are flatly told by their physicians that continued smoking will likely kill them – not only have a higher success rate in quitting than people who are merely advised to cut down or quit, but suffer less in quitting than the people who succeed on the more ambivalent advice. (I believe the difference is between the mental activity of the person who believes himself *to have quit* and that of the person who thinks of himself as *trying to quit*. For the latter there is suspense and the need to decide over and over on the occasions that invite one to smoke.)

What might our menu offer for daydreams? One possibility would be a mechanism to keep my mind from wandering. Often when I try to pay attention to a speaker I hear something that sends my mind on a detour. Paradoxically, the more stimulating what I listen to, the more I miss because of so many opportunities for my wayward mind to pursue a thought and, in doing so, to miss the next one.

The same thing happens when I think to myself. I am supposed to be working on a problem and I wake up to discover that for some unmeasured period my mind has been playing, not working.

Mind-wandering is not about beliefs but about mental behaviour. But there is also make-believe. Children seem better at it than adults. That may be because children can do it together. I spend some time in pure reverie – what my dictionary calls 'dreamy imaginings, especially of agreeable things' – in which I am the protagonist, but I do not usually admit it and would be mortified to recapitulate my daydream for somebody else, and haven't done it as a duet since childhood. Along one dimension the quality has certainly deteriorated, that of believing in the plot. I may be able to imagine vividly an audience that I hold spellbound, but the feeling that I am really doing it is a weak one. Children who make believe out loud together seem to enjoy a higher quality of involvement. That may be partly because they are unabashed about it. Should we wish that the menu contains something to make our daydreams more real? I don't mean make the plot more realistic, just make the imagined experiences feel more like real experiences.

I can think of two different kinds of daydreams to which this notion of enhancement might apply. One is pure entertainment unrelated to the activity one is engaged in or the environment in which one finds oneself. I do it sitting on a bus or on an aeroplane. The other one is – I am a little shy to admit – investing something that I am doing with a make-believe interpretation. People who run for exercise sometimes pretend to themselves that they are in a race or on some heroic errand. There is not much else to do while running; so any mental recreation is at low opportunity cost. A little anaesthesia is welcome. Any arduous task ought to become a little less burdensome if one could dress it up with some make-believe. I refuse to answer whether I would order some instant make-believe if it were available on the market; I would certainly order it only if it came in a plain wrapper. Trying to improve the quality of our daydreams sounds shamefully childish; the childishness of our actual daydreams is, fortunately, known only to ourselves.

So we come to the final item under 'daydreams' on our menu, the daydream suppressant. If daydreams are a childish waste of time, a bad habit, might we like to be rid of the habit? Are daydreams merely low-grade entertainment, as involuntary as preoccupation with something on a TV screen that the management won't turn off? If we can't improve our daydreams, would we like them turned off? Whether we would like it may depend on what it is we are going to do instead. If we daydream to escape thinking about what we are supposed to be thinking about, eliminating the daydreams may just make us find some other escape. Until I know what that other escape is, I'm not sure whether I would rather stick with my daydreams. If it means I will get my work done more expeditiously, I should welcome it. If I am facing a long bus ride and the alternative to daydreaming is studying the upholstery on the seat in front of me, or looking for the letters of the alphabet in the billboards we pass, it may be better to improve the quality of the dreams than to reduce the quantity.

The human mind is something of an embarrassment to certain disciplines, notably economics, decision theory and others that have found the model of the rational consumer to be a powerfully productive one. The rational consumer is depicted as having a mind that can store and process information, that can calculate or at least make orderly successive comparisons, and that can vicariously image, imagine, anticipate, feel and taste, as well as simulate emotion, in order to compare and choose. To decide whether to risk being caught in bad weather on an off-season mountaineering expedition, whether to face immediate embarrassment or to get a reputation for running away, whether to have another child, whether to change to a pleasanter occupation at reduced earnings, whether to go without wine to save money for a stereo system or even just to choose a restaurant meal over the telephone, the mind has to be capable of somehow sampling the pleasures and discomforts, the joys and horrors on the basis both of remembered experience and description and creative extrapolation.

Just how one decides whether one is in the mood for broiled salmon or roast duck isn't the concern of the decision sciences, at least not unless the way it is done turns out to conflict in some fashion with the rest of the model of rational choice. It sometimes seems to me – to me as a consumer and not as an economist – that I choose dinners from menus rather like the way I used to choose movies from 'coming attractions': I mentally consume a morsel of broiled salmon, register the quality of the taste but erase the taste itself, do the same for the roast duck and let the two sensations feed into an analogue computer that signals my choice. But I can't be sure; if I watch myself and find that that is what seems to happen, it may be the result of the watching.

Now we probably believe, if we bother to think about it, that ultimately the roast duck that I order is enjoyed in my brain. But not in my *mind*. We can say that I consume the roast duck, or we can say that I consume tastes and smells that I produce with roast duck; we could say that I consume chemical and electrical activity in the brain that is triggered by the sensory nerves of taste and smell, but unless our interest is the brain that doesn't add anything. Still, there is mental activity; looking at the roast duck is not eating it, but it is part of the activity, and the visual aesthetics of the meal seem 'mental' in a way that appeasement of appetite does not. Anticipating the roast duck, contemplating the first bite, has a 'mental' quality.

If a gourmet host dawdled for thirty minutes choosing the grandest meal of his career, looking at the raw meat shown him by the chef, discussing wine with the wine steward, watching it brought to the table and tastefully served; smiled at the friends assembled around him, delicately sampled the wine and nodded his approval and watched the first course served impeccably onto everybody's plate and died instantly of a heart attack, we'd be tempted to say that the last half-hour of his life was perhaps the best half-hour of his life. More than that, we might say it was the most enjoyable meal of his life, one of the best he had ever 'consumed'.

If instead he didn't die but proceeded to the more conventional enjoyment and two days later described this superb meal in mouth-watering details to a few of his gourmet friends, we might be tempted to judge that he enjoyed the meal as much in the telling as in the eating, much as a person who barely wins a bitterly fought tournament enjoys the winning more in reflecting back on it than on the hot afternoon on which he nearly lost it.

These observations bring me to the notion of the mind as a *consuming organ*. We consume with our mouths and noses and ears and eyes and proprioceptors and skin and fingertips and with the

THE MIND AS A CONSUMING ORGAN

nerves that react to external stimuli and internal hormones; we consume relief from pain and fatigue, itching and thirst. But we also consume by thinking. We consume past events that we can bring up from memory, future events that we can believe will happen, contemporary circumstances not physically present, like the respect of our colleagues and the affection of our neighbours and the health of our children; and we can even tease ourselves into believing and consuming thoughts that are intended only to please. We consume good news and bad news.

We even – and this makes it a little like traditional economics – spend resources to discover the truth about things that happened in the past. People wish to know that children dead for many years died without too much pain or died proudly. It gets very compounded. If an estranged child makes a painful and urgent journey to arrive at a parent's bedside in time to become reconciled just before the parent dies, all that the parent gets is an hour's love and relief before leaving this world. Whatever the worth of a single hour of ecstasy, compared with vicariously enjoying Dorothy's trip to Oz, it is entirely a mental consuming. The days away from work and the airfare the child spent to be at the dying parent's bedside is a consumer expenditure, a gift to the parent. If the parent dies too soon and never knows that the child is on the way, the investment is largely wasted. If the trip succeeds, the child may consider it the most worthwhile expenditure of his consuming career. One hour's mental consumption.

Furthermore, others will want to know, and will care, whether the child made it to the bedside. There are some who care enough to make large expenditures to hasten the child's arrival or to prolong the parent's life long enough for the reconciliation to take place.

And, finally, the whole story can be fiction. We can be gripped with suspense and caring as we wonder whether an entire lifetime is going somehow to be vindicated by an ecstatic discovery that, after barely an hour, will be extinguished by death.

So we have at least two distinct roles for our minds to play, that of the information processing and reasoning machine by which we choose what to consume out of the array of things that our resources can be exchanged for, and that of the pleasure machine or consuming organ, the generator of direct consumer satisfaction. Actually, like a television set that can frighten small children or bring grief in the form of bad news, the mind can directly generate horror as well as ecstasy, irritation as well as comfort, fear and grief as well as enjoyable memories, reflections and prospects. But that is partly because of still another characteristic of the mind; namely, it doesn't always behave nicely.

Just as it may fail us when we need to remember, or panic when we need all our faculties, the mind can remember things that cause grief, with flashbacks that spoil our appetite, by remembering ugly things it insists on associating with beauty, or humming interminably a tune we'd like to get out of our minds. It is like a complex piece of machinery that has a mind of its own, and is not disposed to be our obedient servant. Or possibly we just have not learned how to get the right service out of our mind. In our culture we stress the importance of the mind as an auxiliary instrument, the information storage and retrieval and articulating mechanism that performs intellectual tasks like communicating and reasoning, and we do not emphasize learning to make our minds produce the thoughts and memories and exploratory previews that bring joy and comfort, and to screen out or expunge the other kind.

The mind evolved as an organ of many uses and many capabilities, an imperfect organ, an organ whose imperfections along some dimensions are compensated or adapted to by the mind's development along others. The dimensions that we associate with analytical thought and speech, even the orderly filing system of our memory, are fairly recent in human evolution;[8] they may not have achieved the autonomy that is assumed in some decision theories and philosophies. Consider the question whether a person can be said to have values and to know his values, and to make choices in accordance with those known values. When it is time to make a decision, that is, when beset by certain stimuli that call for a response, the rational individual is supposed to be able to illuminate and scrutinize his preference map in order not only to calculate how to achieve a particular outcome but to remind himself which outcomes he prefers. His brain may not only selectively transmit information but selectively illuminate his preference map. We know that people are incapable of keeping their eyes from focusing on potato

---

[8] More recent than the *Iliad*, if we can believe the fascinating argument of Julian Jaynes (1982), *The Origin of Consciousness in the Breakdown of the Bicameral Mind*, Houghton Mifflin.

chips, sexy pictures or animated cartoons; we know that both externally administered and internally secreted chemicals can suppress or anaesthetize certain activities; we have little empirical basis for believing (and much for not believing) that the mind will neutrally and indiscriminately process information and scrutinize memory to permit a person to make a choice unaffected by momentary stimuli, whether related to food, fear, sex, affection, aesthetic pleasure or attractive violence. The unconscious accommodation of one's beliefs to achieve a reduction in 'cognitive dissonance' is often treated as a defective or undesirable process, one to be on guard against. Maybe it is to be welcomed, like the reduction of other annoying dissonances. At least, the mind is *trying* to help!

This is all apart from the fact that the mind is a wanderer, a source of fantasy and an easy captive for puzzles, mysteries and daydreams.

As far as I know, it's all the same mind. Marvellous it is that the mind does all these things. Awkward it is that it seems to be the same mind from which we expect both the richest sensations and the most austere analyses.

There is an interesting question of perspective. Like the question, do creatures reproduce themselves by way of genes, or do genes reproduce themselves by way of creatures: do I navigate my way through life with the help of my mind, or does my mind navigate its way through life by the help of me? I'm not sure who's in charge.

8. Goethe's *Faust*, Arrow's Possibility Theorem and the individual decision-taker*

IAN STEEDMAN and ULRICH KRAUSE

> Two souls, alas, do dwell within his breast; The one is ever parting from the other.
>
> GOETHE, Faust, Part I

> Faust complained that he had two souls in his breast. I have a whole squabbling crowd. It goes on as in a republic.
>
> BISMARCK

> There is no reason why one person should not combine a number of distinct want-systems.
>
> J. R. HICKS

> Every human being is just a mass of contradictions.
>
> ANON

The idea that a single person can be pulled in different directions or can, in extreme cases, even be internally divided in a tragic conflict is far from being the preserve of great literature, or even of a statesman attempting to unify a nation when he cannot even unify himself; rather it is an everyday experience, as is witnessed by Anon. It is a common-place that a given individual can feel the force of conflicting considerations, some telling for and some against a particular action, whether it be a trivial one or one of great significance. Yet when we turn to economic (and other) theory concerned with individual decision-takers, we find that the 'individual' of the theory is represented by a single, complete, transitive preference ordering; if there are 'many souls', if there has been inner conflict and contradiction, then this has been transcended and the individual is represented simply by the final, *unified* ordering.

*We should like to thank J. M. Buchanan, J. M. Currie, D. Elson, M. Farmer, N. Geras, P. Halfpenny, R. Hartley, M. Hollis, A. Hylland, H.-D. Kurz, H. Lesser, S. Parrinello, P. Pettit, H. Steiner and participants in seminars at the universities of Bremen, Bristol, Manchester, Newcastle, Rome, Stirling and York, for help and/or encouragement of various kinds.

The purpose of this chapter is to consider how – and, indeed, whether – such a unified ordering can come to represent, in an adequate manner, the decisions of a typical, multi-faceted individual; or, in other words, to open up the 'black box' constituted by the rational individual of economic theory in order to display more clearly what lies inside. It must be emphasized at once that it is no part of our purpose here to throw doubt on the general characterization of individuals as rational, that is, as acting for reasons, in the light of beliefs and purposes. Nor do we seek to reject the idea that important aspects of rational decision-making can usefully be represented by means of complete, transitive preference orderings. On the contrary, we shall picture a typical, multi-faceted individual as having *many* such orderings over alternatives, these different orderings representing the different 'points of view' from which such an individual will assess those alternatives. Our concern is to consider how an individual may finally decide to act on the basis of these various – and sometimes conflicting – partial judgments and whether the *overall* decisions can be represented by maximization with respect to a single, overall ordering. Even if one were to answer this last question negatively, therefore, one would only be rejecting one particular – and especially simple – characterization of rational action; one would most certainly *not* be rejecting the concept of rational action itself. The concept of acting for reasons is far less restrictive than that of action representable by a *single* preference ordering (cp. Sen 1977b, Section 7). It must, of course, be recognized that the representation of a multi-faceted individual's decisions may well be more complex than that needed for the traditional 'rational individual' of economic theory but there is certainly no basis for asserting a priori that pluralism is incompatible with rationality (cp. Sen 1980–1, p. 204; Sen and Williams 1982, pp. 16–18).

Throughout the paper we shall be concerned with a descriptive analysis of how individuals reach decisions or, in other words, how they 'aggregate' the *judgments* reached from different points of view; we shall not deal with either prescriptive analysis or the question how an individual's 'welfare' may be measured (cp. Sen 1977a, Section 1). This reference to the aggregation of judgments will naturally remind the reader of social choice theory and, prompted by Bismarck's observation that 'It goes on as in a republic', we shall bear in mind the analogies between our topic and some of the familiar arguments of social choice theory. Our focus of attention, nevertheless, will be exclusively the multi-faceted individual.

I. Preliminary considerations

Before we enter into our discussion of the many-faceted individual and the attendant issue of integration of those facets, it may be as well to recall that our topic is a very old one; this may help to suggest both that our 'problem' is not an illusory one and that its 'solution' is not obvious. What follows does not, of course, constitute even a brief survey of the relevant material; it is no more than a list of examples, an *aide-mémoire*.

In the *Republic*, Plato presented his doctrine of the *divisions* of the soul – the rational, desiderative and spirited parts – and exploited this doctrine in seeking to account for inner conflict. (It is also relevant for us that Plato – like Bishop Butler in his *Fifteen Sermons*, and many others – drew an analogy between the conflicting 'aspects' of the individual and the citizens of a state and thus between that which integrates the person and the government of a state.) The relation of the Reason to the Passions has been a standard topic for discussion amongst philosophers, even if they have taken very different views of that relation. J. S. Mill's distinction between the higher and the lower pleasures points to different 'parts of our natures'. And Sidgwick (1893) – who queried what maximum happiness can mean if some pleasures are not quantitatively comparable – also drew sharp attention to another aspect of the 'multiplicity' of the person, the temporal dimension; what is the relation between the 'I' that decides now and the 'me' that suffers or enjoys the consequences of that decision in the (near or distant) future? (See further in Section II below.)

Psychiatrists and sociologists also exhibit a strong tendency to picture the individual as a complex structure, rather than as a simple, homogeneous unity. Most obviously, perhaps, the Freudian model sees each person as a structure of interacting id, ego and superego. More generally, psychiatrists are concerned with the integration, or at least cohesion, of the personality; for Wolf (1977), for example, the proposition that 'a cohesive self [integrates] many diverse aspects of the personality' appears to *define* a cohesive self, and certainly psychiatrists take seriously the metaphors of 'falling apart' and 'fear of fragmentation' as applied to their patients. Sociologists often give great emphasis to the analysis of the individual as a *set* of social roles (see, e.g. Dahrendorf (1968) for a particularly firm statement of this approach). This way of seeing the individual as a 'multiplicity' is not, however, necessarily incompatible with the economist's emphasis on the individual as a *decision*-maker, first because *no* social role is fully defined – but rather is open to the individual's interpretation and, in any case, may well be defined in an inherently contradictory manner – and secondly because the individual has many *roles* and can, within limits, make choices as between them (e.g., over how much effort is put into different roles).

More abstractly, then, there are many different dimensions to, and expressions of, the possibility of seeing each individual as a multi-faceted unity, having different 'aspects' and being alive to different types of consideration which may be difficult, or even impossible, to render readily commensurable. There are many reasons for and ways of seeing the individual as multi-faceted, as a structure, as subject to inner conflict.

Yet the more one presses these points, the more insistently the questions come back, 'And what is *it* that has these many facets? why do the parts make *a whole*, rather than just being independent entities? where/what is *the person*, the site of decision and responsibility?' It will be clear both that we are heading straight for the deep waters of 'personal identity', the concept of 'the self', etc., and that we *must* follow the advice of the Scottish preacher to stare these issues in the face and *rapidly pass on*. It is notorious that Hume, on inspecting the theatre of his mind, failed to capture his ever-fleeting self and, like others, denied the existence of a permanent, identical 'I'. But if we are to discuss *the* decision-taker, in a recognizably 'economic theory' manner, then we must inevitably retain a distinct concept of *a person* as a unified centre of decision and responsibility; we must follow Mayo (1956) who, in drawing an analogy between Rousseau's 'General Will' and *the* will of the individual, writes,

Now we can hardly state dogmatically that the human being is a unity or is a plurality. But there are at least certain purposes for which it is convenient to regard him as a unity and not as a plurality.

And it is because it shows him as a unit in action that the term 'will' is often useful. This last point is so important that I think it would hardly be overstating the case to say that the will 'is' this unity.

We shall use such terms as agent, person, individual or decision-taker to refer to the unity. It is less easy to decide how to refer to the multiplicity (the citizens of the Bismarckian 'republic'), but we agree with Williams (1976, p. 202) that it is *not* helpful to talk about the agent's different 'selves' and with Thomas Reid's blunt statement that 'A part of a person is a manifest absurdity.' Any social choice analogy will inevitably and strongly suggest the idea of representing the multiplicity of the person in terms of homunculi and 'the homunculus metaphor' (de Sousa 1976) has indeed received strong support from Dennett (1978), Hofstadter (1981) and Lycan (1981), who all argue in favour of picturing the agent as a hierarchical structure of ever-simpler homunculi. We shall *not* use this language because it overemphasizes the separateness of the 'aspects', not least because, as de Sousa stresses, *beliefs* might be thought to characterize *the person* (the unity), not the separate 'aspects'. It thus seems best to refer to multiplicity with such terms as facets or aspects of the person, or the 'different sides' of our nature or even to refer to *the* agent considering a choice 'from different points of view', or making different partial judgments.

II. A Faustian decision-taker

To provide a more specifically 'economic theory' motivation for the analysis of subsequent sections, we consider here an individual decision-taker who has many sides to his nature, who can and does assess alternatives from various points of view and whose preferences in any particular dimension i can be represented by a utility function $u_i(\ )$. What sorts of interpretation may plausibly be given to these various $u_i(\ )$? Perhaps there is no closed list of answers to this question; any normal human agent has access to so many different possible assessments of alternatives: as a parent, as a spouse, as a snooker player, as a (self-perceived) defender of high culture, as a self-indulgent person, as a would-be ascetic, as a serious person, as someone who values light amusement from time to time, as a second-hand car salesman, as a second-hand car salesman who hopes to become the owner of a chain of garages, as a person aware of others' needs and values, as someone who likes to be left alone (but also values company), as . . . Perhaps the list is endless *in principle*, even for a given agent? We shall suppose that it is *not*, in order to simplify the discussion. We suppose also that each individual $u_i(\ )$ represents a reflexive, transitive and complete ordering over the full set of relevant alternatives. (All the orderings are contingent on the agent having the beliefs he does; for the relevance of this, see Sen 1979.) For the most part, each $u_i(\ )$ will be thought of as purely ordinal.

It was implied in the above (purely illustrative) list of possible bases of assessment, that some of the standpoints from which a given agent may assess alternatives are standpoints concerning the implications of those alternatives for other people. Taking account of other people's viewpoints (which is, of course, a perfectly normal part of individual decision-taking) involves an attempt to assess alternatives *from their* point of view – necessarily, as 'understood' by the decision-taker – and/or in the light of general moral principles, codes of social conduct, etc. Any normal 'self' will be concerned with many dimensions of assessment which are not 'selfish' in any non-tautological sense of the term and our Faustian individual may (or may not) be alive to altruistic and/or malevolent considerations (cp. Collard 1978), to the claims of rights and other ethical principles and to his political rights and responsibilities (cp. Margolis 1982). Of course, more immediately personal dimensions of assessment, of many kinds, will no doubt be part of his make-up, as well; our purpose is to emphasize the complexity of the typical agent's criteria for assessing alternatives, not to emphasize some criteria at the expense of others.

The alternatives between which an individual has to decide may be actions, or states of affairs or intricate combinations of actions and consequences. But it may be useful at this stage to consider the simple case of an individual's choice between alternative quantities of commodities (or characteristics) which are constrained to lie within a convex set. Fig. 1 illustrates the case with two 'goods', the chosen quantities of which cannot lie outside the convex set bounded by CS and the two axes, and two alternative points of view, or forms of assessment; I_1 is the highest indifference curve achievable with respect to the first ordering (point of view) and I_2 that for the second ordering. For any *given* ordinal representation of $u_1(\ )$ and $u_2(\ )$, as we

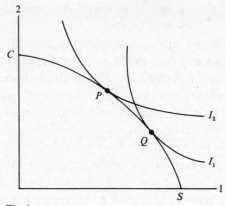

Fig. 1.

notionally travel from S to C in Fig. 1, we may trace out, in the direction of the arrow, the 'utility possibility frontier' shown in Fig. 2; points p and q in the latter figure naturally correspond to P and Q in the former. (The reader may readily work out how Fig. 2 would change if, in Fig. 1, P and Q coincided or P coincided with C and/or Q coincided with S.) Reflection will show that such a 'utility possibility frontier' for the individual will also obtain in the more general case of many 'goods' and many bases for judgment. We shall not pursue, at this stage, the question how the individual might choose a position on the 'utility possibility frontier' but need only note that the position chosen need not necessarily lie on pq in Fig. 2; an increase in $u_1(\ )$, for example, represents an improvement from the point of view of one aspect of the

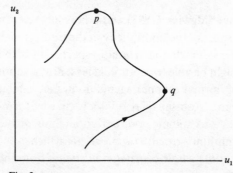

Fig. 2.

agent's character, but that may be an aspect which is *viewed negatively* by the agent.

Suppose now that CS in Fig. 1 is linear, being an ordinary budget constraint, and that the agent views each aspect positively. It will be clear that we can derive a 'partial' demand curve for each particular aspect ordering and that the actual quantity of a commodity purchased at a given price will lie between the highest and lowest quantities defined by the 'partial' demand curves at that price. We can, in other words, derive, if not a demand curve, then at least a demand 'band'. (We avoid the term 'demand correspondence' on the grounds that the agent *may* have a higher level decision process for choosing amongst the quantities defined by the 'band'.) The same kind of argument may be used to adapt the familiar Edgeworth–Bowley exchange box arguments (concerning the contract curve, agents' offer curves and the relations between competitive exchange equilibrium and Pareto-efficiency) to the case of multi-faceted individuals. It will be clear that the consideration of multi-faceted individuals, far from sweeping aside the familiar tools of microeconomic analysis, here requires merely a flexible approach to their application.

To reinforce this last point, we now turn to a consideration of intertemporal choice, to show how the analysis of the multi-aspect decision-taker might indeed assist in reconciling conflicting views about time preferences; for this purpose we shall provisionally abandon our usual 'ordinal' stance and adopt a cardinal view of utility.

Intertemporal choice

It was noted in Section I that Sidgwick (1893) and others have drawn attention to the temporal aspect of the multiplicity of the 'self'. It may therefore be of interest to consider whether a 'multi-aspect' view of the individual decision-taker might be able to capture, at least in part, both the 'Benthamite' view that normal *rational* agents do in fact exhibit pure time preference and the 'Ramsey–Harrod' view that it is *irrational* to do so. We might, for example, present an analysis of the familiar 'choice of consumption stream' problem, in which $u_i(\ )$ represents the assessment *of the whole consumption stream* from the standpoint of the agent as he will be in period i; the various $u_i(\ )$ will here be treated as *cardinal and comparable* and a function $w(u_1, u_2, \ldots, u_n)$ will be introduced to represent 'the' agent's overall assessment of the complete consumption stream. Each $u_i(\ )$ function might exhibit a 'Benthamite' concern with propinquity, whilst the $w(\ )$ function could capture the element of 'Ramsey–Harrod' time neutrality by treating all the $u_i(\ )$ equally. We capture, in this way, the idea that prudence 'arises from the human capacity to view the present simultaneously as "now" and as a particular time, tenselessly specifiable' (Nagel 1970, Ch. V). The overall function expressing *w as a function of the elements of the consumption stream* both would exhibit elements of pure time preference (insofar as the individual $u_i(\ )$s do so) and would not (insofar as the various $u_i(\ )$ all enter $w(\ )$ symmetrically). If one likes such metaphors, the $u_i(\ )$s might be said to represent the more impulsive, myopic elements of the agent's character and the $w(\ )$ his more dispassionate judgment. It will be seen below that each $u_i(\ )$ is taken to involve not only a positive (but incomplete) discounting of subsequent consumptions but also *incomplete* discounting of *previous* consumptions.

(Before continuing our own brief discussion, we may draw attention to three relevant papers. Elster (1977, Section V) interprets the existence of positive pure time preference as a form of *akrasia* and argues that it must be irrational since it can be the cause of subsequent *regret* and (hypothetical) reconsideration. Schelling (1980) considers the various stratagems which 'we' employ in order to achieve *self-command* over 'ourselves'. Thaler and Shefrin (1981) also discuss behaviour over time in terms of 'self-control' – noting that that term would be paradoxical if the agent were a simple unity.)

Consider then a very simple Debreu-like analysis, involving three time periods $(0, 1, 2)$, with decisions taken at the beginning of period 0. Since the example is purely suggestive, we may as well adopt very simple additive functions. Let

$$u_0 = u(c_0) + f u(c_1) + f^2 u(c_2)$$

represent the evaluation of the consumption stream (c_0, c_1, c_2) from the perspective of the agent *in period 0*, where $u(\ )$ is a 'normal' utility function and f is a forward discount factor $(0 \leqslant f \leqslant 1)$. In similar vein, let

$$u_1 = b\,u(c_0) + u(c_1) + f\,u(c_2)$$

$$u_2 = b^2\,u(c_0) + b\,u(c_1) + u(c_2)$$

represent the period 1 and period 2 evaluations of the consumption stream, where b is the backward discount factor $(0 \leqslant b \leqslant 1)$. Now let $w(u_0, u_1, u_2)$, representing the agent's dispassionate treatment of his various temporal aspects be of the simplest, symmetrical kind

$$w = u_1 + u_1 + u_2$$

or

$$w = (1+b+b^2)\,u(c_0) + (1+b+f)\,u(c_1) + (1+f+f^2)\,u(c_2) \tag{1}$$

To lighten the notation, let us rewrite (1) as

$$w = a_0\,u(c_0) + a_1\,u(c_1) + a_2\,u(c_2);$$

how will the (a_0, a_1, a_2) values compare with one another? The answer is shown in Fig. 3, in which the curves have the equations $b = f^2$ and $b^2 = f$; it will be noted that only in the upper left-hand area does $a_0 > a_1 > a_2$ hold good. More specifically, we can ask when (a_0, a_1, a_2) form a geometric progression; the answer is 'Only in the rather trivial cases $b = f = 0$ or $b = f = 1$.'

To repeat, the above example is not meant to be taken too seriously, but the idea behind it does perhaps merit further consideration; it does

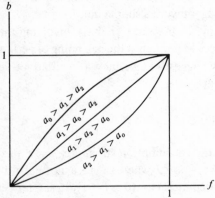

Fig. 3.

at least make perfectly *consistent* (i) a 'Benthamite' attention to propinquity, (ii) a 'Ramsey–Harrod' concern for neutrality as between the agent's various temporal aspects and (iii) the difficulty of finding empirical evidence for *pure* time preference. A more serious analysis along these lines would, of course, allow for various points of view/dimensions of assessment *in each* time period, but we hope to have shown in this section that the analysis of the Faustian decision-taker, whatever his different bases for judgment might be, is not completely alien to traditional microeconomic ways of thinking.

III. Aggregating judgments

It has been urged thus far that there are good grounds for conceiving a typical individual decision-taker as forming judgments in many dimensions, from many points of view. If this is accepted, and if one accepts also the usual insistence of economic theorists that an individual's orderings $R_1, R_2, \ldots, R_n$ can (at best) be represented only by *ordinal* utility functions, then one must inevitably consider whether Arrow's Possibility Theorem has a meaningful interpretation for the multi-faceted individual, thus ruling out the existence of a complete, transitive *overall* ordering for that individual. Or, to put the same thing differently, one must ask what assumptions could reasonably be made in order to render Arrow's theorem inapplicable and to make the existence of an overall ordering compatible with the individual's multi-faceted nature. The purpose of the present section is not to suggest that a mechanical application of Arrow's theorem can prove that a typical individual has no complete, transitive ordering, but only to stress that any theorist wishing to maintain simultaneously (a) the multi-dimensional view of individual judgments, (b) the rejection of cardinality and (c) the representation of the individual by a single all-purpose ordering, does have to *show* how (a), (b) and (c) are mutually compatible.

Since it goes without saying that Arrow's conclusions concerning the existence of a process leading to a complete, transitive ordering would hold good if the familiar (U, P, I, D) conditions were accepted, our question becomes 'Do the U, P, I, D conditions have meaningful application to the case of the multi-aspect person, and, if not, why not?'

The *no-dictatorship* condition (D) could be accepted on formal or on substantive grounds. The formal grounds are that without it we should have nothing to discuss, Faust having only one soul and Bismarck having subdued the republic and installed an all-powerful monarch. From this formal standpoint, then, the simple decision-taker, with only one aspect/point of view/ dimension of evaluation, constitutes the *special case* in which D is violated. More significantly, it is one aspect of most people's characters that they do not wish to become *complete* fanatics, to become purely *one*-dimensional. It is thus meaningful to accept condition D.

It was noted in the previous section that an individual could conceivably attach a *negative* value to the enhanced fulfilment of some particular ordering; it is also possible that he would at first value positively and then, after a certain stage, value negatively such greater fulfilment of an ordering (cp. Sen 1980–1, p. 214, n. 42, where the Aristotelian view of the 'mean' is referred to as an example of the second phenomenon). But if such cases can be dealt with by reversing negative rankings or by breaking up the more complex rankings into 'sections', then it will still be the case that the individual's overall judgment of alternatives should respond positively to the degree of fulfilment of each of his (thus reformulated) orderings R_1, R_2, . . . , R_N. By construction then, the *Pareto* condition (P) must be met by any overall ordering.

Consider now the *unrestricted domain* condition (U). There would seem to be a presumption in favour of maintaining this third condition, too, in an analysis of the multi-faceted person. Decision-making can be difficult, even for an individual, precisely because alternatives do arise such that the individual aspect/point of view orderings can conflict sharply; consider, as one example, the rankings of today's and tomorrow's consumptions by the agent's different temporal aspects (as a young and as an old person). Even if there were something to be said for the speculation that *too much* 'aspect heterogeneity' is incompatible with the integration of the personality, this would hardly justify some version of 'single-peakedness' in aspect orderings. So, condition U is meaningful in the context of the multi-aspect individual.

Can we escape Arrow's looming embrace by rejecting the *independence* of irrelevant alternatives condition (I)? This condition has two aspects to it, the irrelevant alternatives aspect and the ordinality aspect. A major function of the former is to back up the latter by blocking approaches to cardinality via comparisons with 'other' alternatives (Sen 1970, Ch. 7; MacKay 1980, pp. 8–9, 32f). On the other hand, the independence aspect is also important in reducing the construction of a ranking to a sequence of *pairwise* choices and, in particular, in ruling out of court the use of 'global' information, for example, 'x_{17} is preferred to *all* other available alternatives'. (*N.b.*, this statement is *not* exhaustively reducible to a sequence of pairwise statements – MacKay 1980, p. 93.) In the present, individual agent context, is it reasonable to insist that the agent's overall ordering should depend only on the aspects' *ordinal* rankings? that inter-aspect 'utility' comparisons are not allowed? that 'global' information should be rejected? that irrelevant alternatives should be ignored for some other reason?

MacKay (1980, p. 87) has shown that one implication of the I condition is that the 'aggregating device' should be what he terms 'non-creative', that is, roughly, that 'the device' should play a purely *passive* role with respect to the inputs (e.g., votes in the social context). Is it part of our conception of an agent, an individual decision-taker, that, the alternatives having been ranked by various preference orderings, R_i say, the overall ordering, R say, simply follows passively via some set procedure representable, in principle, by a computational algorithm and utilizing only pairwise comparisons? *If* we answer affirmatively, and if we insist that *only* ordinal rankings count as relevant information, then it seems that we have to accept the I condition (in addition to the D, P and U conditions accepted above) and hence an Arrow-like conclusion: there is no process by which the agent can arrive at a complete, transitive overall preference ordering and therefore he has no such ordering. Needless to say, that conclusion cannot be rejected out of hand (with the implication that one or more of the D, P, U, I conditions must be inappropriate after all); it is *not* a known fact about any agent, past or present, that he had or has a complete, transitive preference ordering. (And certainly it would not be intellectually respectable to reject any of D, P, U and I in order to avoid the conclusion, i.e., without good *independent* reasons.)

Obviously enough, even if one can legitimately reject the bundle (D, P, U, I), further questions remain to be considered. That bundle is usually regarded as a rather weak set of *necessary* conditions on choice processes, not a sufficient set; to show good cause for dropping one or more of (D, P, U, I) is one thing, while to show that (and if so, how) the agent can construct an R out of his many 'point of view' orderings is quite another. There may well be *further* conditions which might reasonably be expected of the 'integrating' process. On the other hand, it may be interesting to pursue, in the multi-aspect agent context, Sen's concept of a 'choice function' (1970, Ch. 4) – as opposed to a full ordering – which requires only reflexivity, completeness and 'acyclicity' (a much weaker condition than transitivity). Also to be considered is the question whether completeness is plausible for every individual R_i and, if not, what follows for the agent's decision-taking. There are, indeed, many other questions to be considered in the context of the multi-faceted individual and many different ways in which Arrow's result can be avoided (although some of these latter would involve abandoning an overall ordering for the agent in any case. It might be suggested, for example, that as the agent's concerns and foci of attention change, different subsets of $R_1, R_2, \ldots, R_N$ come into play; or, again, that the individual has no need of a constant 'constitution'). As was stressed earlier in this section, our purpose here has not been to 'prove', via Arrow's Theorem, that individuals do not have overall orderings, but to emphasize that their having them is not *obviously* compatible with non-cardinality and multi-dimensional judgment-making. The following sections will therefore consider in more detail the conditions under which 'rational action' can be represented by a single ordering and some of the implications for individual decision-taking when those conditions are not met.

IV. An agent's character

Based on the considerations set out above, we shall now develop a model which treats more systematically some features of the process of decision taking by a multi-faceted individual. In Sections I and II, on the one hand, we emphasized the different aspects or 'points of view' pulling the individual in different directions, thus making him a Faustian decision-taker. In Section III, on the other hand, we discussed the individual's integrating or fusing process of the many different aspects. Both the aspects taken into consideration by the individual and the integrating procedure employed are much more related to the individual's character as a whole than to some particular feature: his intellectual capacity, for instance. Consider, for example, intertemporal choice as discussed in Section II. The action taken depends first on the possible configurations (u_0, u_1, u_2) of evaluations for the three periods taken into consideration by the agent. Secondly, the action taken depends on the agent's overall assessment $w(u_0, u_1, u_2)$, which in our example was given by adding up the u_is. In any case, the agent has to apply some integrating procedure, which in itself has nothing to do with choosing between alternatives but with evaluating preferences on a meta-level according to the agent's specific character. It may be, as in our example, that the agent is able to make inter-aspect utility comparisons, but we cannot expect that this will be so in general. Hence, beside such cardinal characters as the utilitarian one, where w is given by adding up the u_is, or the Rawlsian one, where w is given by the minimum of the u_is, we have to take into consideration also ordinal characters, where the integrating procedure depends only on the aspects' ordinal rankings.

To make things clear, let us give a formal description of an agent's character. Let A denote the set of alternatives, R the set of all (binary) relations on A and O the set of all orderings on A. In assessing alternatives, the agent considers a certain (for simplicity a finite) *number of aspects n*, say aspect 1, aspect 2, . . . , aspect n, to be relevant for him in taking decisions. Of course, $n \geq 2$ is the case of the Faustian decision-taker we are interested in. Assessing the alternatives under a certain aspect i, the agent arrives at a certain relation R_i on A. In order to simplify the discussion and not to confuse two different problems, we shall assume that R_i is an ordering, whereas the same assumption will not be made with respect to the agent's overall assessment of the alternatives. It might be argued also, that the ordering property is more likely for single aspects than for an overall assessment. Hence the evaluation of the alternatives with respect to all aspects results in a bundle $(R_1, R_2, . . . , R_n)$ of n aspect-orderings. What the agent then wants to obtain from such a bundle is some single overall evaluation R on A. Now, speaking of an agent's character means that R is related to $(R_1, R_2, . . . , R_n)$ according to some rule, specific for that character. It may be that the agent applies this rule not to all bundles which are logically possible but only to a certain subset of all these bundles. This subset reflects the extent to which the agent admits conflicts between the different aspect assessments and will therefore be called the agent's *domain of conflict D*. On this domain then the agent's integrating process or *formation rule F* is defined, giving for every bundle $(R_1, \ldots, R_n)$ in D a certain overall assessment $R = F(R_1, \ldots, R_n)$. Of course, R is a relation on A but, warned by the discussion of Arrow's Possibility Theorem, one cannot expect that R is always an ordering. Thus F is a mapping from D into R. Putting things together, we model the *character of an agent* with respect to decision taking by the triplet (n, D, F), where n is the number of aspects, D the domain of conflict and F the agent's formation rule.

As the reader will expect, there is a huge variety of possible characters. Perhaps the most important part of an agent's character is the formation rule employed, which, if specified, singles out a certain *type* of character. In the following we list only a few types, where the number of aspects is n and the domain of conflict may be any subset of all logically possible bundles. (Note that we conceive relations as subsets of $A \times A$, which permits us to apply set intersection '$\cap$' and set union '$\cup$' to relations.)

Pareto-type: $p(R_1, \ldots, R_n) = \bigcap_{i=1}^{n} R_i$

The outcome of this formation rule p is always reflexive and transitive but in general not complete.

Counting-type: $(x, y) \varepsilon c(R_1, \ldots, R_n)$ if and only if the number of i such that $(x, y) \varepsilon R_i$ is greater than or equal to the number of j such that $(y, x) \varepsilon R_j$. The outcome is always reflexive and complete, but not transitive in general.

Sen-type: $s(R_1, \ldots, R_n) = \bigcap_{i=1}^{n} R_i \cup \bigcup_{i=1}^{n} P_i$

The outcome is always reflexive and complete, but in general not transitive. However, the outcome is always quasi-transitive in the sense that the strict relation corresponding to $s(R_1, \ldots, R_n)$ is transitive (cp. Sen 1970, Ch. 5 and 5*). Note that P_i represents *strict* preference.

Hierarchical-type: $h(R_1, \ldots, R_n) = \ell(R_{\sigma(1)}, R_{\sigma(2)}, \ldots R_{\sigma(n)})$ for some fixed permutation σ of $\{1, 2, \ldots, n\}$. Thereby ℓ denotes the (ordinal) lexicographic rule defined by $\ell(R_1, \ldots, R_n) = P_1 \cup (I_1 \cap P_2)$ $\cup (I_1 \cap I_2{}^n P_3) \cup \ldots \cup (I_1 \cap \ldots \cap I_{n-1} \cap P_n) \cup (I_1 \cap \ldots \cap I_n)$. The outcome of h is always an ordering.

All these types, although different from each other, portray not implausible integrating procedures for an agent when faced with many different aspects. The Pareto-type is a very cautious one, in that some alternative is considered at least as good as another one if this is true with respect to all aspects. This type will often be indecisive, therefore, as was the case with Hamlet. The other extreme is presented by the Sen-type which considers some alternative at least as good as another if even just one single aspect favours the former over the latter. Between these two extremes lie the other two types. The Counting-type prefers one alternative to another if more 'arguments', that is, aspects, count for the former than for the latter. The Hierarchical-type, finally, is perhaps the most appropriate one for everyday life in that he evaluates alternatives first according to the aspect he considers the most important and thereafter according to aspects of minor relevance. (Unfortunately, it might be very difficult to order aspects according to their 'relevance'.)

From the types above, additional types may be obtained by 'mixing' some or all of them, taking intersections or unions of relations. That is to say, if F and G are two formation rules, then by the intersection or union of $F(R_1, \ldots, R_n)$ and $G(R_1, \ldots, R_n)$ a new formation rule on $(R_1, \ldots, R_n)$ is defined. For example $F(R_1, \ldots, R_n) = \ell(R_1, R_2, \ldots, R_n) \cap \ell(R_2, R_1, \ldots, R_n)$ defines a formation rule which is different from all the above rules. Another class of types arises if aspect orderings are mixed directly in the following manner:

$$\textit{Mixed-type}: m(R_1, \ldots, R_n) = \bigcap_{j=1}^{k} \bigcup_{i \varepsilon Ij} R_i$$

where for $j = 1, \ldots, k$ I_j is a subset of $\{1, \ldots, n\}$.

The outcome of m is always reflexive, but in general neither complete nor transitive. The Pareto-type is an extreme case of this mixed-type by taking $I_j = \{j\}$ and $k = n$. Another extreme case $F(R_1, \ldots, R_n) = \bigcup_{i=1}^{n} R_i$ is obtained for $k = 1$ and I_1 equal to $\{1, \ldots, n\}$. According to this formation rule one alternative is already preferred to another if this is the case for any single aspect. A further extreme case is obtained by putting $k = 1$, $I_1 = \{j\}$ for some j. The corresponding formation rule $F(R_1, \ldots, R_n) = R_j$ portrays a fanatic taking only aspect j into consideration.

Characters are also provided by cardinal aggregation devices $w = w(u_1, u_2, \ldots, u_n)$, where real valued functions $u_1, u_2, \ldots, u_n$ defined on the set A of alternatives are merged into one single real valued utility function w on A. But we have to be careful here, because different utility functions may induce the same ordering on A (if A is finite, these utility functions must be strict monotone transformations of each other). Let us therefore select from each class of utility functions inducing the same ordering an arbitrary but fixed representative. If such a selection is made, we can associate with a cardinal aggregation device $w = w(u_1, \ldots, u_n)$ a character (n, D, F) as follows. The domain of conflict D consists of all bundles $(R_1, \ldots, R_n)$, the R_i's being induced by the u_is of a bundle $(u_1, \ldots, u_n)$ on which the aggregation device is defined (in most cases D will consist of all bundles of n orderings). For $(R_1, \ldots, R_n)$ in D, $F(R_1, \ldots, R_n)$ is defined as the ordering induced by $w(u_1, \ldots, u_n)$ on A. Because of the selection of representatives F is well defined. As every selection of representatives defines a character in this way, we obtain in general a whole family of *characters (types) associated with a given cardinal aggregation device*. These characters show the following particular features. Every character associated with a cardinal aggregation device yields on every bundle an ordering as outcome, which may be an advantage. But on the other hand, the characters associated with a given cardinal aggregation device are in general different from each other and may show completely different behaviour, as will be seen later on. Examples of cardinal aggregation devices much discussed in the literature are the utilitarian-device $w = u_1 + u_2 + \ldots u_n$ and the Rawls-device $w = \min u_i$ $(1 \leqslant i \leqslant n)$. Concerning characters associated with one of these devices, we will speak of *utilitarian-characters* and *Rawls-characters* respectively.

It seems quite natural that, once the black box of individual decision-taking has been opened, a whole range of different characters will jump out. The huge variety of possible characters may itself constitute an interesting field for further investigations. But to make contact with the important traditional notion of rational decision-taking, one has to restrict the range of possible characters. For this it is desirable to have answers to the following questions. Is there a common feature to most or perhaps all of the characters mentioned thus far? Does there exist perhaps some domain of conflict on which all the above formation rules yield the same outcome? Can we single out from all the characters some which show a certain kind of rationality? The rest of this section is devoted to answering the first two questions. The third will be tackled in the next section, where the notion of rationality involved will also be defined.

Let us take up first the issue concerning the existence of some common feature to different characters. We say a character (n, D, F) (or the corresponding type resp. formation rule) is *sensible* with respect to aspects, if it has the following property: if for any two alternatives x and y and for any bundle $(R_1, \ldots, R_n)$ in the domain D, x is preferred to y with respect to all R_i, then x is also preferred to y with respect to $F(R_1, \ldots, R_n)$; moreover, if in addition x is strictly preferred to y with respect to some R_j, then also x is strictly preferred to y with respect to $F(R_1, \ldots, R_n)$. It turns out that almost all characters mentioned thus far are sensible in this sense. More precisely, we have the following proposition:

Proposition 1. All characters mentioned hitherto, with the exception of some mixed-types and some Rawls-types, are sensible. Furthermore, arbitrary intersections and unions of sensible types are also sensible. (For reasons of space, proofs of propositions have had to be omitted; they are contained in a mathematical supplement, available on request from U. Krause).

That the mixed-type is not sensible, in general, can easily be seen by looking at the fanatic-type. That Rawls-characters are not sensible, in general, can either be verified directly or be seen from the fact that for a bundle $(u_1, \ldots, u_n)$ of utility functions satisfying $u_1 \leqslant u_2 \leqslant \ldots \leqslant u_n$ the associated Rawls-type coincides with a fanatic one.

Now we come to the question whether there exists a domain of conflict on which the various characters coincide. If we allowed for all characters, then coincidence would be possible only on a trivial domain (see the example below and part (d) of Proposition 3 in the next section). But considering only sensible characters, a non-trivial domain of coincidence can be found, as is shown by the following proposition:

Proposition 2. The formation rules of all sensible characters yield the same outcome on a fixed bundle $(R_1, \ldots, R_n)$ of orderings if and only if the bundle is *harmonic* in the sense that, for any two alternatives x, y and any two aspects i, j, it is not true both that x is strictly preferred to y with respect to R_i and that y is strictly preferred to x with respect to R_j. In particular, the outcome of any sensible character on a harmonic bundle is always an ordering.

Of course, all characters mentioned in this section coincide on trivial bundles, that is bundles $(R_1, R_2, \ldots, R_n)$ such that $R_1 = R_2 = \ldots = R_n$. Harmonic bundles however are not trivial in general; on the contrary, they are complex enough to generate arbitrary orderings, even if those harmonic bundles are restricted to a particular kind. To illustrate this and also some other interesting relationships concerning harmonic bundles, we shall discuss in some detail the *case of three alternatives*.

For $A = \{x, y, z\}$, $n = 2$, let R_1 on A be given by $x > y \sim z$ and R_2 by $x \sim y > z$ ('>' for strict preference, '$\sim$' for indifference). The bundle (R_1, R_2) is harmonic and every sensible character yields on this bundle the ordering $x > y > z$. For example, the Pareto-character, the outcome of which is in general not an ordering, gives on (R_1, R_2) the relation $R_1 \cap R_2$ which is equal to $x > y > z$. But neither the general mixed-type nor all Rawls-types coincide on (R_1, R_2) with the Pareto-type. Concerning the former, this can be seen from the fanatic-type, because R_1 and R_2 are different from $R_1 \cap R_2$, or from $F(R_1, R_2) = R_1 \cup R_2$, the outcome of which is not transitive. With respect to the Rawls-type, consider the representations u_1, u_2 of R_1, R_2 defined by $u_1(x) = 2$, $u_1(y) = u_1(z) = 1$ and $u_2(x) = u_2(y) = 2$, $u_2(z) = 1$. The associated Rawls-type yields on (R_1, R_2) the ordering $x > y \sim z$ which is different from $x > y > z$. Moreover, if we select as representations of R_1, R_2 the simple linear transformations $\bar{u}_1 = u_1 + \frac{1}{2}$, $\bar{u}_2 = u_2$ of u_1, u_2, the Rawls-type associated with these representatives yields on (R_1, R_2) the ordering $x > y > z$. This demonstrates that, even on a harmonic bundle and even if they are connected by a simple linear transformation, two Rawls-types can differ. This contrasts sharply with what is true for the utilitarian-types, because by Proposition 2 all types associated with a utilitarian cardinal device (which may be connected by arbitrary strict monotone transformations) coincide on harmonic bundles. In particular, on harmonic bundles Rawls-types and utilitarian-types may or may not coincide.

Finally, far from being trivial bundles, harmonic bundles are complex enough to represent any ordering. This is so even when harmonic bundles are restricted further to some particular kind, which then ensures uniqueness for the representation. This representation, which seems to be useful for analysing rationality, will be presented in full generality in the next section. For the moment we want to illustrate it in the simple case of three alternatives. As the reader will easily verify, the following list exhibits all the orderings possible on the set $A = \{x, y, x\}$:

$E_1 : x > y \sim z, E_2 : x \sim y > z, E_3 : x \sim z > y,$
$E_4 : y > x \sim z, E_5 : y \sim z > x, E_6 : z > x \sim y, E_7 : x \sim y \sim z$ and
$x > y > z, x > z > y, y > x > z, y > z > x, z > x > y, z > y > x.$

The relations termed $E_1, \ldots, E_6$ are all elementary in that they all have the smallest possible (non-trivial) number of indifference classes, namely 2. (There is exactly one ordering having 1 indifference class, namely the trivial order $x \sim y \sim z$ which can be also considered as elementary.) We leave it to the reader to verify that for every ordering R on A there exist uniquely determined elementary orderings E_i and E_j such that (E_i, E_j) is a harmonic bundle and R is the set-theoretical intersection of E_i and E_j. Thus, for example, $x > y > z$ is the intersection of E_1 and E_2, (E_1, E_2) being a harmonic bundle and there is no other bundle of elementary orderings having these two properties.

V. Rational characters

In orthodox economic theory an individual is considered rational if he exhibits a reflexive, transitive and complete preference, that is an ordering, whenever he has to choose between several alternatives. In what follows we want to examine more closely reasons for and limits to this kind of rationality, which usually is simply postulated. As was argued in the previous sections, we have to take into account that the individual is many-faceted. Using the language of the last section, we can capture the above kind of rationality by the notion of a *rational character*, that is a character (n, D, F) whose formation rule F yields on every bundle in D an ordering as outcome. As will be clear from the analysis made thus far, instead of being the general rule, a rational character is a rather particular kind of character. Thus the problem of rationality becomes one of making explicit the assumptions under which a character will be rational. There are three main possibilities, involving, respectively, the three components, n, D and F of a character. With respect to the first component, the *number of aspects*, it is clear that at least all characters mentioned thus far become rational for $n = 1$, because then $F(R) = R$. Assuming only one aspect, all these characters collapse into a single one, which is a rational one for trivial reasons. To exclude this trivial case of rationality we shall assume $n \geqslant 2$. But then, as may be seen from the examples given earlier, rationality cannot be expected in general, unless some assumptions on the domain of conflict and/or the formation rule are made. Concerning the *domain of conflict*, a situation similar to $n = 1$ arises if D consists only of trivial bundles $(R, \ldots, R)$, R any ordering. In that case $F(R, \ldots, R) = R$ for all formation rules considered thus far, which again yields rationality by triviality. It is reasonable to exclude also this case by assuming that D contains some non-trivial bundles. But then, without specific assumptions about the formation rule, the character cannot be expected to be rational. This is so, even if one assumes that D consists only of harmonic bundles, as defined in the previous section. Although in that case, according to Proposition 2, many characters become rational, this is not true, for example, for the mixed-type $F(R_1, \ldots, R_n) = \cup^n_{i=1} R_i$. Furthermore, characters need no longer coincide as in the two above trivial cases (see the discussion concerning three alternatives in the previous section). Let us finally examine possible assumptions about the *formation rule*. Here again a trivial case occurs, namely that of a fanatic-type. But there are other, non-trivial formation rules leading for arbitrary n and D to rational characters. Of the characters considered in the previous section, these are all hierarchical characters and all characters associated with a cardinal aggregation device. The problem with these formation rules is that somewhat artificial abilities of the individual are required to apply the rule properly. Thus, cardinal aggregation devices require not only inter-aspect comparisons but precise quantitative comparisons. The hierarchical rule requires, similarly, not only some loose comparison of the aspects, but a full ranking of them according to some principle of 'importance'. To put it in another way, the agent must be able to select one particular hierarchical rule from all possible hierarchical rules, and there are $n!$ many of them which are different in general. A similar selection problem, and even more difficult, must be solved by the agent in the case of a cardinal aggregation device, because the various characters associated with such a device are different from each other in general. If the selection procedure is not carefully carried out – that is, different rules are interchanged – then rationality may break down.

This brief discussion shows that, broadly speaking, rationality may result from a restriction of the number of aspects and/or of the domain of conflict and/or of the range of formation rules. An extreme case is the case of 'rationality by triviality', that is, there is only a single aspect or a trivial domain of conflict or a formation rule of the fanatic-type. This 'explanation' of rationality seems to be behind the common postulate of rational individuals, if there is any explanation at all (cp. also Sen 1977b). Because we do not want to follow this procedure, we shall abandon the 'rationality by triviality explanation'. As indicated above, there are reasons not to assume a particular formation rule, but instead to have some flexibility with respect to formation rules. Hence one must look for conditions, on both the domain of conflict *and* the range of formation rules, to reconstruct rationality. Let us call a character *harmonic* if its domain of conflict contains only bundles which are harmonic. (As mentioned already, we shall assume that $n \geq 2$ and that D contains all trivial bundles, but also non-trivial ones. Thus, in what follows characters will always be non-trivial.) From Proposition 2 of the last section, we can draw the following *conclusion: every character which is harmonic and sensible is rational. Furthermore, all these characters coincide where they are jointly defined (n fixed).* Some examples (and also counter-examples) concerning harmonic and sensible characters are provided by Proposition 1. From the examples of characters given earlier, it is clear that neither being harmonic nor being sensible is a necessary condition for a character to be rational. Therefore the question arises whether the assumptions made for the above conclusion are too strong for reconstructing rationality. In the rest of this section we shall try to show that this is not the case. We shall concentrate on the question of harmonicity, because sensibleness seems to be a reasonable property concerning many-faceted individuals, which is shared by many different characters. According to Proposition 2, a bundle is necessarily harmonic if one requires that all sensible characters coincide on that bundle. The following proposition provides some further properties leading to harmonicity:

Proposition 3. Let $(R_1, \ldots, R_n)$ be any bundle of orderings.

(a) The bundle is harmonic if and only if the outcome of the Pareto-character for this bundle is an ordering.

(b) The bundle is harmonic if and only if all hierarchical characters coincide on that bundle.

(c) Let $f(x)$ be a real valued function depending continuously on the non-negative vector $x = (x_1, \ldots, x_n)$ and such that $f(x) < f(y)$ whenever $x_i \leqslant y_i$ for all i and $x_j < y_j$ for at least one j.
     The bundle is harmonic if and only if all characters which are associated with the cardinal aggregation device $w = f(u_1, \ldots, u_n)$ coincide on it. (A similar statement holds if only those characters are considered which are, for fixed u_is and arbitrary numbers $a_i > 0$, associated with $f(a_1u_1, \ldots, a_nu_n)$.)

(d) In contrast to (c), for Rawls-characters the following statement holds. All Rawls-characters (or all Rawls-characters associated, for fixed u_is and arbitrary numbers b_i, with $\min_i(u_i + b_i)$) coincide on the bundle if and only if the bundle is trivial, that is, $R_1 = R_2 = \ldots = R_n$.

The significance of the proposition is the following: statement (a) yields immediately that for a Pareto-character rationality is equivalent to harmonicity. Statement (b) demonstrates that the above-mentioned problematic feature of a hierarchical character, namely to require a full ranking of aspects, vanishes exactly on harmonic bundles. Similarly with statement (c), which shows that the selection problem for cardinal aggregation devices, mentioned earlier, vanishes exactly on harmonic bundles. The utilitarian aggregation device is one exam-ple covered by (c), but there are others (e.g. some kinds of modified Rawls aggregation devices such as $w = \min_i \Sigma_j m_{ij} u_j$ with $m_{ij} > 0$).

Statement (d) exhibits in precise form a peculiar feature of the Rawls' aggregation device which we already observed earlier (see the example at the end of the last section). The selection problem for the Rawls-device does not vanish, except, of course, for trivial bundles. Or, to put it in the language of Social or Public Choice, the Rawls' device depends crucially on interpersonal comparison (trivial cases excepted). (In fact, statements (c) and (d) are strongly related to questions raised in the theory of Social or Public Choice. Thus (c) provides a precise answer to the question of a purely ordinal behaviour of the utilitarian device, which is discussed e.g. by Mueller 1979, p. 176.)

The conclusion mentioned earlier can be combined with statement (a) of Proposition 3 to obtain the following *characterization of rationality*: Consider, for fixed n and D, the class of all sensible characters (n, D, F). Then all characters in this class are rational if and only if they are all harmonic. In a final step we want to establish another link between rationality and harmonicity by showing that the outcomes of a rational character can also be described as the outcome of a character which is sensible and harmonic. For this we need the unique representation of orderings by harmonic bundles of elementary orderings, which was discussed at the end of the last section for the case of three alternatives. Assume that the set A of alternatives is finite and let $m + 1$ be the number of alternatives. Call an ordering on A *elementary*, if it is either the trivial one having only one indifference class or if it has exactly two indifference classes. The latter corresponds to a subdivision of the set of alternatives into two classes, one of them consisting of all alternatives fulfilling a certain property and the other consisting of all alternatives not fulfilling this property (yes-no-preference). For a bundle (E_1, ... , E_n) consisting of elementary orderings only, harmonicity amounts to a meta-ranking of the orderings E_i according to the following rule. One elementary ordering is ranked above another one, if the property fulfilled by the former is implied by the property fulfilled by the latter. (For the role played by meta-rankings in general see Sen 1977b). The following proposition could be viewed as a reverse of our earlier *conclusion*:

Proposition 4. Any rational character (n, D, F) can be described by a sensible and harmonic character (m, D^*, F^*) in the following way. For every bundle $(R_1, \ldots, R_n)$ in D, there exists a uniquely determined bundle $(E_1, \ldots, E_m)$ in D^* such that $F(R_1, \ldots, R_n) = F^* (E_1, \ldots E_m)$; where $m + 1$ is the number of alternatives; D^* the set of all harmonic bundles $(E_1, \ldots, E_m)$ consisting of elementary orderings only and such that a trivial component is followed only by trivial ones; F^* any sensible formation rule on D^* (e.g. the Pareto-rule).

In a sense made precise by the above proposition we may therefore 'attribute' rationality as used in orthodox economic theory to a character which is both harmonic and sensible. Thus, provided the analysis made is correct, rationality cannot be considered as a universal feature in individual decision-taking; rather it is linked with a peculiar kind of character. Because other characters, in particular non-harmonic ones, seem quite often to occur in reality, the road is open to go beyond the orthodox principle of rationality. We do not want to take up this issue here systematically, but we shall offer some more informal considerations.

VI. Further considerations

In the hope that the foregoing discussion will have encouraged the reader to take seriously the possibility that we need a more complex model of the individual decision-taker than that commonly used in economic theory – in the theory of consumption behaviour, of saving, of labour supply, of the firm etc. – we turn now to certain issues arising when the individual cannot be represented by a complete, transitive preference ordering. (In doing this we shall *not* be abandoning 'rational man' theory, understood more broadly as the theory of actions based on reasons.) Our discussion will be set out under three headings, but it will be seen that the issues raised under these headings are in fact intimately interrelated.

Completeness and transitivity

Purely in order to simplify the discussion – and not because it is obviously the case – let us suppose that, from any *given* point of view, the agent has a reflexive, complete and transitive ordering of alternatives. (We may nevertheless recall that the existence of an ordering is more plausible at the aspect level.) The overall preference relation, R, may very well be incomplete when the character is not harmonic; consider, for example, a Pareto-character faced by (xP_iy) and (yP_jx). Now such a situation is commonplace – it is one characterized by indecision (which is, of course, very different from indifference). Now consider Arrow's statement (1973, p. 120): 'It is not at all uncommon to find denials of the [completeness] assumption. Sufficiently remote alternatives are held to be incomparable. But I must say I do not find this line of argument at all convincing. If a choice has to be made, it has to be made.' Note first that 'this' *is not* the 'line of argument' we have just suggested; incompleteness may result not from alternatives' being 'remote' but from their being oppositely ranked by different considerations, it being difficult for the agent to 'strike a balance' between those conflicting considerations. Note secondly that completeness of an ordering is not always necessary for arriving at a choice. And, indeed, Sen and Williams (1982, p. 17) have questioned whether completeness is an essential part of 'rationality', suggesting that the property of never forgoing a definitely superior and available alternative is sufficient in this respect. Note finally that it is just not self-evident that decision-making does, as a matter of fact, always wait on the full and final reconciliation of conflicting considerations; it is true that if a decision has to be made, it has to be made, but it by no means follows that completeness of the ordering is a precondition of decision, *even when the incompleteness directly involves the alternatives between which a decision must be reached.*

At this point we spill over into the discussion (below) on creativity, but we can note immediately that any idea that completeness is a precondition of choice stems directly from the passive view of the decision-taker, which supposes that he can be *fully represented* by a preference ordering. As has been recently pointed out by Levi (1982, pp. 238–9), agents 'often face decision problems where the agent is committed to promoting different values which conflict in the way they rank the feasible options', and it is implicit in any representation of choice by the maximization of a single ranking that such *conflicts must be resolved prior* to choice. (Or, alternatively, that the choice be seen as *constituting* the resolution of conflict.) But Levi argues powerfully that 'agents may terminate deliberation and take decisions without having resolved the moral, political, economic and aesthetic conflicts relevant to their predicaments' (p. 246). If this is so, it follows that an individual's decisions *cannot* be represented as the outcomes of maximizing over a single ordering. Whilst the consideration of his various 'aspect orderings' may well be an essential preliminary to decision-taking, the need for *a decision* remains and it falls to the agent to make it.

It has been noted often enough that choices made subject to many alternative criteria are likely to be incompatible with a transitive preference ordering. An example is the counting character, faced by a non-harmonic bundle of orderings. We have nothing to add here except that, parallel to incompleteness, intransitivity does *not* entail the impossibility of decision and that 'intransitivity' over time could be (*not* 'is') the result of *gradually* 'doing justice to' the various considerations involved, if none is judged to be dominant.

How might an agent deal with incompleteness and intransitivity? One way is by ignoring, whether more or less consciously, various aspects which would make the decision more difficult if they were taken into account. *Akrasia*, self-deception (note the phrase and its implications), refusing to acknowledge certain responsibilities etc., can all be seen, at least in part, in this light. The (more or less conscious) simplification of decisions can also take the form of adopting rules of thumb, following precedents, having habits, etc.; this leads, of course, to satisficing characterizations of agents' actions, and it is not surprising that such characterizations have often arisen in the discussion of *obviously* complex 'agents', such as large corporations. They may be just as relevant to (complex) individuals. It is therefore relevant to touch briefly on the supposed criticism of satisficing theories that they are simply 'truncated' optimization theories, in which the costs of the optimal degree of information acquisition are dealt with implicitly and *ad hoc*. We may note that the criticism supposes imperfect information to be *the only difficulty involved* in reaching a decision. It is not – with any *given* amount of information, reaching a decision can be very difficult because different criteria point in different directions. The individual agent, pulled in different directions by incommensurable considerations, may just 'make do', pursuing a 'not too bad' policy, thinking that further time and energy would be ill-spent seeking for an 'optimum' solution (cp. Dennett 1978, p. 293). This has nothing to do with 'information costs'. (Note though that additional information is just as likely, a priori, to make a decision *more* difficult to reach as to make it easier.)

Perhaps de Sousa (1976, p. 222) is right to reject 'the view . . . that the values and preferences of a man at an instant either can or should be capable of being arranged into a single coherent scale determined by the totality of his dispositions to make choices at that instant', and Nozick (1981, p. 407) to ask, 'But how powerful, really, is the general desire to avoid inconsistency?' Nozick suggests that philosophers are too quick to suppose that *everyone* places great value on consistency, partly because they themselves are a self-selected group of people who value it highly. Could the same be said – *half* jokingly – about economists?

Second-order preferences

Economists might be somewhat surprised to read that 'all the animals *except man are rational*, limited to making consistent choices on the basis of what they perceive and of learned or innate patterns of response' (Johnstone 1970, p. 73, emphasis added), but Johnstone is here using the term rational much as economists generally use it and asserting that humans *are too complex* for their actions to be predictable from complete, transitive preference-orderings. His reasons for asserting this will be ignored here, but the assertion itself leads us to the concept of second-order desires. Whilst (non-human) animal behaviour can perhaps be explained in terms of a 'natural science' model involving only first-order wants and beliefs, humans are thought to be responsible agents, possessing capacities for self-control (independently of the fear of unfortunate consequences) and for 'self-intervention', based on self-evaluation involving *second-order* desires, preferences over preferences, wishes to be a certain kind of person, to have certain tastes and interests etc. (Mischel 1977, pp. 5–7). As Taylor (1977) puts it, it is not their having desires and beliefs that makes humans different from (other) animals but their having second-order desires and the ability therefore to make evaluations *of* sets of desires; such 'strong evaluations' as Taylor calls them (by contrast with 'weighting' of desires) can involve genuinely inconsistent criteria. If there are second-order desires and if they cannot be represented within the familiar, single preference-ordering representation of choice and decision, then that constitutes a criticism of such a representation.

Creativity

In the course of discussing how an agent weighs up various reasons in deciding which action to take, Nozick (1981, p. 244) writes, 'The reasons do not come with previously given precisely specified weights; the decision process is not one of discovering such precise weights but of assigning them. The process not only weighs reasons, it (also) weights them.' He goes on to say (pp. 296–7), 'The weights of reasons are incohate until the decision . . . A decision *establishes* inequalities in weight, even if not precise weights' (emphasis added). In our terms, *there does not pre-exist* an overall ordering R, but rather *the decision* establishes, at least partially, what R could be used *ex-post* to describe the decision as the result of a maximizing exercise. *Ex-ante*, however, that R *does not exist* and the decision process cannot properly be characterized as one of passive constrained optimization, involving *given* constraints and objective function. Decision-making, that is, involves an element of creativity. This view of decision-taking is obviously important to various questions raised earlier in this paper. And it underpins, perhaps, the distinction which, for example, Shackle and various 'Austrian' writers have sought to make between 'Robbinsian maximization', on the one hand, and 'genuine choice or decision', on the other. To the (non-negligible) extent that Nozick is right, the 'Arrow problem' for the individual, Levi's insistence on decision without full pre-reconciliation, the infinite regress problems about choices over choices and decisions subject to information costs, the constant complaints that Pareto could *not* just replace agents by photographs of their preference maps – all fall into a consistent pattern. Decision is not fully representable *ex-ante* as constrained optimization over a complete, transitive *or even pre-given* ordering. And yet the concept of a complete, transitive, *ex-ante* ordering *may still be very important* in representing, separately, each of the individual dimensions or aspects of the agent's decision problem.

A creative view of decision-making loops back to our earlier references to choice over time and to second-order desires. An agent can decide 'now' gradually to lose certain desires, to cultivate new tastes and interests, to allocate resources to education (of any kind) in order to become a different person. On the other hand, a decision 'now' which *assigns* certain weights to certain values may create at least a presumption (no more, of course) that those weights will not be too easily rejected in the (near?) future; people do not often change drastically over a very short space of time (which is why one can refer to their characters). If they did so, in a completely unpredictable way, decision would become almost pointless. In both senses, one can say that 'a person is constructed by the choices he has made sequentially through time' and that 'not even individuals have well-defined and well-articulated objectives *that exist independently of choices themselves*' (Buchanan 1979, pp. 109–11, emphasis changed). An agent's decision 'now' is not fully determined by his orderings and those orderings themselves depend on his previous decisions. (See also Buchanan 1982, Section III).

If careful deliberation concerning the various reasons for and against alternative possible actions does not lead to a decision's 'taking itself', if an agent often has to make a decision in the face of unresolved conflict (Levi), and if an agent can, in part, influence his future preference-orderings, then we are led inexorably to take an active, or creative, view of the typical decision-maker. By the same token, we are led to doubt whether the decisions and actions of a typical agent will be completely predictable. The adoption of a more complex, multi-faceted picture of the individual may thus lead one not only to see the agent as active (as is etymologically appropriate), as *creative*, but also to view him as less than fully determined. An enhanced recognition and understanding of the complexity of the individual's 'inner environment' (as H. A. Simon has called it) may thus be associated with a diminished confidence in our putative ability to predict. (Cp. Farmer 1982, especially Section IV.) To any reader who finds this disturbing, we reiterate that we have been led to this conclusion without having given up, in any degree, the picture of rational agents, of individuals who act in the light of reasons. We have given up *only* the particular, restrictive version of that picture which seeks to represent the actions of creative, multi-faceted individuals by the maximization of a single preference-ordering; and we have attempted to show that there are good reasons for abandoning *that* particular version.

VII. Conclusion

It is a commonplace that, in taking decisions, an individual can feel the force of conflicting considerations, some telling for and some against any particular action. Whilst this has been one of the abiding themes of great literature, as in Goethe's *Faust* for example, only limited attention has been paid to it in the theoretical literature. In economic theory, in particular, the so-called 'rational individual' is immediately represented by a single, complete, transitive preference-ordering. Rather than simply postulating such an individual, we have sought in this paper to consider the multi-faceted individual, who evaluates alternatives from various different points of view. One particularly stark example of this phenomenon arises in all intertemporal decision-taking by any but the most myopic, since the individual cannot but be aware of his inescapable future time aspects: but the reality of multi-facetedness extends far beyond the temporal dimension for most individuals. The fact remains, of course, that even a Faust has to come to decisions, which leads to the question how the individual fuses his aspect orderings into an overall preference relation. We therefore raised the possible analogy, for the individual, with the Arrow Possibility Theorem: not in order to show, by a mechanical application of that theorem, that the individual cannot have an overall ordering, but to point out that the existence of such an ordering is far from self-evident. We then introduced the concepts of an agent's character, domain of conflict and integration procedure (or formation rule). There are many more imaginable character types than could be analysed here, so our discussion was directed towards the rational characters of economic (and other) theory. It was shown that the orthodox rationality concept corresponds to a *harmonic* and *sensible* character, that is, to a character whose aspect orderings do not conflict 'too much' and whose overall preference relation is derived from those aspect orderings in a Pareto-like manner. This representation of rationality can, of course, be viewed both as showing the assumptions needed to support the rationality postulate and as indicating the limited field of application of that postulate. With respect to the latter orientation, many interesting issues relating to non-harmonicity, second-order preferences and human creativity open up, or appear in a new light, but it has only been possible here to offer a few hints in that direction. We hope, nevertheless, to have shown throughout this chapter that an abandonment of the 'rational individual' of economic (and other) theory, far from necessitating the desertion of either 'rational man theory' or all standard microeconomic concepts, leads rather to the prospect of a considerable enrichment of individual decision-taking theory. To contribute to that enrichment is the *serious* way to criticize narrow 'rational individual' theory.

REFERENCES

Arrow, K. J. (1973 [1967]) 'Values and collective decision-making', in E. S. Phelps (ed.), *Economic Justice*, Harmondsworth: Penguin.

Buchanan, J. M. (1979) *What Should Economists Do?*, Indianapolis: Liberty Press.

Buchanan, J. M. (1982) 'History, now, and the constrained future', draft paper for the Interlaken Seminar, June 1982.

Collard, D. (1978) *Altruism and Economy*, Oxford: Martin Robertson.

Dahrendorf, R. (1968) *Essays in the Theory of Society*, London: Routledge and Kegan Paul.

Dennett, D. C. (1978) *Brainstorms*, Brighton: Harvester Press.

de Sousa, R. (1976) 'Rational homunculi', in A. O. Rorty (ed.), *The Identities of Persons*, Berkeley, California: University of California.

Elster, J. (1977) 'Ulysses and the Sirens: a theory of imperfect rationality', *Social Science Information* 16, 469–526.

Farmer, M. K. (1982) 'Rational action in economic and social theory: some misunderstandings', *Archives européennes de sociologie* 23, 179–97.

Hofstadter, D. R. (1981) 'Reflections', in D. R Hofstadter and D. C. Dennett (eds.), *The Mind's I*, Brighton: Harvester Press.

Johnstone, H. W. (1970) *The Problem of the Self*, University Park: Pennsylvania State University Press.

Levi, I. (1982) 'Conflict and social agency', *Journal of Philosophy* 79, 231–47.

Lycan, W. G. (1981) 'Form, function and feel', *Journal of Philosophy* 78, 24–50.

MacKay, A. F. (1980) *Arrow's Theorem: The Paradox of Social Choice*, Yale: Yale University Press.

Margolis, H. (1982) *Selfishness, Altruism and Rationality*, Cambridge: Cambridge University Press.

Mayo, B. (1956) 'Is there a case for the general will?', in P. Laslett (ed.), *Philosophy, Politics and Society*, Oxford: Blackwell.

Mischel, T. (ed.) (1977) 'Editorial introduction' to *The Self. Psychological and Philosophical Issues*, Oxford: Blackwell.

Mueller, D. C. (1979) *Public Choice*, Cambridge: Cambridge University Press.

Nagel, T. (1970) *The Possibility of Altruism*, Oxford: Clarendon Press.

Nozick, R. (1981) *Philosophical Explanations*, Cambridge, Mass.: Belknap Press.

Phelps, E. S. (ed.) (1973) *Economic Justice*, Harmondsworth: Penguin.

Rorty, A. O. (ed.) (1976) *The Identities of Persons*, Berkeley, California: University of California Press.

Schelling, T. C. (1980) 'The intimate contest for self-command', *Public Interest* 60, 94–118.

Sen, A. K. (1970) *Collective Choice and Social Welfare*, Edinburgh: Oliver and Boyd.

Sen, A. K. (1977a) 'Social choice theory: a re-examination', *Econometrica* 45, 53–89.

Sen, A. K. (1977b) 'Rational fools: a critique of the behavioural foundations of economic theory', *Philosophy and Public Affairs* 6, 317–44.

Sen, A. K. (1979) 'Information analysis of moral principles' in R. Harrison (ed.), *Rational Action*, Cambridge: Cambridge University Press.

Sen, A. K. (1980–1) 'Plural utility', *Proceedings of the Aristotelian Society* 81, 193–215.

Sen, A. K. and Williams, B. (eds.) (1982) *Utilitarianism and Beyond*, Cambridge: Cambridge University Press.

Sidgwick, H. (1893) *The Methods of Ethics*, 5th edn., London: Macmillan.

Taylor, C. (1977) 'What is human agency?', in T. Mischel (ed.), *The Self. Psychological and Philosophical Issues*, Oxford: Blackwell.

Thaler, R. H. and Shefrin, H. M. (1981) 'An economic theory of self-control', *Journal of Political Economy* 89, 392–406.

Williams, B. (1976) 'Persons, character and morality', in A. O. Rorty (ed.), *The Identities of Persons*, Berkeley, California: University of California Press.

Wolf, E. S. (1977) ' "Irrationality" in a psychoanalytic psychology of the self', in T. Mischel (ed.), *The Self. Psychological and Philosophical Issues*, Oxford: Blackwell.

9. The Buddhist theory of 'no-self'*

SERGE-CHRISTOPHE KOLM

I. Is Buddhist behaviour genuinely maximizing?

Can diminishing one's *dukkha* (suffering, dissatisfaction, etc.), which is the goal and even the definition of Buddhism, really be said to be a maximizing behaviour? To answer this question, a preliminary analysis of the logic implicit in Buddhist discourse is necessary. Closer examination proves that the vocabulary used to describe this 'action' is as varied in Sanskrit as it is in Pali, and this variety is compounded by the translations that there are in other languages. It is quite clear that *dukkha* can be larger or smaller, and that *sukkha*, its opposite, varies accordingly. We can therefore treat these entities in terms of ordinal indices which decrease or increase in relation to each other, with that of *sukkha* being the 'index of utility' familiar to economists (one should bear in mind that 'utility' or 'satisfaction' are to be treated as having a purely logical meaning). Buddhism then speaks of decreasing *dukkha* or of increasing *sukkha*.

But to increase something is not exactly to maximize it, any more than to reduce something is to minimize it. However, Buddhism also uses superlatives, referring to 'the greatest' *sukkha*. Yet it employs them when speaking of a maximum (or minimum) of satiation (in satisfaction), which may be termed absolute and without constraint, *nirvana*, of which 'the' Buddha says that 'all the *buddhas* say that it is the supreme state'. Nevertheless, it is so rarely attained, and with such

---

Editor's note. This article is a slightly edited translation of Ch. 23 in S.-C. Kolm, *Le Bonheur-liberté*. It develops the analyses of an immediately preceding chapter, on 'Buddhism and "economic man"'. The present discussion begins by considering the relation between the Buddhist goal of minimizing suffering (*dukkha*) and the 'economic' goal of maximizing utility.

Translation by Martin Thom.

difficulty that, whilst a good number of *bhikkhus* ardently aspire to it and consciously wish for it, it is as well that constraints exist, even if they can be overcome (with time and effort). Moreover, before the *arahant*, who arrives in *nirvana*, there is the *ariyan* who merely approaches it. Reducing the *dukkha* must certainly be understood to involve reducing it as much as is still possible: it is indeed a minimization or, what amounts to the same thing, a maximization, with constraints. But the most important of these constraints differ from the usual sort analysed by economists. They are psychic constraints within the one who is making the decision, such as a lack of energy, of will, of concentration, of clearsightedness, of understanding or of wisdom.

The instrument is, moreover, of the same nature. It consists essentially of mental processes, such as becoming aware, comprehension, understanding, conscious mastery of one's mental forms, concentration, remembrance, forgetting. The physical exercises themselves only serve to facilitate these mental actions. We are therefore concerned, in the last analysis, with a fairly specific form of 'behaviour'. A 'behaviourist' would not find this term appropriate, since his criteria for its use are not satisfied here: namely, that the phenomenon can be observed by an external observer.

In addition, to wish to minimize one's *dukkha* is not a priori the same thing as actually doing it. But this action and its constraints being what they are, it is in a sense possible to say that intention and behaviour coincide. If an individual who seeks to make his *dukkha* as low as possible does not actually do it, according to the judgment of an outside observer (on the basis of language or of attitudes, etc.), it is because he comes up against certain mental constraints (ignorance, will, etc.), and one can always state that he achieves this minimization insofar as these constraints allow it. It is worth noting, moreover, that economists are quite familiar with interpretations which invoke an intention to maximize. Indeed, ever since Samuelson introduced (in 1945) the notion of 'revealed preference' and thereby caused economists to play at being behaviourist doubting Thomases, epistemological doctrine has referred to 'behaviour'. Yet previously, and often since then, through the hidden motive that the expression (which is sometimes 'a manner of speaking', but not always just that) betrays, they have considered intentions to be maximizing ('the agent aims to maximize his utility' has not always been and is still not always shorthand for 'acts as if he were aiming . . . ').

We should, however, bear in mind that Hindu philosophy, from which Buddhism derives, has not one principle of choice but three, and that they cannot be incorporated into a single synthetic 'maximand', because they are hierarchized and entail orders of precedence. These principles are *dharma*, *artha* and *kama*, which may be translated as duty, profit and pleasure or, in other terms, conformity to the order of the world, profit and wealth, and immediate enjoyment.[1] When there is a conflict between the norms belonging to these different principles, right conduct is not considered to be a compromise between them. It is a question of priorities, with each principle having to take precedence over the next one in this order. Hindu ethical value, as far as behaviour is concerned, cannot therefore be represented by an index (a real number) which is an ordinal maximand. It is a *lexicographic* preference. But the whole is of course representable by a preference ordering. It is even very probable that each of the three principles may be assessed in terms of an ordinal index maximand. This is manifestly the case with *artha*, common enough with *kama*, and probably possible with *dharma*.

Buddhism may fairly be said to be less hierarchized than Hinduism sociologically and, as a consequence, conceptually (*dharma*, *artha* and *kama* correspond to the Brahman, to the King or to the temporal power, and to the others, respectively). To decrease *dukkha* or to increase *sukkha* is its overall and unique goal. How is one to compare this with the other philosophies of man, which have a unified goal, such as hedonism, eudaemonism or the non-ethical part of utilitarianism? This question is important for my present project, inasmuch as the pure maximizer, man as he is in the theory of choice, has his epistemo-logical and historical roots in these doctrines. Indeed, it is usually necessary to refer to the history of ideas to provide a description or to arrive at a genuine understanding, if not of the logic of a theory, at any rate of its more general position in knowledge and society, the relative nature of its point of view, what it is capable of achieving and its implicit intention. The history of the theory of choice is quite familiar. Epistemologically, its history resembles that of all scientific concepts.

[1] Cp., in particular Dumont (1959).

It involves increasing levels of precision, generalization and therefore of abstraction; it entails the jettisoning of what is not necessary, conceptual refinements, extensions of its application. We find, in the wake of the individualist philosophies, and of ancient hedonisms, the utilitarians' 'calculus of pleasures and pains' (that of Jeremy Bentham, in particular), the work of James and John Stuart Mill, 'the maximization of utility', the marginalist formalization of Gossen, Jevons, Léon Walras and Carl Menger, ordinalism (an ordinal index, which was discovered by Pareto and – thanks to Henri Poincaré – by Walras, suffices), and generalization in terms of an 'order of preferences'. This trajectory occurs in the space of less than a century.

II. Hedonism, eudaemonism, utilitarianism

It is possible to distinguish between two types of hedonist, eudaemonist or utilitarian theories. There are tautological ones and there are specific or substantial ones, which depend upon particular definitions of terms such as pleasure, happiness, utility, etc. Tautological theories are always verified and general in application, for they interpret these terms in such a way that it cannot be otherwise. For example, tautological hedonism is based upon an adequate definition of the word 'pleasure', which allows it to assert that everybody is always hedonistic: a person never does anything except for the pleasure that he expects to gain from it, and one can derive pleasure from (masochistic) pain, from 'good actions' (whether one is a scout or a saint), from being charitable, from national greatness, from paradise or from the hope of going there, from conforming to a tradition, etc. The same arguments apply in the case of 'happiness' or 'utility' or satisfaction, etc. But this conception does not get us very far. It may well be nothing more than a play upon words. Epistemologically, a hypothesis of this sort is by definition unfalsifiable, and modern philosophy of science will therefore judge it only too harshly. One may, however, arrive at a theory which is a priori more dubious, and therefore more fruitful, if one restricts the meaning of these terms. (It is worth noting that John Stuart Mill's utilitarianism, for example, belongs to this latter category, for human behaviour, conduct and intention are described by him in such a way as to exclude quite explicitly the influence upon them of ethical conceptions of the person.)

In their tautological form, these theories are certainly in accordance with the notion of decreasing one's *dukkha*. What happens, however, if we define the terms more narrowly? Is Buddhism a *substantial* hedonism, eudaemonism or utilitarianism? To answer this question we need to compare the meaning of the words, that of *sukkha* with those of the others. Unfortunately, the latter are not at all precise (and this lends credence to the tautological forms of the theory), *sukkha* being clearer due to its particular properties, such as the fact that it is always wished for, and due also to the theory's account of what it is that leads to it (assuaging, detachment, the no-self, etc.). Of the pertinent words, 'beatitude' is undoubtedly the one which expresses most deeply the quality of the concept of *sukkha*, but, by contrast with the latter, it is used to describe a final state (just as *nirvana* is) rather than preliminary and partial states. One cannot have more or less beatitude, whereas this, as I noted above, is an essential feature of *sukkha*. 'Well-being' is probably, in the end, the term which is least ill-suited to translate *sukkha* (it is more apt than the usual English rendering, 'welfare', whose connotations are more materialist). 'Happiness' undoubtedly comes next (it seems to give slightly less sense of the calm and inner peace to which detachment gives rise). Many translations render *sukkha* as 'satisfaction', but this is liable to obscure the fact that it is not so much a question of satisfying one's original desires as of modifying them. 'Utility' does not seem at all appropriate. As for 'pleasure', this provokes the most interesting question, for it has occasioned both one of Buddhism's fundamental doctrines (the 'Middle Way'), one of its greatest controversies, and its major heresies (the various forms of Tantric Buddhism, and those *yogas* which involve mortification). This is due to the fact that it can be given a precise specification, pleasure of the senses, the Sanskrit name for which is *kama* which means both pleasure of the senses and a desire for the pleasure of the senses. Besides, although the Buddha's discussions and teachings on this question (in the first Discourse) concern this kind of pleasure, they are, at a deeper level, concerned with desire in the widest sense of the word, since it is desire, in all its forms, which causes *dukkha*. The theory of choice can, as we shall see, shed some light on this debate.

III. The Buddha's theorem, or the Middle Way

There are two ways of lessening the dissatisfaction that the existence of a desire provokes. One can satisfy it or one can suppress it. Which is the good way, the one that is both possible and the most effective? Some sages in Hindu and Buddhist tradition choose the first, others choose the second. Some seek to 'satisfy their least desires' through a complete gratification of the senses (as in Tantrism, and in left Tantrism or Shaktism[2] in particular, where the emphasis is on eroticism, but also in other tendencies in *mahayana* Buddhism, which hold that 'the passions are the same thing as *nirvana*'). Others, on the contrary, strive to suppress desire, and therefore the utility of its satisfaction. Their behaviour is thus ascetic, either because they wish to break their habits or because they are already without desire (Oriental ascesis is not the punishment that Christian ascesis often is, for it does not value pain for its own sake; it aims, rather, to learn how to be rid of it; the Hindu or Buddhist ascetic is the opposite of Saint Anthony, whose deprivations become the more meritorious the more he cultivates the phantasms of his desires).

The two methods may also be combined. Thus, one can suppress some desire and satisfy the rest. The Buddha noted that the two extreme strategies (hedonism in the strict sense, and Oriental asceticism) are not good. He himself tried each in turn, living first a life of ease and gratification in his father's palaces, then enduring seven years with ascetics, sleeping on thorns, sitting only on his haunches and often eating only one grain of rice a day. In both cases, he remained dissatisfied. He therefore condemned these two positions as heresies (i.e., errors). Good conduct, he said, was a mixture of the two: satisfy your desires but desire little. Only thus can dissatisfaction and suffering be extinguished. This is the doctrine of the Middle Way.

The Buddha's solution is not, however, very precise. It clearly rules out the two extremes, but how is one to choose which desires one should suppress and which one should satisfy?

---

[2] Cp. Kolm (1982), Chaps. 3 and 7. The term 'Shaktism' should in fact only be applied to the left Tantrism which features in Bengali Hinduism, and which took its inspiration from Tantric Buddhism (contrary to what is usually asserted), but in which masculine and feminine roles are reversed, the *Shakti* here being endowed with energy, in accordance with the feminine role throughout Hindu mythology (with the male role being marked by wisdom).

The rule may indeed be made more precisely by adding: do not conserve any desire which circumstances do not allow you to satisfy (the fable about sour grapes would be good Buddhism if the result had not been achieved by means of an illusion regarding the object, whereas one must, on the contrary, denounce the illusion of desire). I would also like to add to this: conserve, create even, those desires which you can satisfy.

Furthermore, the satisfaction of a desire may involve scarce resources, starting with the time, energy and attention of the person concerned. The same is true of extinguishing a desire, as is proved by introspection, or by the fact that the *bhikkhus* who undertake this task proceed so slowly and almost never arrive at their final goal. Man is therefore faced with the problem of allocating his resources between these two activities. This also enables us to define more precisely what good Buddhist behaviour is.

To act directly on one's own desires, preferences, tastes, etc. is very much in the spirit of a number of different philosophies. One thinks of Epicureanism and pleasure, of Stoicism and its notion of happiness, of Christianity and its morality, of seventeenth- and eighteenth-century Europe's conceptions of Reason, of Kant, who is the crowning glory of these centuries, of Hegel, for whom man's destiny is to master the nature of which his own inclinations form a part, of Schopenhauer and his Buddhism, and of existentialism, since one can be held to be responsible for these aspects of one's personality only if one is able to exert some influence over them. Economic analysis, by contrast, has never been concerned with such things. It is a tradition which has, by and large, neglected the manner in which preferences are influenced or formed by something else. But a valuable and not insubstantial literature on this subject does exist, and has existed for some time.[3]

---

[3] There is a range of different approaches. It is best to begin with the logical observation that each variable of an 'index of utility' may be considered as a parameter of the form of the function having the same value, but whose arguments are the other variables. Many preferences have thus received, at least implicitly, partial explanations (but all explanation is necessarily partial). For example, when one considers consumptions occurring at a range of different dates, one is also implicitly considering how tastes at one date are influenced by the consumptions occurring at other dates (these factors would include habit, weariness, anticipation, etc.) Or else, when one considers that a person is interested, apart from his own consumptions, in the consumptions of others or in their incomes, one is also implicitly concerned with the manner in which these variables influence his own tastes regarding his consumptions. The influence of another's consumptions upon a person's tastes has been very closely analysed by

Moreover, an important aspect of this subject is implicitly treated in all theories of choice, or of consumer behaviour, for to choose a thing (for instance, to consume a given quantity of thing), will influence one's preferences regarding all the others. Furthermore, some of the economic studies regarding the formation of preferences analyse phenomena, such as habit, which are special instances of the kind that I have just mentioned, in which care is taken to make the time dimension explicit. But the 'rational' consumer then takes the effect of his preferences into account when he makes a decision. This *does* entail acting on one's preferences, a phenomenon which may therefore be said to be implicitly studied. But this effect is a joint product of consumption or action. Buddhism is concerned with such phenomena: for example, if it recommends moderate consumption, it is in order to prevent habituation to such consumption (this would be an 'attachment'). But what I am more directly concerned with here are those actions exclusively aimed at altering one's preferences, through meditation, reflection, analysis, perhaps through auto-suggestion, etc. This has not been studied and, in what has been, the 'joint product', the effect on preferences, has seldom been made sufficiently explicit.

Suppose we take a person. Since his *sukkha* may be more or less great, it may be represented by an ordinal index. The latter is by definition a real number represented by u, and any other real number which is a rising dependent variable of u, $f(u)$, could replace u. This u is a function of the quantity consumed, c. One could consider such a quantity for each good or service consumed, or even all the parameters

Cunyngham, Pigou, Dusenberry, by Leibenstein ('the snobbery effect'), Valavanis-Vail and, taking into consideration all instances, all interdependencies, and the question of general equilibrium in Kolm (1964); note its analyses of the 'Panurge effect', in particular, etc. Normative consideration of this externality and of the logic of its internalization are the subject of Kolm (1972). The consideration of preferences regarding another's consumptions or income, together with one's own, is analysed in Kolm (1966 Biarritz conference on public economies; 1969). Marglin, Sen, and then later Hodgman and Rogers, and many others after them, have been concerned with this question. There is already a vast literature concerning the formation of preferences over time. See, for example, Haavelmo (1944); Georgescu-Roegen (1950); Koopmans (1964); Gorman (1967); Preston (1967); Pollak (1970); Von Weiszäcker (1971); Cyert and de Groot (1975); Hammond (1976); Stigler and Becker (1977). Sometimes researchers use sociology to refer to 'reference groups', as in the remarkable works of Van Praag and others in Holland. Others study how manifest preferences are formed on the basis of deeper preferences and varying information, as in Lévy-Garboua (1978). Even sociobiology has been employed in this manner (Becker 1976, Ch. 13). Finally, Arie Kapteyn (1977) has devoted a work to this question.

of the person's situation or actions, but I shall restrict myself here to an explicit treatment of *c* alone, which may, moreover, be an aggregate of the whole consumption, for this is sufficient for my analysis and may readily be extended, if necessary, to cover more complex situations. The influence of *c* on *u* depends in particular on the length of time that the person spends reflecting upon this relation, meditating upon it, or upon something which affects it, in order to try and influence it. Let t_m represent the time taken by this meditation. Other individual resources deployed with this end in mind could also be taken into consideration, such as energy, will, attention, the capacity to concentrate, effort, along with such material resources as would enable one to be in a good situation or to receive helpful advice, etc. Likewise, one could present an analysis of the apportioning of t_m between the various sorts of meditation or of exercise, by means of a 'sub-optimization'. But in this first analysis I propose that we only make t_m an explicit variable. These three variables are therefore linked by the relation $u = u\,(c, t_m)$ where $u\,(\ ,\ )$ is a function of the two variables. Admittedly, this *u* is also an implicit function of all the other pertinent variables.

To begin with, this formulation shows that there is no logical difference, as far as these choices are concerned, between the two types of action regarding one's preferences, which may be called *ascetic meditation* and *sybaritic meditation*. The first consists in convincing oneself that one can have the same 'satisfaction' with less consumption: thanks to t_m being higher one can maintain *u* at the same level, with *c* being smaller. The second consists in deriving more satisfaction from the same consumption, by thinking deeply and at length of the gratification involved, by remembering it afterwards and by anticipating it beforehand, indeed by anticipating one's remembering of it, by having an attentive and sharpened consciousness of it, by striving to disregard the possible ill-effects of this consumption, by comparing it favourably with other possible situations or with those of other persons, by imagining stimulating associations or contrasts and by refining and cultivating one's taste, etc. Thus, thanks to a higher t_m, one can have a higher *u*, with the same *c*. To combine these two forms of meditation is a subtle matter. Sybaritic meditation is obviously employed by the tantrisms noted above. Yet the Buddha was obviously concerned with ascetic meditation. Sybaritic meditation may also be considered in terms of 'consumption time', as we shall see below.

It is very common for the acquisition of c to take time too, given the labour involved in producing it or the need to earn the wherewithal to buy it. Let this length of time be t_a. The quantity c is in general an increasing dependent variable of this variable, so that $c = c\,(t_a)$. We then have $u = u[c(t_a), t_m]$. Time may in general be transferred between t_m and t_a. What is the optimal allocation between these two variables? It may perhaps be $t_m = 0$, where there is thus no time for meditation and the whole time is devoted to working for consumption. This is the Western conception of life. But it is perhaps also $t_a = 0$, where in general $c = 0$, with the 'grain of rice' begged and survival thereby guaranteed. The Buddha says that the optimum is neither of these two extreme cases, but rather an intermediate one: some meditation, in order to lower the desire for this consumption, and therefore also to be satisfied with less of it, and some consumption nevertheless (and therefore the labour that it entails). This is the 'theorem of the Middle Way'. It therefore follows that, in the optimum case, if we suppose the functions to be derivable and if we define u_c and u_m as the first derivatives of u, we arrive at $c' = u_m/u_c$, that is, *the marginal productivity of labour involved in producing consumption is equal to the marginal efficacy of the meditation involved in economizing upon consumption without altering satisfaction* (labour and meditation being measured here in terms of their duration).

The Buddha is concerned with ascetic meditation. If, however, a sybaritic meditation was involved, the problem would, as we have seen, assume much the same form. In the optimum, we would undoubtedly not have $c = 0$, since there would no longer be any consumption to savour (it would be purely and simply a dream). We would then not have $t_a = 0$, if, as is frequent, $c\,(0) = 0$. If, in addition, the optimum is not $t_m = 0$, the previous formula remains valid.

In neither of these two problems did we suppose that the other form of meditation did not exist; we merely did not consider it explicitly. Consequently, these results remain valid if both these forms of meditation are practical.

But the time involved in sybaritic meditation may well be considered to be within the time devoted to consuming this consumption in general. Indeed, there is no clear or straightforward way of distinguishing between them. Some durations, such as the time involved in tasting things, are apparently liable to belong to both of the two classes. Let this consumption time be t_c. One can often increase the satisfaction given by a consumption by taking more time to enjoy it. If one writes this out in full one has $u = u[c(t_a), t_c, t_m]$. Let us suppose that time is transferable between t_a, t_c and t_m. The previous result remains valid. Besides, some time is always required for the consumption of a quantity c if it actually is consumed, that is, if $c > 0$ is actually consumed, $t_c > 0$. Now, this is the case with the Middle Way. Let us define u_t as the derived function of u in relation to t_c. In the optimum it is then also true that $c' = u_t/u_c$; that is, *the marginal productivity of the labour involved in producing consumption goods is equal to the rate of substitution of amount of consumption for consumption time.*

With some consumptions, it may happen that consumption time is strictly tied to the quantity consumed. Let us define this relation as $t_c(c)$. We then have $u = u\{c(t_a), t_c[c(t_a)], t_m\}$, hence, in a Middle Way optimum, $c' = u_m/(u_c + u_t \cdot t'_c)$. This result may be interpreted in the same way as the first one was, with the proviso that the economizing on consumption to which meditation gives rise, in order to provide a given satisfaction, acts also by economizing upon consumption time.

It is, moreover, frequently the case that the activity of acquiring consumption (labour), and therefore the time devoted to it (t_a), may in themselves give rise to satisfactions or annoyances or distress. In order to take account of this in our analysis, we must add t_a to the range of variables of the function u. Let us call the corresponding derived function u_a. All the previous discussions and results then remain valid if we add u_a/u_c to c', whenever we come across it.

We have already dealt with a wide range of different cases. Yet none of them can be said to represent Gotama's human experience. For he never worked. Throughout his life, $t_a = 0$. As mentioned earlier, he ate very little for seven years, he begged with the success of a famous apostle afterwards and, previously, when he ate a great deal and over a long period, everything was provided for him in his father's palaces! When he referred to his own experience in order to decree the Middle Way, t_a could have had no place in it. The only durations involved were therefore t_c and t_m. The quantity consumed, c, was not a constraint. It may or may not be strictly tied to consumption time. *Sukkha* may then be $u(t_c, t_m)$, or $u[c(t_c), t_m]$, or $u[c(t_c,), t_c, t_m]$, the first two being

244 SERGE-CHRISTOPHE KOLM

variants of the third and more inclusive form. But there is not really any significant analytic difference between them. The 'theorem of the Middle Way' states that, in the optimum case, neither t_c nor t_m are null: meditate *and* eat, $t_c \cdot t_m > 0$. So, $u_c \cdot c' + u_t = u_m$ (with, as a possibility, $u_c \cdot c' = 0$ or $u_t = 0$).

Finally, if we consider the various sorts of consumption, is it possible to state how Buddhist meditation or action upon oneself is liable to affect the structure of preferences? Which desires are first singled out to be corroded by its acid? This Buddhist practice consists essentially in lowering one's sense of one's 'self'. Now, the self is basically a social product. There are, moreover, forms of consumption whose aim, or one of whose more important aims, is to promote or to satisfy this self-in-society, that is, the image that others have of oneself, or that one has of oneself in relation to others. There are conspicuous consumptions ('I spend, therefore I am', Veblen's man would say), consumptions between rivals (keeping up with the Joneses) and those that are tied to status or standing ('maintaining one's rank'), etc. Thinking that the 'self' is an illusion may well erode at first the needs that are based upon it, or the forms of consumption which are intended to create or to sustain it (all the more so given that the others are *a fortiori* at least as illusory). This has particularly significant social and economic consequences, since consumptions between rivals are in some sense self-sustaining – if each person wants to have more than the other, it is impossible for everyone to be satisfied.[4] It is clear how far the question of growth, for instance, is affected by this fact.[5].

IV. Buddhist egoism, its limits and its meanings

All the above Buddhist precepts are strategies aimed at improving one's personal situation. Thus, they are entirely egoistical, as is most of ordinary Buddhist practice. In terms of most Western morality which holds that one only becomes altruistic by ceasing to be egoistical, the ethical doctrine of Awakening and the Buddhist sage seem to be cynically egoistical. The doctrine has subtler ramifications however.

[4] For a detailed analysis of these questions, see Kolm (1972).
[5] Observations of this kind have been made recently in the West, in the 1920s in particular, by the economists R. Harrod and J. M. Keynes.

First, the detachment to which Buddhists aspire implies a diminution in, and then a cessation of, feelings of hostility towards other human beings, of malevolence, hatred, spite, cruelty, envy and jealousy in particular. This represents a lowering of negative attitudes towards others rather than an enhancement of positive attitudes towards them, but it is a general tendency of Buddhism to consider the negative rather than the positive aspect of things. In many respects, Buddhism takes negation to be more real than affirmation. It is no small thing, after all, to reduce these hostile sentiments. At least no Buddhist has ever killed another man in order to win salvation or happiness for himself, his victim, man in general or any idol whatsoever.

Moreover, even if we discount his attitudes, his knowledge alone prevents a Buddhist from entertaining negative feelings towards another human being, since the *self*, and therefore that of another, is merely an illusion. One cannot hate something which does not exist, nor can one detest or despise it. This in itself is something of an achievement. But one cannot love it either. At most one can 'love one's neighbour as oneself', since 'one' does not exist either. But if it is a *yoghin* who favours mortification who follows this precept. . .

However, the Buddha's teaching calls upon one to develop compassion (*Karuna*) alongside wisdom (*panna*). The former term does not refer to a sentiment or an attitude, as it is often said to do in the West. The sentiment of friendship towards everyone is *metta*. *Karuna* refers to an action undertaken with a view to helping another, where a fairly wide range of intentions and attitudes are involved, including tolerance, forgiveness, benevolence, goodness, affection, pity, charity, etc. The Buddha then explains in detail what form this compassion in one's conduct towards others should take, namely, *sila* or moral conduct. This is realized in words, acts and modes of life (which ought not to harm others either directly or indirectly). It thus involves three of the eight of the paths of the 'noble eightfold way' of good Buddhist behaviour.

Buddhists will invariably point to this aspect of their doctrine when Westerners accuse them of egoism. One cannot help feeling, however, that this 'compassion' is important more for the goodness it represents in the person who displays it than for the benefit of the one who receives it, as an attitude rather than as a good deed. Buddhists will then point out to us that it prevents the former from simply living in a state of pure wisdom and therefore of withering up, and in some sense it moistens, oils and anoints the state of wisdom, kneads it with affection and good intentions and gives it its emotional dimension. One becomes somewhat sceptical, in particular, when one hears that this 'compassion' must be extended not only to all human but to all animal beings. Friedrich Nietzsche, a Westerner with no direct knowledge of Buddhism, who could only have known a small number of texts, but who had sufficient perspicacity and intuition to remedy this deficiency, had a good understanding of this. He wrote of the Buddha that 'He understands benevolence, being kind, as health-promoting'.[6]

It is also worth recalling that, of the two great forms of Buddhism, *mahayana* Buddhism places more emphasis on altruism than *theravada* Buddhism does. This is one of the main distinctions between them. In *mahayana* Buddhism, the 'saint' is the *bodhisattva* who so loves others that, when he arrives on the threshold of *nirvana*, he refrains from entering it so that they may rejoin him and he may help them by lending them some of his numerous merits. However, it may certainly be asserted that *theravada* Buddhism is the purest form, being closest to the origins and therefore more properly the 'true' Buddhism.

For example, Buddhist monks must live off alms, and others must give them alms. What more altruistic gesture is there than charity of this sort? But the purpose of this begging is to enable the monk to devote himself to advancing along the Way, without cares or material ties. No one should expect to be thanked for the alms that they give. This, quite simply, is how *theravada* Buddhism regards the relation between giver and receiver. *Mahayana* Buddhism, on the other hand, has stressed its altruistic side. I would point out, however, that the true Buddhist, the monk, is he who receives and not he who gives! And even the moral advantage gained from the gesture is actually reversed, with the *bhikku* or *lama* having to use it in order to love the 'benefactor' who feeds him, through a particular form of recognition: he receives both the rice and the *sila*, both food and an object of 'sympathy'. *Mahayana* Buddhism, moreover, has now almost abandoned begging.

It is nevertheless the case that, for a monk to receive, someone else has to give. And, conversely, if there is some thing he does not have,

[6] Nietzsche (1968).

another person must by implication have it. Now, a *bhikku* owns little, very little indeed (although he may use the goods owned by his community), and the Buddhist is exhorted to dispossess himself of everything or to acquire nothing. This applies both to objects and to rights and social situations. If these are rare and can be transferred to others, to renounce them or to do without them *in fact* amounts to giving them to someone else. The *mahayana* places value on both of the two consequences of renunciation, that of being less attached and that of allowing someone else to have more: 'If I eat, what will I have to give?' (Chantideva). But even in the case of the *theravada*, which is only concerned with the first consequence, this abstinence in some way constitutes an implicit and involuntary altruism in its own right. The essential point in Buddhist ethics is therefore that 'a thing should not be mine'. Seen more altruistically, the essential point is that it should go to someone else. Now, in many circumstances, the first point implies the second, or enables it to occur. Buddhist behaviour thus often appears to be altruistic in practice. One can imagine a Buddhist Saint Martin ridding himself of half of his cloak because it is for him an 'attachment' that he can do without; he certainly would not prevent the poor person who was cold from picking it up.

Also, in one of his arguments designed to show that 'all is suffering', the Buddha, while recognizing an altruism which he transforms into a second-degree egoism, states that 'something agreeable to one person may bring suffering to another'. This may occur in several different ways, one being the deprivation of another, such as I have discussed above. Through each of these links, one's abstention will make others happy while one's enjoyment will cause them pain. But, the argument goes on, empathy often causes one to feel the suffering of others, and thereby to suffer oneself. A form of altruistic sentiment is thus recognized. What, however, does the Buddha do? Does he value it in ethical terms? Does he oblige us to cultivate it? He merely says that, because of it, one suffers certain ills which one may transmit to others by attachment to things or by consumption of them, and for this reason one is recommended to abstain from these attitudes or forms of behaviour. Altruism thus becomes the tool of egoism![7] It is worth

---

[7] There is a formalization of this question, which takes into account all individuals and all the effects induced (the pleasure which your pleasure gives me gives you pleasure, and so on), in Kolm (1969).

recalling here that Pali and Sanskrit even have a word, *muditha*, which refers to the pleasure that one derives from the pleasure of others, and which one has caused.

However, the edifying stories of the *djatakas* (the previous lives of the Buddha) have been shown to contain a plethora of charming or touching anecdotes which stress the value of gifts, of devotion and of sacrifice for others. But Westerners, Bible in hand, undoubtedly live out the most fervent egoism of all. It is best, therefore, to rely upon observation of men rather than upon traditional stories.

If someone acquainted with the reputation for egoism that Buddhism, and *theravada* Buddhism in particular, has long had among Western observers, attends one of the *theravadins'* sessions of spiritual exercises, he will be surprised to see that they usually begin with a long meditation upon *metta*. Indeed, it is the case that numerous forms of behaviour intrinsically connected with Buddhist life, and often with Buddhist doctrine, appear to be altruistic. First, there is the Buddhist form of welcome, the physical opening of the temple to begin with, but above all, if the visitor is truly interested, the welcome into the *sangha* (community), the hospitality, the benevolence and sympathy displayed towards him, and the patient manner in which he is treated. The communal practices which are in themselves a part of the monastic search imply some recognition, at the least, of the mutual aid which the searchers can give each other. More specifically, Buddhism holds that, in practice, one cannot advance very far along the Way without the advice of someone who is wiser, who will point out the more opportune strategies and who will, to begin with, transmit the concepts appropriate to the psychic phenomena involved, so that these latter may be perceived, understood, influenced and even created. Now, such advice may require much time and availability, and it is always given to those who are truly interested and willing, and it is always free. There could even be said to be an ardent desire in Buddhism to teach the extinction of desires and, more generally, the Way, that is, to teach others to suffer less. This implies a concern for the other or, at least, a concern which operates by way of the other. There is, then, in accordance with the Buddha's own injunctions, a Buddhist proselytism, which is sometimes very intense but in its own very calm and serene way, and whose most striking feature is its complete respect for others. Its education, its sermons and, *a fortiori*, its 'conversions', are never, and have never been, imposed upon others. Jains take this respect so far that they refuse even to strive to have influence and therefore to preach. That is the opposite of the Crusaders' killing love.

More generally, non-violence (*ahimsa*) is, from the point of view of society, an essential feature of these doctrines, a principle which Buddhism and Jainism have in common and which various forms of Hinduism have revived. Even when the ultimate objective is felt to be that of safeguarding one's store of Karmic merits, or its purely psychic equivalent, the result is the same. And the Buddha extends the principle of *ahimsa* to cover all the indirect consequences of acts (no arms dealing, for instance). It is, admittedly, only an altruism in negative, through prohibition rather than through expansive love – which may rapidly become 'all-conquering'. But it bears on a fundamental aspect of relations between humans. All-consuming love, love as absorption, is perhaps less altruistic than simple respect for others.[8]

[8] Buddhism has been swept from India by successive waves of white Huns, then by Brahmanism, and finally by Islam, because the *bhikkus* let themselves be murdered without resistance by the Hephtalites, the Hindu brahmans of Shankaracharaya, and by the Persian mudjahiddins of Bakhtiar. It is true that, taking everything into account, the non-violent doctrine of the Awakened One did not conquer the subcontinent in an entirely innocent manner either. The great Buddhist King Ashoka, the unifier of India, used imperial decrees to make Buddhism the official religion in the third century BC. He had to kill hundreds of thousands of persons to carry out his conquests (the body-count is his own). But he was careful to safeguard his own consistency and morality, along with that of Buddhism, by practising perfect timing. For he only became a Buddhist after he had done these things and, later, when he had to crush some rebellion or round off some frontier, he would abandon Buddhism for the period necessary to carry out these imperial duties. Once he was victorious, Ashoka lost no time in preaching Buddhism to those of the defeated who had survived, placing special emphasis upon the duty of *ahimsa*, i.e. non-violence with respect to men and animals (and emperors). He inscribed this on huge steles and rocks scattered throughout the country, which may still be read today. He was not, however, so brazen as to saddle the Buddha with the responsibility for these macabre hypocrisies, nor did he promise *nirvana*. And he certainly desisted from tampering with the caste and class system. If you think that I am slandering a great king, who did so much to further the cause of wisdom and knowledge, listen to his visitor, the Greek diadoch Ptolemy Philadelphus, who came from Egypt to see him at Patna: 'He is skilled in saying one thing and thinking another.' You can imagine how easily, therefore, he might engrave one thing and do another! He was involved in many other subtleties too. For example, he had, in his role as emperor, to levy taxes. But, being a *bhikkhu*, he was not supposed to take anything from anyone else. However, according to the rule of the *sangha*, he had to accept everything that was given to him. The solution which he arrived at was very simple. He decreed that taxes would no longer be called by that name but would from then on be termed alms. Saint Louis might have thought up that one! But others have been known to dream up such things too. Herodotus tells us that the Persians used this trick with the Arabs who, being a proud nomadic people, were much happier if they could describe the tribute they had to pay as

This respect for others is intrinsically linked to Buddhist philosophy. There is no notion of dogma or of sin in Buddhism; truth and error are the only things that count. The Buddha says what he believes to be true, but he basically offers a psychological explanation, which each person is invited to come to terms with through introspection. He recommends that one be guided by no tradition, custom, textual or personal authority, hearsay, appearance, speculative pleasure, etc.: 'when you know for yourself that certain things are unfavourable, false or bad, renounce them, and when you discover for yourself that certain things are favourable and good, accept them and follow them' (Epistle to the Kalama). The Buddha exhorts one to place everything in question, to criticize everything, to search for the true (which includes the good) by oneself, as he himself did. This is Cartesian doubt, but without God and not sparing the 'I', it is Protestant autonomy with its inner world serving as its sole Bible, it is Sartrean liberty, but one that is not negated by responsibility and engagement. It is, to begin with, extreme respect for the liberty within each person.

Likewise, since there is no evil in itself apart from the suffering which is one's own retribution, Buddhism knows nothing of sin. Nor, more generally, does it know of good or bad *moral* conduct, where this term is taken to imply a transcendence of man and even, in most cases, only of the individual. Buddhism therefore does not stir up a bad conscience or guilt feelings, whereas many religions feed off these, just as vampires feed off the blood of men. On the contrary, it actually fights against them and, when it wins, suppresses them, since they are sources of moral pain, quite clearly tied to the *self*, to its relations with the rest of the world, to agitation etc., in accordance with Buddhist psychology. Now, who then can be truly said to *love* the other better: he who says 'you are a wretch but I pardon you because I love you' (and sometimes I burn you alive), or he who gives him advice as to how to rid himself of the ills of living, without leaving life itself?

Do not however expect the Buddhist, for all his 'compassion', to sympathize with you in your misfortunes. At best he will pity you for being still sufficiently 'attached' to suffer from what happens to you. Why should he suffer from your pain when he is striving with all his

a gift. The most recent instance of this brings us back to the question of massacres, and to Buddhism, though in this instance it is its obliteration that is intended. The Khmer Rouge suppressed taxes, but replaced them with 'voluntary contributions'.

soul (if he has one) not to feel his own? He is capable of imagining himself in the situation which makes you suffer, but the more successful he is in his own search the less such a thing will make him suffer. Buddhist 'empathy' does not work because 'pathos' is not Buddhist. A Buddhist cannot pity his fellow any more than he pities himself. He could, however, go through the motions of expressing sympathy with you, in order to console you and thereby to lessen your pain. But he would be rendering you a disservice, for the cure thus effected would be superficial and short-term rather than definitive. You would be no further along the road to an effective and lasting cure; in fact it would lead you to a dead end. Worse still, it might well reinforce your illusion regarding your *I*, and thus distance you from the proper solution and entrench you yet more deeply in this suffering and in that of others. Furthermore, why should a Buddhist take a genuine interest in your being when he is marshalling all his intelligence in order to logically understand that such a being does not exist, and furthermore all his sensibility in order to become aware that the being who might be interested in it does not exist either? A Buddhist does not sympathize with the misfortunes of others, not because there is no misfortune (in fact that is all there is), but because, in reality, *others* no more exist than *the self* does. He may therefore often seem to be extraordinarily insensitive to the misfortunes of others and, in this sense of the word, inhuman. But this is precisely what a Buddhist strives to be towards all things of this world. It is his wish, his only wish even, to reduce misfortune. But he wishes to reduce misfortune in general, and to do so effectively and thoroughly.

This last observation would seem to account for a good part of the apparently egoistical aspects of Buddhist behaviour. To show how it is that this egoistical conduct stems from an intention which is not egoistical, I will cite an instructive example. It derives from the letter of Buddhist teaching, and it seems to me that it is lived by a number of *bhikkhus* and other Buddhists, although they may not be very conscious of the fact. This is how it works. The object of Buddhism is indeed to lessen suffering, and not exclusively, or even particularly, one's own. But this latter is part of the overall suffering, and Buddhist psychological and therapeutic theories hold that it is basically on this part that the individual can act effectively and deeply. Through making an effort on myself, I am able to detach myself, to humble or suppress my desires, but I cannot hope to have the same effect on you and yours; it is you and you alone who can do that and the best I could do would be to point you towards therapeutic theories or prescriptions which you could then apply yourself. Consequently, in order to reduce the suffering of the world, the Buddhist is led to concern himself essentially with acting on his own self. Hence his egoistical behaviour.

If I give you a good or 'render' you a service, you will derive relief or pleasure from it. But that will not give rise to an effective or lasting lowering of your dissatisfaction, for you risk becoming habituated to it or attaching yourself to it, you will fear future privation and will be ill prepared for it, you will want something else. The only way in which you can be lastingly and deeply satisfied is to control your desires and their birth. This is something that you alone can do, and with this end in view all I can do is to supply you with advice and wise words. We have thus to do with an altruism largely restricted to ideas. But these pieces of advice are the good ones, their hints are effective. The well-known Chinese story which holds that it is better to teach someone how to fish than to give him a fish is a Buddhist apologue. Only help another if you do not know how to advise him to help himself. Tangible generosity and devotion are last resorts reserved for ignorant people incapable of speaking well. Only in the last resort should good action be substituted for good speech.

Once again, it was Nietzsche who perceived this: 'In the teaching of the Buddha egoism becomes a duty: the "one thing needful", the "how can *you* get rid of suffering" regulates and circumscribes the entire spiritual diet.'[9]

This interpretation of Buddhism is both in strict accordance with its expressed teachings and logically compatible with the doctrine of the no-self. All Buddhist doctrine speaks of reducing suffering, but practically only provides few indications as to how one is to lessen one's own. The writings of the 'ancient school of wisdom' state quite unambiguously that 'No one can be saved by another'. This has been taken to mean that Karmic merits cannot be transferred, and in this respect it has been to some extent breached by *mahayana* Buddhism, but the deep psychological meaning of *karma* actually lends credence to our present argument. It has also been observed that the not-self that implies the concept of suffering exists on its own. Buddhaghosa, for

[9] Nietzsche (1968).

instance, says: 'Only suffering exists, but there is no sufferer.' Understood in these terms, the ethical objective and criterion of Buddhism – to lessen overall suffering – comes to seem effectively identical to that of ethical utilitarianism – to maximize the 'sum' of individual utilities. But one can in general increase this latter 'sum' by transferring riches from one person to another whereas for a Buddhist, this would be a futile way of attempting to increase the well-being of persons. What is required is that they should sever their attachments to the world: namely, their desires. And one cannot transfer the will not to wish for things; one can at best transfer the knowledge of its importance, along with techniques for its manipulation.

In this conception, Buddhist egoism is purely instrumental: it does not belong to the realm of ends, and is in no sense an egotism. We have even seen that, in a fundamental sense, Buddhism formed its doctrine in opposition to egoism, just as the great moral systems of the West had done. But these doctrines define the contrary of egoism quite differently, so that they actually seem opposed to each other. In the West, we have altruism, charity and fraternity, in the East, the no-self. In the former case the opposite of the me is the *you*, in the latter it is the *not-me*. I have just observed, admittedly, that Buddhist practice contains many altruistic features. But they always seem to be a means or a consequence stemming from the basic quest, which is the effacement of oneself.

Western ethics may also involve an attenuation of the *ego*, but in general as means rather than as an end, and it never pursues this to the limit. The renunciating of one's attachments is a value in the West, but it exists as a means to help or serve others or God better (one distributes one's 'worldly goods' to 'the poor') not, as is the case in Buddhism, as a direct means to achieve the absence of suffering. The individual may also be devalued in comparison with the social class of which he is a member, but the Buddhist will retort that in fact such an individual does not exist, that he is merely an illusion. Humility, as when one says that the self is small when compared with God, is largely a way of increasing God's stature by relying upon a very resilient self for support. In fact, a Buddhist will reply, none of that exists, neither God nor self (or, more precisely, there is undoubtedly no God for the *theravada* Buddhist and there is definitely no self for all Buddhists).

Finally, we can grasp most vividly the fact that Buddhism has chosen altruism, not as a primary and self-evident attitude and form of behaviour (since the diminution of suffering has preempted it), but as a consequence of a mature reflection and a conscious and deliberate decision to pursue this end (first of all, by way of education), by considering the famous episode in the Buddha's life known as 'the descent from the mountain'. Having found Awakening under the Bo tree, that is, having found the cause of suffering and a radical means to abolish it, Guatama took refuge on the mountain, in order to apply this remedy to himself. He then asked himself if he ought to share his discovery with other men, and try to instruct them in it. Would they be capable of understanding it, would they have the strength to put it into practice? He finally decided that it was worth trying. Then, 'full of compassion', 'Sakyamuni came down from the mountain' towards the other men, in order to tell them of his discovery. He sought out his five former companions in his quest, intending to inform them of what he had found, and they, apostles five centuries before Christ, were to transmit this knowledge to the others. They constituted the kernel of the *sangha* which organized and perpetuated advanced knowledge and which would spread it throughout the world, to all men who were prepared to listen to the answer to their own questions.

V. Badness, unhappiness and the self: the great illusion. Buddhist ontology

For Buddhism it is clear, therefore, that *badness is unhappiness*. The true unhappiness, however, is not poverty but attachment, which is virtually its opposite, and the bad that there is in attaching oneself consists not in the attachment but in the self that is attached. Fortunately, however, this 'self' does not really exist, it is merely an illusion. One simply has to become aware of this for one's attachments, and therefore one's miseries, to cease.

In order to prove that the 'self' does not exist, Buddhism employs a fairly impressive argument. It consists in considering the person as a set of simple elements which has no reality in itself but only in the mind of the observer. And one is advised to apply this perspective to oneself, whilst taking great care to ensure that the corresponding knowledge is itself a set of elements belonging to those that it uncovers. If one genuinely succeeds in bringing off this ploy, all discomfort would seem to disappear. One would also seem to require more than one life to understand it, and several to apply it, declares the *tathagata* Guatama (the Tibetan Milarepa, a long time after him, is the only one to have effected this in a single life). All the more reason, then, to start straightaway.

One begins by acknowledging that a person is composed of several elements. The profane person would see this as a 'decomposition' of the still perceptible person into several elements. One would then make him see that what he believed to be a person *is only* this set of elements that he stubbornly persisted in regarding as a whole: there is nothing else, the world is empty of 'self'.

The West has long been habituated to such analytic dismantling of being. From Plato, through Descartes to Freud, we find a division between appetite, reason and mind, or we hear of the ghost in the machine, or of id, ego and superego, or of conscious and subconscious, or of conscious, unconscious and preconscious, or of the cognitive, the conative and the affective, etc. But the dismantling that the Buddha (a century before Plato) proposes is infinitely more refined than the crude divisions into two or three elements imagined by Westerners. Even when Hume says, much as a Buddhist would, that 'the mind is only a bundle or collection of different perceptions' linked by causalities, he only grasps one out of the six *skandhas* (it may be that he employs the word 'perception' in a slightly wider sense, but he is hardly explicit about this).

Buddhism is concerned with elementary or simple, indecomposable elements, ontological 'atoms', as it were, which are said by it to be the only things enjoying any reality, and which are called *dharmas* in Sanskrit (*dhammas* in Pali). This word also refers to the Buddha's doctrine, a double reference which is frequent in Buddhist language (*dharma* has many other meanings also, and although most Buddhist terms have several meanings it is probably the richest of them all). As a consequence, the first two words of the Buddhist *credo*, *ye dhamma*, mean both 'I follow the doctrine' and 'I am only [composed of] simple elements.' If these two apparently very different meanings coexist, it is because the deepest meaning of *dharma* is 'ultimate reality' (or 'ultimate truth'). These *dharma* elements occur in many different forms. The elementary manuals in the monasteries describe several dozen of them, but several hundred are said to exist. These types of *dharma* are classed in different ways, according to different criteria. Before being ordained as *bhikkhus*, the novices must learn three of these classifications: in terms of *skandhas*, in terms of *ayatanas*, and in terms of *dhatus*. The most famous is the classification in terms of *skandhas* or 'aggregates' (of *dharmas*), which are five in number. To begin with, there are the ten properties of matter, of material things which, where a person is concerned, means his body and the things which he owns, with the body referring also to his ideas, thoughts and mental images. Then there are the sensations of the six senses (the sixth sense involves perception and sensation of ideas, thoughts and mental images by the mental and cerebral organ – an expression that John Locke was later to reinvent). Then there are the fifty-eight volitions, impulses or 'mental formations'. Finally, the conscious-nesses of all the above crown the whole series. The classification into *ayatanas* obeys a cognitive criterion; its twelve categories are the six senses and the things that they know, the latter being the sixty-four types of mental *dharma*. The division into *dhatus* serves to describe the 'current' (*santana*) of causal relations between *dharmas* which seem to constitute an 'individual' (*pudgala*). It consists of eighteen classes, adding the consciousnesses of the corresponding properties–percep-tions–sensations to the twelve of the preceding classification. But Buddhism sometimes puts itself at the level of modern scholarship by distinguishing three categories, matter, spirit and forces, a classifica-tion which it teaches to small children and to them only. The dual division between spirit and matter is also present.

The important point to note is that, once the person is dissolved in this way, Buddhism sees no reason to reassemble these elements into so-called individuals. It dismantles the human machine conceptually, and with great finesse, but then it disdains to put it together again. Man remains in detached and scattered pieces. A Buddhist observing you will see a pile of elements, a bag containing several hundred types of things, an aggregate of aggregates, a flux of events, a current of causal relations, but not *you*. The Buddhist gaze is a ray which disintegrates being. It is fortunate, then, that it is himself that a Buddhist will spend his time thus scrutinizing.

What thus is this thing which so interests people, which activates their passions, which they care for so intensely, about which they talk so much, their 'self'? It is a concept, a construction of the reason and of the imagination, a way of seeing and of composing the world, but not an entity which really exists. In other words, it is an *illusion*. But does not man excel most at transforming his ideas into suffering? The idea of the 'self', Buddhism says, is the heart of all pain. The worst possible thing to do would therefore be to reassemble the robot, and to believe that this montage on the part of the mind has a real existence.

The idea of the 'self' is not the only thing, Buddhism generously adds, to which this argument applies. The same is true of every mental construction. For instance, a cart consists of wheels, shafts, frame, etc. It *is* these elements; the entity 'cart' is a creature of the mind, an illusion. Or, to put it another way, one must not say that this fruit *has* this form, this colour, this smell, but rather that this fruit *is* this form and this colour and this smell and so on. Likewise, the mind doesn't *have* sensations, sentiments, ideas, volitions, etc., but what one calls 'mind' is these things. And the 'self' is that plus material elements. But to believe in a cart or in a pear does not have the same consequences as believing in oneself.

The main conclusion we can draw from this is that the 'self' is a mental construction, and by realizing this one may suppress pain. Precise analysis of the causes of suffering, of the perceptions which bring it, of its sensation of the consciousness of these facts, enables one either to remove this conscious sensation or to take a detached and objective view of it, and thereby to remove the pain. It is worth noting that Buddhism claims that this latter method is its own peculiar achievement, arrived at thanks to the no-self (the cutting off of sensation, reputed to have been the means employed by the Buddha's last *guru*, did not satisfy the Buddha, inducing him to search for his own answer by embarking upon a long meditation, from which he was to emerge 'awakened' to the solution.) At any rate, more or less training is required to produce these results. This is particularly the case with physical sufferings, where one has to overcome the danger and the fear that its absence would deprive us of the warning that the body is incurring some serious destruction. And things are much easier in the case of self-love, jealousy, hatred, pride, and of shame, honour or love! When one understands the causes and mechanisms of suffering, when one becomes aware of their basic sequences, suffering ceases. In the West, Spinoza (in his *Ethics*, in particular) had certain intuitions about this phenomenon, but he provided no account of the precise mode of functioning, or even of the structure of the psyche such as would enable one to understand it, and such as Buddhism provides. One is tempted, however, to improve the latter doctrine by saying: only strive to dismantle mentally those things which do you harm; attach yourself when it is possible and painless or agreeable, disengage yourself when it ceases to be so; opt for the agreeable side of things, and only analyse the rest in a Buddhist manner! This should be all the more possible that Buddhist psychology provides all the warning and knowledge which are required in order to prevent that a voluntary attachment turns into a sadistic master.

In this diagnosis of the cause of human unhappiness, and therefore in the therapeutic practice which derives from it, Buddhism proves to be the exact opposite of the Western tradition (which includes both Marx and Freud). The latter sees unhappiness, despair, neurosis, alienation, etc. in human beings who are divided, in fragments and internally dismembered, and equilibrium, the necessary condition for happiness (and a concept reminiscent of that of *nirvana*), in the integrated personality. Buddhism, by contrast, regards the latter as the cause of all ills. In order to remedy it, it shatters man (the illusion of man in man's eyes) and is only too glad to leave him in pieces. Is there then a fundamental contradiction between these two theories, each of which is firmly anchored in a tradition? The important thing to note is that the divisions of the personality identified by these two traditions are by no means the same. In Buddhism, the elements are psychological categories which, although connected, belong to different planes, whilst for Freud, for example, the superego and id may collide head-on over particular choices.

To be more precise, however large the number of 'things' (or, more exactly, of 'facts') Buddhism sees in an 'individual', there is one which he will not find there, namely, the 'I', the heart of being, which would be at once the subject of volitions and the object of suffering, and therefore a link between desire and *dukkha*. Chapter 19 in Kolm (1982) analyses precisely and in detail this question of the 'I', and it explains that Buddhist advanced philosophy considers in fact many kinds of 'I', some of which are real by definition or by nature and some of which are illusory. It is the illusion of the 'I in itself', both based upon and providing the basis for desires and attachments, which

Buddhists hold to be the specific cause common to all sufferings. Critical examination of the 'self' enables one to show that an individual contains no entity of this sort. When, therefore, one has succeeded in realizing this and in convincing oneself of it, both desires and pains fade away.

Having thus presented a more detailed account of the Buddhist conception of the self, we are now in a better position to gauge whether it can be reconciled with the theory of choices. If the 'self' is simply an illusion, what reality can the 'order of preferences' have? If it is composed of various 'aggregates' and specified elements, can the whole of behaviour be explained in terms of this ultra-simple entity? If everything is provisional, 'impermanent' and in a perpetual flux of change, as Buddhism declares it to be, what can the stability of these preferences be worth? If 'everything has a cause' and 'everything is determined', which is another base of this philosophy, it applies to individual's actions, and can one then speak of a person's free choice, or even of choice at all? And if 'I' do not exist, who is it that does the choosing?

An illusion is something quite real for the person observing someone who is in a state of illusion (his theoretician, as it were), and if this illusion guides or influences its victim's acts, one can perhaps describe this effect in terms of the theory of choices. But, for a Buddhist, the illusion of the *self* has a crucial effect on the decisions of a non-Buddhist or, more exactly, on non-Buddhist decisions. Only an *arahant*, because he has understood, is an exception to this, but he is a rare phenomenon and undoubtedly acts very little. On the other hand, the action entailed by the theory of choices is indeed caused by constraints and preferences, which are themselves caused by something else. The instability of preferences, for its part, does not obstruct the pure theory of choices which dates them; it may, however, hinder certain of its practical applications. Buddhism states that everything changes, everything disappears, without specifying the speed of this process or the delays that occur. It may take a lifetime, or an aeon. Finally, the fact that out of five 'aggregates' one may only derive one 'self' does not necessarily imply that one cannot derive an order of preferences from them. For the *perceptions* of the available alternatives produce more or less agreeable sensations, and this gives rise to an order which is a *mental and volitional formation*, all of this being liable to be more or less *conscious* (with certainly a higher degree of rationality in the sense of transitivity the more conscious it is).

VI. Buddhist methodology. The dialectic of knowledge, action and cure. The threefold relation to oneself: self-reference, self-production and self-destruction

There is nothing more fascinating than the Buddhist method and logic of knowledge, action and cure. It is the very essence of Buddhism. It is fairly difficult to explain, and it is not presented as being easy to understand, still less to apply. Buddhist doctrine simply asserts that it is possible to understand and to apply it in various degrees, and even completely with enough time, effort, luck and inspiration. The difficulty arises from three linked features: *relation to oneself* (self-reference and self-production), *negation* (or criticism), and the mixture of genres or *multi-dimensionality*. I would hasten to add that, as well as giving rise to difficulties, these features also account for Buddhism's success. Reference back to oneself signifies that the aim of Buddhism is to cure oneself, the means it employs being action upon oneself, and this action in turn is effected by means of knowing oneself (which itself is, as I shall try to show below, a prerequisite for cure, the result of all this being the disappearance of the 'self'). The second feature is negativity: in order to suppress suffering, one criticizes conceptions and denounces illusions, beginning with that which oneself constitutes. Finally, by the mixing of genres I mean that this process implies all the dimensions of man and man's thought about himself, in a very interlocked manner.[10] At the level of knowledge, Buddhism thus mobilizes all its logics, psychology, physiology, ontology, epistemology, methodology, ethics and eschatology, in such a way that these cannot be distinguished one from the other. Western categories are therefore not very relevant here. Thus it is clear that

---

[10] In Hindu thought, knowledge is not something purely intellectual, as it is liable to be in the West. 'Pure' knowledge, sometimes fuelled by 'fundamental research', is an alien conception to it. Hindu knowledge is, on the contrary, a priori meant to guide action, it is meant to be effective and considers itself to be such. It conceives itself as being by and large a know-how. Its spirit thus is not very far, by its type of intention, from that of contemporary economic science. If Marx had been Hindu, he would undoubtedly have felt no need to give a dialectical account of the relations between theory and practice.

Buddhism succeeds in being, in the extreme, an analytic phenomenology[11] of the sort that the West has gambled upon producing, as well as a practice. The most remarkable aspect of this venture, and the key to its success, is the relation to oneself.

Let us consider how this works. The aim is to suppress suffering. To achieve this, one must act (on oneself in this case). To act effectively, one must understand the mode of operation of the thing one wishes to influence (and therefore why it operates as it does), that is, one must find remedies for suffering and thereby understand its cause. But, in order to understand, one requires a calm, clear, lucid and penetrating mind, and one may only achieve this by freeing oneself from suffering.

Is this impossibly contradictory? There are several reasons why it need not be taken to be so.

First of all, the sequence works out in such a way that, by setting up the conditions for an end to suffering, the objective is actually realized. Therefore, by seeking to set up these conditions, one reduces one's suffering. By doing what is required to understand the causes of suffering, the suffering itself abates. Understanding suffering implies that one is master of it, although the mastering of suffering also implies that one understands it. The two cannot help but advance together. If someone teaches the cause of suffering, he clearly enables his pupil to combat it effectively; but if he teaches a process, however mechanical it may be, which reduces suffering, he thereby enables his pupil to understand it and therefore to act by himself in relation to it. La Fontaine's fable, 'The labourer and his children', is a good single illustration of this Buddhist dynamics. Look out for the treasure. You will not find it, because it does not exist – there is no 'I' which suffers. But it is the activity of looking for it which will in the end give you what you are looking for – wealth, in the case of the labourer's children, the end of suffering, in the case of those who follow the Buddha. The end is immanent in the means. The means are the end.[12]

On the other hand, the circle described above is not necessarily a vicious one, for there are degrees of both knowledge and assuagement. A little knowledge enables one to reduce one's suffering a little more, which enables one to increase one's knowledge, and therefore to

---

[11] And relatively anti-Husserlian, negating any 'transcendental ego'.
[12] Psychoanalysis seems here, as in much else, to present a sketch, albeit a vague and incomplete one, of what Buddhism is. See, for example, Jung (1959).

reduce one's suffering still more, and so on. The process could, a priori, be blocked, either at the start or in the middle. But it is Buddha's hypothesis that this does not necessarily occur. The progression may reach a 'fixed point', an 'equilibrium', between the two relations of suffering to knowledge and vice versa, and this is described as perfect knowledge, the absence of all suffering, *nirvana*. The various stages of the progression are described in terms of the successive 'lives' of the metempsychosis.

Another example will serve to show how self-reference is coiled at the very heart of the problem. What kind of knowledge is in question here? 'I suffer.' Why? Let us begin at the beginning. Why do we say 'I'? The 'self' turns out to be a set of 'aggregates' and even of 'elementary phenomena', of *skandhas* and *dharmas*. It itself is merely an illusion. It is worth noting that one could ask whose illusion it is, and one could answer that it is my own, I, who am an illusion. It is therefore an illusion of an illusion. And so on. Even if there is an infinity of interlocking illusions, they will still have no real existence. This illusion (or these illusions) is in fact a set of *dharmas*: some 'idea of oneself', a 'sensation of oneself' and awareness of these facts, exist without there being a 'self', or rather they are the things which constitute it, along with other *dharmas* of sensations, perceptions, volitions, sentiments, matters and awarenesses of all these things. If I know that this is how it is, what is this 'self' which knows? It is a set of *skandhas* or of *dharmas*, etc. More precisely, this knowledge is a set of *dharmas*: ideas, sensations, consciousnesses, 'mental formations', etc. But what is it to know all that? A set. . . Everything is simply *dharmas* and relations between *dharmas*. The *self* does not exist.

We can draw the following lesson from this example. Plato, with his 'Know thyself', is a Buddhist too, and this injunction is the Buddha's advice, remedy, basic activity and his goal (since to know is, as we have seen, to cure). But, in analysing oneself, what does one discover? That one does not exist. To know oneself is to deny oneself, to destroy oneself, to register 'one's void', and thereby even to cure oneself, since the hooks of suffering no longer have anything to hook on to. It is an implosion of the husk of the illusion of the 'self' in its inner void. This image is, moreover, the Buddha's own, since the word *sunna– sunya*, which is translated by 'void', means 'hollow' and, still better, 'swollen'. The ego is a painful abrasion, and the source of all pains; the self is a painful swelling; it is a balloon which explodes under the *dharma*'s piercing gaze.

As well as being in many ways self-referential, Buddhism is also self-productive in the extreme. If to know is to change oneself, what is one to say of one's knowing oneself? To know oneself is first to have a conception of oneself, therefore, in Buddhist terms, to make oneself, but only for the purpose of becoming aware that one is merely this conception, which is constructed upon a basis that does not imply it. Buddhism, however, places more emphasis upon necessity: to know oneself implies to make oneself and vice versa, if only because one must calm one's mind, exercise one's perception and refine one's intelligence, and because to achieve these things one must know oneself. A man who is advanced in Buddhism is certainly more nearly his own creator than anyone else is. But he is, rather, his own destroyer, since, for him, to make himself is to unmake himself. In order to change itself, being must understand itself; and by changing itself, it understands itself, including with the traditional deep require-ment – such as stated in the West by Croce for instance – of being the maker of the object of the understanding; but this change is a dislocation and what is understood is that there is nothing and no one to understand (no 'self' which could be an object of knowledge nor, at any rate, any 'I' which could know). Will erases representation.

Buddhist ontology somewhat resembles the snake that catches its own tail, gulps it down and disappears by swallowing itself; even if it cannot go right to the end, its apparent self may at any rate diminish drastically in length. Or it could be said to resemble the Yellow Submarine's suction-cleaner which, having sucked up the countryside, sucked itself up as well. But it is possible to produce, at least for parts of the 'theory', more precise models. The causal loops which I have described, for example, in the case of the triad knowledge–action–well-being, along with the large number of others presented in Buddh-ist doctrine, and their interrelations also, may be analysed with cybernetic concepts, as much in terms of a qualitative analysis as (particularly for the dynamics) by specifying more the variables.

REFERENCES

Becker, G. (1976) *The Economic Approach to Human Behavior*, Chicago: University of Chicago Press.

Cyert, R. M. and de Groot, M. H. (1975) 'Adaptive utility', in R. H. Day and T. Groves (eds.), *Adaptive Economic Models*, pp. 223–46. New York: Academic Press.

Dumont, L. (1959) 'Le renoncement dans les religions de l'Inde', *Archives de Sociologie des Religions* 7, 45–69.

Georgescu-Roegen, N. (1950) 'The theory of choice and the constancy of economic laws', *Quarterly Journal of Economics* 64, 125–38.

Gorman, W. M. (1967) 'Tastes, habits and choices', *International Economic Review* 8, 218–22.

Haavelmo, T. (1944) 'The probability approach in econometrics', *Econometrica* (supplement) 12, 1–118.

Hammond, P. (1976) 'Changing tastes and coherent dynamic choice', *Review of Economic Studies* 43, 159–73.

Jung, C. (1959) *Modern Man in Search of a Soul*, London: Routledge and Kegan Paul.

Kapteyn, A. (1977) *A Theory of Preference Formation*, Drukkerij.

Kolm, S.-C. (1964) *Introduction à la théorie économique de l'Etat*. Paris: IFP.

Kolm, S.-C. (1969) 'The optimal production of social justice', in J. Margolis and H. Guitton (eds.), *Public Economics*, pp. 145–200. New York: St Martin's Press.

Kolm, S.-C. (1970) *Le service des masses*, Paris: Dunod.

Kolm, S.-C. (1970) *L'Etat et la système des prix*, Paris: Dunod.

Kolm, S.-C. (1971) *Justice et equité*, Paris: CNRS.

Kolm, S.-C. (1972) 'La taxation de la consommation ostentatoire', *Revue d'Economie Politique* 82, 65–79.

Kolm, S.-C. (1980) 'Psychanalyse et théorie des choix', *Social Science Information* 19, 269–339.

Kolm, S.-C. (1982) *Le Bonheur-liberté*, Paris: Presses Universitaires de France.

Koopmans, T. (1964) 'On flexibility of future preferences', in M. Shelly and G. Bryan (eds.), *Human Judgments and Optimality*, pp. 243–54. New York: Wiley.

Lévy-Garboua (1978) *Information et formation des choix du consommateur*. Paris: CREDOC.

Nietzsche, F. (1968) *Twilight of the Idols and the Anti-Christ*, transl. R. J. Hollingdale. Harmondsworth: Penguin.

Peston, M. (1967) 'Changing utility functions', in M. Shubik (ed.), *Essays in Mathematical Economics in Honor of Oscar Morgenstern*, pp. 233–6. Princeton: Princeton University Press.

Pollak, R. A. (1970) 'Habit formation and dynamic demand functions', *Journal of Political Economy* 78, 745–63.

Stigler, G. and Becker, G. (1977) 'De gustibus non est disputandum', *American Economic Review* 67, 76–90.

von Weiszäcker, C. C. (1971) 'Notes on endogenous change of tastes', *Journal of Economic Theory* 3, 345–72.

Index of names

Sternbach, R. A. 138
Stewart, Kilton 180
Stigler, G. 134, 137

Taylor, C. 225
Thaler, R. 5, 17, 134, 138, 205
Timberlake, W. 136
Tversky, Amos 5, 6, 8, 27, **35–57**, 134, 138

Valéry, P. 93, 105, 110, 111
Veyne, P. 4
Voltaire 110

Walras, Léon 236
Wasson, C. 138
Williams, B. 198, 201, 223
Winston, G. 17, 134n
Wolf, E. S. 199